The Battle for the Rhine . . .

The Siegfried Line was "impregnable"—the most deadly combination of fortresses, tank traps, mine fields and artillery that Hitler's generals could devise.

The Allied commanders were split—the hottest debate on strategy since D-Day was boiling up to a showdown between Eisenhower and Montgomery.

The battle was a man-killer—a bloody, brutal yard-by-yard advance of men and tanks through blasted concrete bunkers and shattered cities. It ground forward for mile after mile, and it lasted six months—the most massive collision of armed might on the Western front.

R. W. Thompson, war correspondent and historian, saw it happen. In BATTLE FOR THE RHINE he reveals the doubts of commanders, the agony and courage of fighting men in the last great battle that annihilated the German Army.

More Ballantine War Books
You Will Enjoy

R. W. Thompson

BATTLE
FOR THE RHINE

Ballantine Books • New York

© 1958 and © 1959 by R. W. Thompson
Library of Congress Catalog Card No. 58-59598
First American Edition: February, 1959
Second Printing: July, 1967
First Canadian Edition: June, 1967

Printed in America.

BALLANTINE BOOKS, INC.
101 Fifth Avenue, New York, New York 10003

Contents

ACKNOWLEDGEMENTS

I WISH to record with pleasure and humility my thanks to the Chief of Military History, Department of the Army, Washington, D.C., for his helpful attitude towards my work. I have also to thank most warmly all those busy people who have found time to aid in checking facts, in finding source material, and discussing many aspects of the actions in this campaign. I am again especially grateful to H. A. Cordery, Esq., the Archivist of the Historical Section, for placing at my disposal the relevant War Office records.

I am grateful also to President Eisenhower, William Bradford Huie and Major John North for permitting me to quote from their work, and for replying so courteously and promptly to my letters.

The extracts from *The Supreme Command* by Forrest Pogue, and from *Objective Schmidt* by Charles B. Macdonald in *Three Battles,* are used by permission of the Chief of Military History, Department of the Army, Washington, D.C.; from *Triumph and Tragedy,* vol. VI by Winston S. Churchill by permission of Lord Camrose and Messrs. Cassell & Co. Ltd.; from *North West Europe, 1944-5* by John North, and *Grand Strategy,* vol. VI by John Ehrman, by permission of Her Majesty's Stationery Office; from *The Execution of Private Slovik* by William Bradford Huie, by permission of the author and Messrs. Jarrolds.

To all those others, some among my friends, others previously unknown to me, others known only by way of correspondence, who have all given me encouragement in various ways through a very difficult time, I offer my warmest thanks. I embarked upon this task because circumstances had combined to give me a unique personal view of these battlefields. I wish I had the talent to do justice to the opportunities I have enjoyed.

FOREWORD

IN *The Eighty-Five Days* I argued my belief that the main line of attack after the break-out from Normandy should have been the Antwerp, Breda, Moerdijk, Rotterdam line, and not Brussels, Nijmegen, Arnhem, Zuider Zee. I thank those professional soldiers and historians to whom this argument seemed valid, and worth stating.

The book was also an attempt to relate major strategy to the lot of the common soldier on the battlefield, to show what happens to "Jones" when, in the conventional phrases of generals, armies are flung across rivers—or flung back. So far as I know it was, and remains, a task not before attempted in this way.

This second volume. *Battle for the Rhine,* argues the vital importance of Schmidt in relation to the Rhineland battle, and to the whole front north of the Ardennes. I believe the argument that the front north of the Ardennes should have been one front is unanswerable.

I have not been able to find anyone who has considered Schmidt in this context, and very few soldiers in this country who have heard of Schmidt at all.

In a more ambitious way than in *The Eighty-Five Days* I have attempted to relate major strategy to the soldier on the battlefield, and to reveal in a new perspective the facts behind the long arguments which bedevilled relations between the Allied generals.

It is inevitable in work of this kind, and at this distance, that men should begin to assume a human shape. In the midst of the passions and distortions of war it was not surprising that the real worth of many commanders was obscured. Some of them seemed to cast gigantic shadows, and the shadows were mistaken for the men. It lent courage to ordinary people to see them in such a fashion.

But we were served by men, not Gods—or "Sacred

Cows". These men faced tasks of a magnitude far greater than any in that field which had previously confronted human beings, and far beyond anything in the experience of any one of them. It is not surprising that they made so many mistakes, but that they made so few.

In the history of war from Alexander the Great to Mao Tse Tung the world had not produced more than a handful of men of genius capable of commanding armies. The name of Napoleon springs to mind. Hannibal, perhaps. The magnificent "Pippins", Charles Martel and Charlemagne. Marlborough? I doubt it. Such men are not thrown up generation after generation.

It is certain that nothing approaching genius touched the generals who gave of their best in the Allied cause in N.W. Europe in 1944-5. If these men are to have their just dues they must be seen as men, wrestling with giant tasks bravely, and often boldly. Human stature must be restored to them.

Perhaps of them all only George Patton was truly capable of commanding an army. Not one could manage a group of armies.

It would be a travesty to suggest that Field Marshal Montgomery was "commanding" the left wing of his armies engaged in the battle of the Scheldt, and an even greater travesty to suggest that General Bradley's right hand knew much about what his left hand was doing.

It may be true that the very magnitude of the problems confronting these men forced them to think of themselves in outsize terms, lest by realizing their own true stature they might quail. A senior staff officer once remarked to me: "Even generals wet their knickers". I doubt whether that was true of the commanders of armies and army groups.

The Supreme Commander, General Eisenhower, is exempt from these particular criticisms—if they are criticisms. He did not face these tasks. He has been criticized by some, his own countrymen among them, in that he acted as "a Chairman", and did not exercise his powers of command and enforce his will. It is not, I think, a valid criticism. He had to be a chairman. Short of a Napoleon being available that was the very best we could hope for, and we were fortunate to find a man at once able in that role, and of unimpeachable integrity. The defects of his virtues, if I may say so, have become apparent in his subsequent role as President of the United States of America.

It is not reasonable that we should expect men suddenly called to such tasks to become gods. It is stupid to continue to insist that they were gods.

In subjecting many battles to critical and detailed analysis certain constant factors in command have become apparent to me. I found that I was not alone in observing that following the promotion of battalion commanders to command brigades the timings of brigade movements were always too fast. The battalion commander, knowing perfectly well in his mind the composition of his new command, could not at a bound span the gulf between the possibilities of movement of a battalion and a brigade.

It was said by Guderian, I think—or it may have been von Manteuffel—that Hitler was never capable of visualizing anything larger than a division. That was the cause of many of his gravest mistakes. I think it is true of almost all generals: the command of a division represents the limit of the abilities of most very able men.

Field Marshal Montgomery, for example, commanded a division extremely well. It is probable that he made a good job of commanding the Eighth Army—I cannot speak with authority, for I have not studied it. He might have been a very good commander of the 2nd Army—and so might General Sir Miles Dempsey.

The Montgomery-Dempsey relationship is interesting to compare with the Bradley-Patton relationship.

I venture to bring up some of these points with great diffidence, not only because of my admiration for men like Montgomery, and for others whose roles made less monumental demands upon them, but also because I am aware that we do not inhabit a world of reason. The sharp division of the world into two harsh spheres has made itself felt right down the scale, perverting and inhibiting all normal criticism and expressions of opinion on a wide variety of subjects. When I wrote *Cry Korea* I was said to be "anti" all those things for which I was prepared to give my life, and for which I have often risked it. On the

slender basis of any criticism of the U.S.A. men are sai
to be "anti-American".

Since these are the kind of epithets experience has le
me to expect, I deny them in advance, and in my tur
brand the users of such terms as evil men and wome
among the foremost enemies of mankind. Such peop
are threatening the vital freedoms of thought and expre
sion which the communists deny openly, and which th
West denies under the counter. But these are among th
values for which tens of thousands fought and died on th
battlefields I attempt to portray. In common with tens (
thousands of others I owe a personal debt to my frienc
and my companions, who died to preserve, among man
other things of greater importance, my right to write wha
I believe to be true.

Unhappily, certain passages in this book have been sup
pressed. Their loss is not great, save as a symptom (
the most pitiful and craven fears afflicting this great Na
tion. But I add that these passages, relating to U.S
troops, were unquestionably acceptable to the American
as valid and genuine criticism, without malice. The att
tude of the American authorities to historical inquiry i
not only beyond all praise, but also not the least of th
hopes of mankind in a wider sphere. They are not afrai
of the facts of history.

PART ONE: THE CHECK

THE BACKGROUND TO VERITABLE

i.

T FIVE o'clock on the morning of February the 8th, 945, four months after the original date planned, the ritish 30th Corps, two hundred thousand strong and acked by one thousand guns, advanced southeast out of ie narrow Nijmegen bridgehead against the powerful orthern hinge of the Siegfried Line in the Reichswald rest. The 30th Corps was under command of the 1st anadian Army, while the British 2nd Army planned the hine crossing and guarded the line of the Maas.

To the north the Canadians launched infantry in am-hibious attacks over the floods that had made a vast land lake of all the country north of the Nijmegen-leves road to the Rhine banks opposite Emmerich. To ie south, covering the right flank of the British, seven ifantry and three armored divisions of the U.S. 9th rmy, under command of Montgomery's 21st Army roup, faced the Roer River in flood from Julich to üren, timed and ready to assault on February 10th, and converge as the right arm of the embrace to crush the nemy back upon the Rhine at Wesel.

For two weeks, not according to plan, but according to ll probability, the 1st Canadian Army fought alone, draw-ng virtually the whole German army in the north to its hallenge. As at Caen in Normandy, again in the Reichs-ale forest, it fell to British troops to fight the second nd last of the great battles of the "hinge" and to open the ay.

From the Rhine floods in the north to the Swiss frontier ighty-five German divisions faced an equal number of llied divisions on the last battlefield in the final struggle hich was to destroy the Nazi power west of the Rhine.

This great battle for the Rhineland was the climax of a

long winter of discontent. The high hopes of the lat
summer and early autumn of 1944 had evaporated i
frustration, and through all the winter army group an
army commanders jockeyed for supplies, each one takin
advantage of every opportunity to impose, or to carr
forward, his own ideas.

The events in which they were caught up were great
than themselves.

ii.

The four months delay in the final launching of th
Rhineland battle is the measure of the remarkable re
covery of the German armies in the West and of the failur
of the Allied command to appreciate and react to th
situation in early September. On the British 21st Arm
Group front the battles of the Scheldt and Arnhem shoul
have been avoided. In the south General Patton shoul
not have been permitted to use up vast quantities of am
munition (in dangerously short supply) in abortive action
which resulted in heavy losses in men and materials with
out compelling the enemy to give ground, or to move s
much as a reserve division.

In November the Supreme Commander, General Eisen
hower, startled the Western Allies with an urgent broad
cast appeal for increased production of ammunition.

At Aachen the U.S. 1st Army was held after a penetra
tion into German territory south of the city on Septembe
13th. Even two months later the vital importance of th
whole Hürtgen Forest area was inadequately appreciated
or disregarded. Seven dams at the head of the river Roe
south of Düren in the Hürtgen Forest area controlle
160,000,000 cubic meters of water, and the Germans, i
the words of the military historian John North, could sen
"a calamitous flood cascading into the ravine-confine
Roer down to Roermond." A complete water barrie
would thereby guard the Cologne plain. The existence an
potential of these dams was no secret. It should have bee
clear to anyone that here was the vital key to any of
fensive action on the front north of the Ardennes.

As it was, through all the dismal month of November
1944, the U.S. 1st and 9th Armies battered away in mud
flood, ice and snow, and torrential rains, measuring thei
total gains in yards, and without improving their posi
tions. Unknown even to itself, the U.S. 1st Army held th

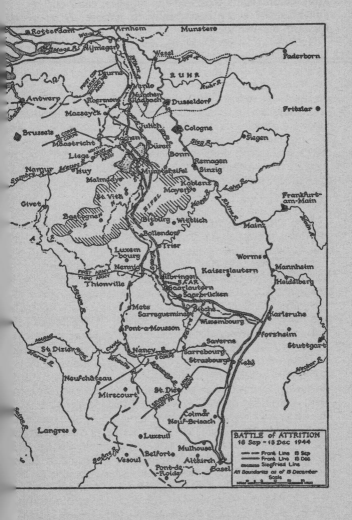

BATTLE of ATTRITION
16 Sep ~ 15 Dec 1944

Front Line 15 Sep
Front Line 15 Dec
Siegfried Line

All Boundaries as of 15 December
Scale

key to the northern Rhineland in its grasp and let it go in a
disastrous battle, badly appreciated, carelessly planned,
hopelessly organized, and almost unheard of, at a place
called Schmidt.

South of the Ardennes, the U.S. 3rd Army entangled
itself for weeks in the wilderness of Metz and its sur-
rounding fortresses, and by the end of November the
Germans, having teetered on the brink of utter defeat in
August, could claim Arnhem, the Scheldt, Aachen, and
Metz as defensive victories.

But for a continuous and sustained failure to appreciate
the extent and nature of the German recovery, the Battle
of the Ardennes might not have been launched. As it was
the Germans defeated themselves by their "all-out gam-
ble," and heavily underlined the "strategic reverse," hotly
denied by the Supreme Commander, but which had occurred through the autumn of 1944.

iii.

The whole pattern of the autumn and winter battles in
northwest Europe and all the bitter frustrations and arguments between the Allies derive from the events of the
month of August, 1944. It was then, at the moment of
seeming victory, that the unbalance in strength between
the United States and Britain began to assert an overwhelming influence upon the campaign. The immense
toll of war, long sustained, had reduced Britain to the role
of junior partner even before the production and manpower of the United States had reached their peak, and
because of that fact alone it may be that August, 1944
not only marked a vital turning point in the campaign in
northwest Europe, but also in world history.

In the midsummer of 1944, Britain, having withstood
the siege and contrived at last the springboard into Europe, lacked the power to be the architect of the victory
she had made possible. It was this fact above all that was
at once the inspiration of Montgomery's dreams of quick
victory, and the reason why they were impossible of at-
tainment. The peak of production attained in 1943 could
not be regained. The labor force was declining, and the
call-up of new age groups could no longer meet the demands of the army. It was no longer possible to do more
than make up new brigades, and it was necessary to rob
the Navy and Air Force to keep the Army going.

In March, 1944, the numbers in the field had been ared equally by Britain and the United States, but by e beginning of July the disparity had grown to forty-eight .S. divisions against thirty-eight British. Six months later e gap had widened to seventy-eight U.S. against forty-ght British.

But these difficulties were as nothing to those faced by e enemy. In June, July, and August, 1944, the Germans ad sustained the colossal total of 900,000 casualties on e Eastern front. In the West, in these same months, the nemy had lost 300,000 killed, wounded, and missing and ad been forced to man her fortresses with 230,000 of-cers and men, 85,000 of them drawn from the armies in e field. All these performed a static role until finally aptured.

The Allied achievement was in fact remarkable. Within wo weeks of August 18th the Allies had crossed the eine, cleared all northern France, Belgium, and Luxem-ourg, and advanced a full 200 miles to the German order. That was the end of possibility, for "in hardly ny respect (wrote Forrest Pogue) were the Allies pre-ared to take advantage of the great opportunity offered hem to destroy the German forces before the winter . . . irtually the whole intricate military machine was geared o a slower rate of advance than that required in late August. Unfortunately the period of the great opportunity asted only a few weeks and there was not sufficient time, owever vast the effort, to make the necessary readjust-ents in the logistical machinery which would ensure peedy victory."

But the scent of victory was overpoweringly strong for he commanders in the field. The SHAEF G-2 summary t the end of August stated: "The August battles have one it and the enemy in the West has had it. Two and a alf months of bitter fighting have brought the end of the var in Europe within sight, almost within reach." In the ollowing week the summary gave its opinion that the German army was "no longer a cohesive force, but a umber of fugitive battle groups, disorganized and even emoralized, short of equipment and arms."

One of the very few to hold a more sober and realistic iew—a view shared by the Supreme Commander—was Colonel Koch, General Patton's Chief of Intelligence. His

3rd Army G-2 estimate of August the 28th reads a
follows:

"Despite the crippling factors of shattered communica
tions, disorganization and tremendous losses in personne
and equipment, the enemy nevertheless has been able 1
maintain a sufficiently cohesive front to exercise an overa
control of his tactical situation. His withdrawal, thoug
continuing, has not been a rout or mass collapse. Numer
ous new identifications in contact in recent days hav
demonstrated clearly that, despite enormous difficultie
under which he is operating, the enemy is still capable c
bringing new elements into the battle area and transfer
ring some from other fronts.

"It is clear from all indications that the fixed determina
tion of the Nazis is to wage a last-ditch struggle in th
field at all costs. It must be constantly kept in mind tha
fundamentally the enemy is playing for time. Weathe
will soon be one of his most potent Allies as well as te
rain, as we move east to narrowing corridors . . . bu
barring internal upheaval in the homeland and the re
moter possibility of insurrection within the Wehrmacht, i
can be expected that the German armies will continue t
fight until destroyed or captured."

This magnificent piece of foresight went unheeded, ye
by the end of September the Germans had given clea
proof of their ability to continue in the fight, and winte
was fast approaching. Antwerp, the major port that migh
have spelled Germany's doom remained, lamentably, unde
German control. An army of 100,000 men, which shoul
have been trapped beyond all hope in the Pas de Calais
had made an orderly retreat, safeguarding the bulk of it
equipment and artillery, and was strongly entrenched t
deny the Scheldt estuary to the Allies for weeks. The
neck of the Beveland Isthmus was sealed, and the road t
Rotterdam closed.

In the north the enemy lay in strength along the line o
the Nederijn and Ijssel in time to deny Montgomery hi
bridgehead and his hopes of turning the Siegfried Line
The great barrier of the Maas was intact.

In the south Hitler had conceived powerful counter
attacks against the long-extended flank of the U.S. 3r
Army on the Moselle.

Eastward then lay the West Wall, the Siegfried Line, the
battles of attrition, and the long winter of discontent.

2: THE RE-APPRAISAL

i.

THE MAIN business at the Brussels conference of October 18th was to make a sober re-appraisal of the possibilities in the light of the enemy recovery. The hope of quick victory had gone. Every task all along the front from the Channel to Metz had been underestimated, and it was recognized that any major offensive must wait upon the opening of Antwerp. The effect of Antwerp could not be expected to make itself felt upon the battlefield before December, and at that time also U.S. reinforcements would be arriving. It was, therefore, Eisenhower's purpose to keep the enemy stretched as fully as possible everywhere and to prevent him from strengthening his defensive positions.

It was agreed that Field Marshal Montgomery should launch his battle of the Rhineland on November 10th, but that the effort should be subsidiary to the main thrusts of Bradley's 1st and 9th Armies aimed through the Aachen Gap on Cologne and Bonn. The 9th Army would swing northeast across the Roer upon Düsseldorf and Krefeld.

With this plan the main thrust was moved for the first time to the south of the Ruhr, and the British role would be to fight down between the rivers to link up with the Americans.

Before the plan could be implemented, the Germans counterattacking strongly, knocked the northern armies off balance at the point of contact between the British and the Americans, and the position was not restored until the end of the month. At the same time the resolute enemy defense of Aachen thwarted the hopes of the U.S. 1st Army. The city did not fall until October 21st, and this was merely the outer gateway. The "moat" of the Roer river and its great dams high in the forest country to the southeast of Aachen remained an impassable barrier.

Meanwhile General Patton, disliking a secondary role for his 3rd Army, had become understandably restless, urging Bradley to agree to full-scale attack against the Saar as soon as weather permitted. There was no possible warrant for General Bradley's agreement to Patton's demands, but he gave his agreement.

ii.

It was ironical that in the first week of November, when Montgomery had his feet firmly on the ground for the first time since August, Bradley should choose to shift the strategic center of gravity south of the Ardennes. November opened with the worst weather for fifty years all along the line, and set the tone for the winter. In the north Montgomery was able at last to gather his armies together, to regroup and to face east. All southwest Holland was clear, and the successful final assault upon Walcheren Island on November 1st promised the opening of the Port of Antwerp by the end of the month. December, therefore, might see the opening of the Rhineland battle.

But on November 8th, in appalling weather, Patton ordered Manton Eddy to attack with the U.S. 19th Corps northeast from Nancy upon the Saar line. Twenty-four hours later Walton Walker's 20th Corps moved to encircle Metz. It was not until November 23rd that Metz, a smouldering wilderness of iron and steel, which seemed to writhe under the leaden sky in a tortured Gorgonesque confusion, was finally won. The 12th Corps was less fortunate. Before them the enemy defense in depth, backed by the West Wall, absorbed their attacks, and at the end of the first week of sheer slogging misery and death a maximum of fifteen miles of ground, strategically worthless, had been won at great cost.

On the Moselle, Patton's engineers were seeing their bridges swept away by the torrential waters, and were "sitting down in the mud and bawling like babies" in General Patton's own words. The Siegfried defenses of the Saar withstood all the 3rd Army assaults until the end, and by the middle of November huge stocks of ammunition and supplies had been consumed to no purpose. The Saar offensive had failed even to force the movement of reserves away from the U.S. 1st Army front.

The Saar attack must be condemned as one of the most irresponsible actions in the campaign. The alternative to the attack north of the Ruhr could only be an attack by the U.S. 1st Army south of the Ruhr. The whole weight of the 12th Army Group resources behind the U.S. 1st Army at this time might have achieved real success, and by such a success the tempo and pattern of the campaign could have been changed.

Perhaps because of these major happenings the events of the week beginning November 2nd have escaped notice and have never been assessed in their context.

It is time to leave major strategy and to consider the impact of some of these things on the men on the battlefield. On November 2nd the 112th Regiment of the U.S. 28th Infantry Division of the U.S. 1st Army advanced in a fog of ignorance upon Schmidt, there to suffer one of the most tragic disasters ever to befall American arms.

3: SCHMIDT

i.

EARLY IN November the U. S. 1st Army planned to launch its main offensive with the 7th Corps south and southeast of Aachen upon Düren and thence across the Roer river to the Rhine at Bonn. A massive air bombardment would precede the offensive.

As a preliminary, the 5th Corps would launch a flank attack with the main purpose of protecting the flank of the 7th Corps from counterattack. The objective of the 5th Corps attack was a small town called Schmidt. From thence the intention was to drive southwestwards to take in the rear the strong enemy defenses of Monschau in conjunction with a frontal assault by the 5th Armored Division.

The task of taking Schmidt and of advancing subsequently upon Monschau was given to the U.S. 28th Infantry Division. The Division moved into the line east of Rotgen to take over from the U.S. 9th Infantry Division on October 26th. It was an unhappy experience. The 9th had had a hard time and showed it. The troops were unkempt, dirty, unshaven, and unutterably weary. Above all they showed signs of prolonged strain, dull-eyed, morose, nervous. They had been badly shaken. The sight of them had a depressing effect upon their successors, and so also had the ground. Behind them and in front of them, surrounding them on all sides, they saw dark rain-saturated forest. It had the feel of some nether region, foul with the offal of war. The broken muddied trails were pock-marked and heavily cratered by shells and mines. The splintered trees added to the sense of ruin. Rotting, sodden garments clung to hideous scraps of green flesh that yet bore an obscene resemblance to the living. Cans, helmets, boots, tools, spent cartridges, and old mines lay about in that dark and muddied confusion that only great poetry or painting may hope to convey to the uninitiated. In it there seemed the breath of despair.

The forest rose steeply to heights of more than one thousand feet, embracing closely narrow belts of open field round the villages and small townships which, here and there, lay upon the high plateaus and in the deep folds. The heavily wooded and precipitous gorges were threaded with fast-running streams and small torrents, emptying the one into the other, and many of them into the Kall River gorge, which joined its waters to the main stream of the Roer at a point some five miles due east of the American forward positions.

Such was the first prospect of the Hürtgen Forest. In the area of the U.S. 28th Division it comprised also the forests of Rotgen and Gemund, part of a thickly wooded mass of high ground extending southeast from Eschweiler to join with the Ardennes. Simply as a strip of difficult country nullifying American superiority in armor and in the air it was of great value to the enemy.

The U.S. 9th Division had breached the outer defenses of the Siegfried Line at Rotgen and had penetrated into the Hürtgen Forest proper, but by holding Aachen for a month the Germans had gained time to add to and strengthen their main belt of defenses running through the whole forest and north through Düren to Geilen-kirchen on the right flank of the British 2nd Army.

The whole forest area was thickly studded with powerful pillboxes and strong points, sown with mines and booby traps, and covered by mortar fire. Artillery, well sited on ridges both east and west of the Roer river, dominated important objectives and road junctions.

Through all October it had been the scene of bitter and desperate fighting, ending in virtual stalemate. Isolated villages had become heaps of muddied ruins, losing identity, changing hands from day to day, even from hour to hour, in that battered no-man's-land on the fringe of the German main defensive line.

The U.S. 28th Division took up its positions with its leading companies just forward of the Wittscheide-Germeter-Reichelskaul-Raffelsbrand road. The 109th Regiment on the left, the 112th Regiment in the center, and the 110th Regiment on the right. These dispositions and the roles of the regiments were dictated by 5th Corps. In the center the 112th Regiment would attack and take Schmidt. On the left the 109th Regiment would attack to the north to secure the dangerous flank and shield against the heavy counterattacks which must be expected out of the Hürtgen Forest. On the right the 110th Regiment, less one battalion held as divisional reserve, would move southeast through thick forest to seize the enemy strong point at Simonskall and secure the road from Schmidt to Strauch.

For this task the 28th Division was reinforced by battalions of tanks, self-propelled guns, 4.2-inch mortars, and an engineer combat group. Field artillery battalions of 4.5-inch, 105-mm, 155-mm, and 8-inch guns of the 5th and 7th Corps would reinforce the divisional artillery and fire the most extensive barrage the slender supplies of ammunition would allow. The attack was timed to go in on October 31st.

Appalling weather, allied to the natural difficulties of terrain and the close proximity of the enemy, inhibited patrol activity. The divisional headquarters staff studied 1:25,000 maps and disliked what they saw. Air photographs added very little to their knowledge, for the trees and the narrow gorges masked the important trails.

Immediately ahead of the 112th Regiment lay the village of Vossenach, served by a hard-surface road out of Germeter and approached over a narrow belt of open fields enclosed by the forest. Forward of the village the ridge lay bare and exposed to the enemy batteries sited on the Brandenburg-Bergstein ridge overlooking the position. No troops could be spared by the 5th Corps for an attack on the German batteries, but they would have to be neutralized.

Vossenach was the first objective of the 112th Regiment in its assault on Schmidt, and as soon as the village was taken the main assault must go through. A road ran south out of Vossenach to cross the Kall River gorge and to link the village with Kommerscheidt and Schmidt immediately beyond. A road ran north-south at the foot of the gorge, but nothing could be seen of the trail leading down the steep and thickly wooded slopes, across the Kall River and up again on the other side. But that was the only way to Kommerscheidt and Schmidt, and there could be no other until the road from Strauch might be won and opened.

The responsibility of establishing and maintaining a line of communications over the Kall River gorge would be a heavy one. It would be the one possible lifeline, the one possible channel for supplies to reach those who might get across, the one possible way of retreat. This vital task was assigned to the 20th Engineer Combat Battalion, and its grave importance emphasized.

The responsibility of 28th Division Headquarters was limited to the details of the plan, for the 5th Corps had dictated the roles of the troops, the attack missions having been dictated by the U.S. 12th Army Group and U.S. 1st Army. It had been arranged that the 9th Tactical Air Command of the 9th Air Force should isolate the battlefield, but this would be a task of great difficulty, largely governed by weather.

Fog and rain forced the postponement of the operation, but there was little margin of time to spare, and on the cold and misty morning of November 2nd the leading troops of the 28th Division, in a state of innocence most terrible to contemplate, and beset by vague fears, advanced out of its positions under fire.

Even with his very limited knowledge of the battlefield, and in profound ignorance of the true position, Major General Norman D. Cota, commanding the 28th Division, considered that the operation had no more than "a gambler's chance." In fact, it had no chance at all.

ii.

The township of Schmidt lies within one mile of the great Schwammenauel dam, the principal dam controlling the flood waters of the Roer river. This was the most vital and sensitive point in the German defenses over the whole front from the Swiss border to the North Sea. While the dam remained under German control, troops crossing the Roer could be isolated piecemeal and destroyed. A wall of water could be sent roaring down the river to wash away all bridges, and render the river impassable for some days. In the event of threatened disaster the Germans could release an immense torrent to flood the whole Cologne plain, thereby meeting disaster with disaster. The Schwammenauel dam was therefore the essential—and obvious—pre-requisite to the offensive of the U.S. 1st and 9th Armies.

The great importance of the strongly held enemy pocket of the Maas at Venloe and in the Roermond-Heinsberg triangle is evident, and easily understood, in relation to Schmidt, for it is at this point that the effective defensive potential of the Roer comes to an end. It is the second gateway to force in order to open the way for the battle of Rhineland.

All this topography had been the subject of intensive scrutiny over many weeks, yet the 112th Regiment launched its attack on November 2nd without any knowledge of the Roer dams. Colonel Carl I. Peterson, commanding the regiment, stated categorically that the "Roer dams never entered the picture." It is equally certain that all his battalion commanders were equally unaware.*

This is a startling fact, yet it is even more startling that the dams are not mentioned in 5th Corps orders or in 28th Division orders for the battle. The intelligence estimate of 28th Division reveals no awareness of the real importance of Schmidt "fundamental in the German scheme for preventing an Allied break-through to the Rhine."

In a footnote to *Objective: Schmidt* Charles B. MacDonald comments, "Just when the American command fully realized the importance of the dams is not clear." But in the U.S. 1st Army operational report covering the period August, 1944, to February, 1945, there is a passage referring to a plan by 5th Corps "to seize the two large dams on the Roer river."

Throughout all October the enemy had reacted with the utmost violence to all attacks in the sensitive Hürtgen

---

*It is probable that no single action in the history of war has been subjected to an investigation as thorough and meticulous as that which followed the battle of Schmidt. Almost every survivor from generals to G.I.'s was interviewed and carefully questioned. The war diaries and intelligence summaries of 12th Army Group, 1st Army, 5th Corps, 28th Division, of the regiments and all supporting arms and services involved have been carefully examined.

See: *THREE BATTLES*, Office of the Chief of Military History. Dept. of the Army, Washington, D.C.

Forest area, immediately to the north, and had observed all allied dispositions and troop movements in the Rotgen area with great care. The arrival of the 28th Division had been noted, and the expected attack had been confirmed to the enemy by U.S. artillery preparation. The Germans believed that the attack could have no other purpose but the taking of the dams.

In those few days between the arrival of the 28th Division and its attack on Schmidt the position had taken on an even greater importance for the enemy. It was not only the linchpin of the Rhineland defenses, it had become also the vital point on the northern flank of Hitler's planned offensive to drive through the Ardennes, to cross the Meuse, and thence on to Brussels and Antwerp. With the defenses of Schmidt and Monschau in allied hands, such an attack would be prejudiced before it began. At that stage also the dislike of von Runstedt and von Manteuffel for the Ardennes plan had led them to suggest an alternative which would involve pinching out the Americans in the whole Aachen salient. This secondary plan enhanced the value of Schmidt.

The Allies knew nothing of these things at the end of October, but they did know—or they should have known —everything about the Roer dams.

iii.

The morning of November 2nd dawned cold and clammy with mist under a dirty sky like the inside of a rough iron casting. There might be snow, or sleet, or bitter cold rain. The temperature was within a degree or two of freezing point. The woods were thick with mist, curling round the trees, hanging heavily. At eight o'clock the whole of the 5th Corps front erupted with the stabbing flame and thunder of guns, and the men of the 28th Division lay under that harsh turbulence, waiting and listening. Shortly before nine o'clock the barrage came down on close targets, and the change in the pattern registered instantly in the ears. There were fifteen minutes to zero.

In the hours before dawn, engineers had cleared lanes through their own defensive minefields. At nine o'clock the 2nd Battalion of the 112th Regiment began to advance out of its outposts and into the wilderness of mist and smoke. On their left and right the 109th and 110th

egiments were going into action on the flanks, but in
e center the 2nd Battalion moved out alone to prepare
e way for the main attack of the regiment. Most of
em did not know this; many of them did not know
eir regiment; too many had been rejected a year before
s unfit for "combat" service. They went into battle.
even tanks supported the left-hand company, and three
nks moved forward with the right-hand company. The
enter company would move up as soon as the right flank-
g company had cleared a distance of three hundred
ards, and mop up the little township of Vossenach
hich lay dead ahead. The gaunt skeleton of the church
teeple stood up above the tower out of the mist. The
1ap showed that it stood at the crossroads, facing west,
 massive bastion barring the way to the main street of
Vossenach.

The men moved close up behind the tanks, keeping in
heir tracks for safety against mines. But safety was gone.
Jpon the instant, as the barrage lifted, the enemy artil-
ery came down upon the forward positions all along the
ine, accurate and deadly, killing and maiming men as
hey rose up from cover to go forward.

On the left, the lanes through the minefields were
oorly marked, and at the outset one of the tanks leading
G Company hit a mine and lost a track. Almost at once
 second tank bogged down. The going was bad, soft and
ludgy in patches over open fields. The command tank
noved forward to take the lead. The five remaining tanks
vent on steadily, shielding the riflemen, firing steadily and
oncentrating on the tower of Vossenach church. The
ire of supporting machine guns crashed into the fringe of
he woods to the north. 81-mm. mortars put down a
:reeping curtain of high explosive one hundred yards
ahead.

The enemy in Vossenach had sustained an immense
veight of artillery fire, but had not been silenced. Mor-
ars, automatic weapons and small-arms fire sought out
he men as they moved through the minefield. The short
lelays at the loss of the tanks had been costly. One man
tepped on a booby trap, and a second, moving to pick
im up, stepped on another, touching off a chain of five
nti-personnel mines. Twelve men of the headquarter
group were killed or wounded in the minefield within four
aundred yards of the start. The leaders of the machine-

gun platoon were casualties. The riflemen paid a stead
toll, but the attack went doggedly on.

Sergeants took over as lieutenants fell; corporals le
in place of sergeants. There was no cover, but after it
initial difficulties G Company made good progress, ha
assed by enemy artillery, mortar and small-arms fire. It
role was to skirt the township of Vossenach and to tak
up positions on the bald nose of the ridge forward an
close up to the forest line.

On the right F Company had a more complex rol
Advancing astride the Richelskaul-Vossenach road,
met direct enemy resistance from machine gun posts an
anti-tank guns. The bulk of the enemy had withdraw
from Vossenach, but strong pockets remained, ready t
hold their fire, to let the leading platoon pass, and t
take those who followed by surprise. Nevertheless by earl
afternoon F Company occupied most of the townshi
and had established itself at the eastern end. The men c
G Company no longer felt so alone in their foxholes o
the bare eastern ridge.

By three-thirty in the afternoon the mopping-up com
pany had come up through the center of Vossenach
blasting small groups of enemy out of houses with gre
nades, and consolidating the gains of F Company. But i
its experiences there had been ominous undertones. Th
Company had met with delay at the outset, owing to th
failure of F Company's reserve platoon to move out. Th
platoon had not been called upon, and awaited orders
The mopping-up company had assembled too soon, an
in those minutes of doubt on the start line the men stoo
exposed to the enemy artillery fire, and suffered casualties

The main body of the company then moved forwar
behind a platoon of tanks and with an attached sectio
of machine guns. The 1st platoon, with the role of pro
tecting the right flank, got away well in advance of th
main body, but took the wrong line out of Richelskau
and came at once under heavy machine-gun fire from th
forward edge of the woods to the south. Enemy mortar
at once concentrated on the men where they lay. Brav
individual attempts to go forward in rushes failed. Finall
the few survivors managed to withdraw, and to go int
Vossenach behind their company.

Nevertheless this opening phase of the action designe
to clear the way for the main attack of the 28th Divisio

ainst Kommerscheidt and Schmidt, had progressed
iftly and successfully, despite severe casualties. With
ossenach held, the northern flank was secure and the
immediate route opened to the crossing of the Kall River
rge.

At noon, H-plus-three hours, the 1st and 3rd Battal-
ns mounted the main attack of the 112th Regiment, the
t Battalion leading in column of companies to cross the
all River gorge and seize Kommerscheidt, the 3rd Battal-
n to pass through and take Schmidt. Both battalions
ould then prepare to attack towards Steckenborn and
rauch. Schmidt was the objective, not the object.

The 1st Battalion advanced out of Richelskaul on time,
tending to take a line through the wooded slopes to the
uth of Vossenach. A rough track leads out of the vil-
ge to join with the Simonskall road at a point about one
arter of a mile out of Richelskaul. At that point the
ading platoon ran head on into concentrated fire from
tomatic weapons and small arms, losing its platoon
ommander. It went no further. A concentration of fire
om the 81-mm. mortars failed to dislodge the enemy.
second platoon tried to move forward and failed de-
ite brave efforts by its severely wounded platoon com-
ander.

No other company was committed, and the main at-
ck was called off. Under cover of darkness the com-
any withdrew.

The attacks of the 109th and 110th Regiments on the
anks had also failed. The 109th, with the role of gaining
start line for an attack against Hürtgen and of protect-
g the northern flank, was halted mainly by minefields
ithin five hundred yards, and there finally "holed in" for
e night. The 110th came up against the powerful pill-
ox and concrete defenses built into the hillsides, cover-
g the vital area of Steckenborn and the rear of Mon-
hau. The 110th Regiment suffered heavy casualties. No
rogress was made towards the Schmidt-Strauch road.

The attack of the 28th Division on this opening and
ital day "had been pushed with a surprising lack of
igor . . . it had set back considerably the hour by which
chmidt might be taken."*

The weather had greatly hampered the hoped-for air

*Objective: Schmidt, Charles B. Macdonald.

support, but this failure could not have attributed to th
failure of the 28th Division to press home its main a
tack. The first aircraft were unable to leave the groun
until well after noon. Only one mission out of five su
ceeded, fighter bombers attacking the Bergstein ridge an
targets on the Roer. One squadron bombed U.S. artiller
at Rotgen causing twenty-four casualties, including seve
killed.

The night of November 2nd was quiet and bitter col

iv.

The 112th Regiment revised its plan of attack durin
the night, and at seven o'clock in the morning the 3r
Battalion moved out of Germeter in a column of com
panies into Vossenach. On the right the company of th
1st Battalion, which had bloodied its nose on the enem
strong point athwart the original line through the wood
put in a diversionary attack, hoping to mask the new lin
of approach. The 1st Battalion attack was timed to cor
form with the progress of the leading battalion.

Sunrise was at thirty-two minutes past seven that morn
ing, but the event had long since lost its happy promise
At seven o'clock it was still dark, even in the east. Th
night mist was heavy, indistinguishable from drizzlin
rain, seeping steadily through clothing to chill the bone
Again the temperature was a degree or two above free
ing.

Behind the lines in Germeter, Reichelskaul, Wit
scheide, stoves were roaring, and cooks were boiling u
coffee. That was another world.

The men strung out at five-yard intervals, companie
staggered three hundred yards apart, signal, machine-gu
and headquarters jeeps keeping position, the thin ste
rods of their aerials curving like slender masts, the a
tennas of the troops' radio sets squawking with muffle
voices. Supporting tanks and heavy vehicles churned th
sodden earth to a morass.

Except for intermittent, harassing fire, the artillery wa
silent, so that the noises of men and vehicles on th
move over the sludgy ground, the dull clank of arms an
equipment, and the squelch of feet became predominan
The enemy guns were silent. They had been silen
through most of the night.

At half past seven o'clock the leading company of th

d Battalion reached the road junction at Vossenach
hurch, and prepared at once to move out south on the
all River trail to the woods. One company of support-
g tanks moved forward to the bare ridge where the ad-
ance company of the 2nd Battalion had watched out the
ght, huddled in their foxholes and miserably cold.

The first platoon of tanks reached its position safely,
ut the leading tank of the second platoon struck a mine
ree hundred yards east of Vossenach Church. It seemed
o spark off a chain explosion, for almost at that precise
oment the enemy guns opened up from the Branden-
urg-Bergstein ridge to bring down a fierce concentration
f fire upon the battalion assembly point, forcing the men
o scatter for cover. The armor moving into position
pened fire on the woodland line to the southeast.

The enemy fire lifted as suddenly as it had begun, and
e leading company of the 3rd Battalion assembled
viftly and moved off sharply to gain the woods. The sky
ooked like mud. The saturating mist lay in the trees as
hick as wool. Sporadic fire came down upon the men in
e open, but they moved steadily on into the woods,
ver the rough Kall trail, slithering down, slipping on the
utcropping rocks. Their supporting tanks lifted their fire
o concentrate with their hull guns on Kommerscheidt
cross the gorge.

Harassed constantly by tree bursts the leading com-
any negotiated the steep trail. Snipers caught the signal
ne-layers, and brought death to stragglers. The forward
couts met a small enemy pocket at the Kall River cross-
ig, and blasted it out of the way. At nine o'clock the
orward platoon of the 3rd Battalion forded the river at
 point to the south of a water mill, Mestrenger Muhle.
here was a stone bridge, probably capable of bearing
anks. The bridge must be tested by the engineers. The
rater was icy cold, but safer. The bottom was hard rock.

It is a steep climb up to the crest of the Kommer-
cheidt ridge, yet the ridge is lower than the high point
outhwest of Schmidt itself. The men went up the trail in
ilence, saving their breath, listening to the gunfire of their
upporting tanks fluffing overhead from Vossenach.

When they reached the ridge and came out of the
voods, they saw their shells falling on Kommerscheidt.
A short burst of small-arms fire challenged them across
he open fields in front of the township, but the scouts

deployed, moving fast at the double. The tank fire lifted
and within half an hour the leading company of the 31
Battalion was in Kommerscheidt, almost unopposed.

Schmidt sprawled on the eastern slopes a thousand
yards ahead, and to the forward company it appeared to
hold little of menace. They could see the houses strag
gling along the Harscheidt road to the east, and the Has
enfeld road to the south. A small group of cottages lay
between them and their objective at a curve of the di
road. The dark woods enclosed the broad, high clearing
on all sides with narrow spears and bulges of woodland
thrusting inwards marking the re-entrants.

On the left the 2nd Company of the battalion was at
ready in position, having crossed the Kall River gorge a
a point some three hundred yards north of the stor
bridge. Keeping pace with the leading company, it ha
come into Kommerscheidt from the east. The third com
pany had also made good progress. At noon the 1st Ba
talion had moved out of Germeter to follow up throug
Vossenach and over the trail.

All companies and supporting arms, especially movin
out of Vossenach, had sustained casualties from enem
shelling and mortaring. Tree bursts continued over th
trail all day, and the woods had an ominous feel. An oc
casional sniper's bullet testified to the eyes of the enem
That was all.

A heavy concentration of enemy artillery forced th
leading company to take cover as it prepared to mov
out of Kommerscheidt, warning them that their presenc
was known. An hour later Schmidt was taken. A score o
so of enemy had been surprised, some eating and drink
ing, one or two riding bicycles casually down the mai
street, apparently unaware of danger threatening. A fe
shots came out of isolated houses and were quickly stilled
A machine gun opened fire from a small group of house
along the Hasenfeld road. By dusk the battalion had o
ganized all round defense for the night. There had bee
too little time, but they had done the best they coul
Mines had been placed out on the roads in full view, b
covered by bazookas. The mortar men and the machin
gunners, toiling along the trail, under their heavy wea
ons, had had an exhausting day. It was dark before the
could set up their weapons.

The 1st Battalion in Kommerscheidt gave a solid fee

g to their backs. Along the Kall trail a battalion of en-
neers would be working against time all through the
ight to open a supply route from Germeter through
ossenach to Schmidt. Above all it was vital to move
rmor over that steep and narrow trail.

Long after dusk, machine gunners and mortar men
ontinued to lug their heavy weapons forward to the
.ommerscheidt-Schmidt ridge to wait for the dawn.

v.

The difficulties and extreme vulnerability of the Kall
River gorge had not been sufficiently appreciated. In the
.lanning phases of the action the opening, maintenance
nd defense of the supply route, had been allotted to the
.ngineer Combat Group, and the security emphasized.
3ut the emphasis had been lost in the break-down of the
.lan. The engineer plan, issued on October 30th, failed
o allot the defense precautions to any of its units and
nerely observed that *local* security would be required.
.he plan with this wording was seen and approved by
.8th Division. The 20th Engineer Combat Battalion went
o its task of opening up and maintaining the trail, un-
.ware that it needed to do more than keep a sharp look-
ut. North and south along the main gorge road, and
hrough all the thick woods, the enemy could move at will.

Through that first night of intense and ferocious en-
leavor, with jeeps, weasels, trailers, slewing, slithering
ff the trail, with medical officers, supply officers, and
nany others striving to reconnoitre routes for their ve-
.icles and services, the work of three men in particular
vas outstanding. These were Lieutenant Muglia, a med-
:al officer, Lieutenant William George, the 3rd Battalion
.otor officer, and Lieutenant Raymond Fleig, a tank
latoon commander. The names of these three men weave
 bold and coherent pattern through seven days and
ights of growing disaster. They are not only brave, but
:sourceful and tireless. In all the broken strands these
.ree strands hold.

Muglia had gone ahead with the leading troops, and
ad found a dug-out built into the rock and reinforced
ith logs. There he gathered medical supplies and es-
.blished his main aid station on the trail.

By midnight on the night of the 3rd-4th, Lieutenant
.eorge had wrestled a supply train of three weasels over

the trail, and dumped the stores safely in Kommerscheid
He had then made the return journey with wounded, an
again returned with anti-tank ammunition. By then it wa
nearing dawn, and armor blocked the trail.

The task of coaxing Sherman tanks over the Kall tra
cannot be exaggerated. It would have been dismissed a
impossible by many, but it had to be possible. The trac
was nine feet wide, a shelving out of the rock wall an
with open shoulders from which the woods fell awa
steeply. Rocks outcropped in dangerous patches, a men
ace above all to armor, which could easily belly dow
upon them. Hairpin bends turned angles of 180 degree
and were too shallow even for weasels to turn withou
shunting. Trailers had to be manhandled. At such point
the rock wall bulged to lessen the usable width of th
trail. In places it was precipitous. It was mined
booby-trapped, sniped, and shelled constantly with tre
bursts.

At dusk on the afternoon of the 3rd two tank captain
went forward to make a reconnaissance. At one point
weasel blocked the trail. This was Lieutenant Muglia'
weasel. He had been forced to abandon the vehicle an
carry his medical supplies forward with the help of his or
derly. Engineers were getting down to hard labor, sweepin
for mines, assembling tools, and trying to blast away th
rock bulges with German Teller mines. The trail wa
the exact width of a Sherman tank, with not an inch t
spare. Wherever the rock wall bulged even slightly th
heavy armored vehicles would be forced out on the ope
shoulder.

Mines and shell fire had accounted for three tanks ou
of sixteen in Vossenach during the day, and the remain
ing thirteen of the company assembled ready to attemp
the crossing of the Kall. Their presence had given som
comfort to the riflemen on Vossenach ridge, but no
much. The men had found that any attempt to leave thei
foxholes in the hours of daylight brought down heav
concentrations of fire upon them. They were cramped
The damp cold gripped their bones. They lay sleepless,
few dozing fitfully but without rest through the secon
night, awaiting their third day.

In contrast, across the Kall gorge, the men of the 3r
Battalion in Schmidt were in good spirits, buoyant afte
their easy victory, confident of success.

Soon after midnight Lieutenant Fleig led his platoon of Sherman tanks onto the trail. His tank hit a mine missed by the engineers in the first two hundred yards, and blew a track. Using the towing cable of the damaged tank, and the tank itself as a pivot the platoon sergeant, Spooner, contrived to winch his tank round Fleig's and winch it back again onto the trail. The armor was blocking the life line, and he was deeply aware of it, yet a moment of impatience might have cost hours and brought disaster. Behind them enemy shelling was making it uncomfortable for all those who waited.

As soon as the platoon sergeant's tank was well on the trail, Lieutenant Fleig took over and went on. He had a picture of men without armor in his mind, and he was resolved to beat the dawn. Behind him on the trail the tank crews winched, towed, side-slipped off the crumbling shoulder, lost tracks, refitted, and fought their way by inches down to the gorge, and all the cavalcade piling up through Vossenach into Germeter, the signal wires and all the air sizzling with urgency.

Fleig went steadily on, talking to his driver softly, guiding, never faltering. He knew that his outer track was crumbling the open shoulder, but he judged vehicles would manage. In any case he had to get through. The stone bridge across the river was sound. Fleig coaxed his driver, and the heavy vehicle, rocking blind up and down switchbacks, moved on. As the first light came into the leaden sky, Fleig's Sherman roared up over the last ridge into Kommerscheidt. At that precise moment a hail of enemy shell fire hit Schmidt, crashing into the American positions, traversing the town from end to end, weaving a pattern of fire from which it seemed there could be no escape.

Communications were already bad, and they swiftly became worse. Enemy shell fire constantly clipped the signal wires back from Vossenach to Germeter. Communications were also bad forward. The companies in Schmidt kept contact with their perimeter defense platoons by runners, but runners had very short lives.

In the fringes of the woodland the men in the forward foxholes thought they saw movement, the milling of many men, preparing to attack. They were sitting athwart the enemy's main line of communications to his powerful defenses at Steckenborn and behind Monschau. Knowing as little as they did about Schmidt, the battalion commanders and company commanders knew that, and it seemed to them enough. No man doubted that the enemy shelling heralded the assault.

As the dawn broke the 3rd Battalion in Schmidt braced itself for battle while behind them over the Kall River trail two tanks of Lieutenant Fleig's platoon were steadily gaining ground, and a host of men toiled without rest to keep the pulse of supplies beating. Far behind on the trail the second platoon of armor met Fleig's abandoned tank on the trail. Believing that the tank must have been by-passed, and not realizing that the leading platoon had winched its tanks, the second platoon slid off the trail. Enemy shelling killed the men as they left the leading tank to investigate. Five tanks in all were disabled on the trail, and behind them four others waited, unable to move.

4: COUNTER-ATTACK

i.

THE NEWS of the advance on Vossenach and the start of an attack by the U.S. 28th Division, was brought to the notice of Field Marshal Model, commanding *Army Group B,* while in the course of a "map study" conference with his commanders at Schlenderhan Castle, near Quadrath on the Urft. The Commander of the German *74th Corps* returned at once to his command while the U.S. attack and its probable developments became the subject of study for the generals. A real problem had fortuitously replaced a hypothetical one.

The task of appreciating the U.S. intention appeared to present little difficulty. The intention must be to take the Schwammenauel dam, to open the way for an offensive across the Roer into the Cologne plain, and to outflank and cut the communications of the Monschau-Steckenborn defenses. None of this could be tolerated.

The U.S. attack was expected, but in the early stages the method was obscure. Nor did it become less obscure at any time. With ample forces at his disposal the enemy awaited developments before committing his main striking power to counterattack.

The *275th Infantry Division* was responsible for the defense of the Hürtgen area, with the *12th Volks-Grenadier Division* on its right, and the *89th Infantry Division* on the left. The presence of Field Marshal Model at the map conference probably accelerated the movement of a Kampgruffe of the *116th Panzer Division* from *Army Group B* reserve near München Gladbach.

The German principal intention, which was to remain throughout, was to pinch off the U.S. attack along the base line, the Hürtgen-Germeter road. For this reason the attack of the 109th Regiment on the American left towards Hürtgen was at once held, while the Vossenach attack and its later developments were followed closely.

The weather favored the enemy, and unless an unlooked-for break occurred, U.S. air power would be unable to exert a major influence. The whole area of Vossenach, Kall River, Schmidt lay under the German guns.

Holding both ends of the north-south Kall gorge road, with many concealed positions in the woods lining the gorge, and with powerful defenses covering Steckenborn and Strauch, the enemy's first task was to hold the flank attacks and to observe the 112th Regiment as it climbed steadily out onto the long slender limb, from which it appeared there could be no going forward and no going back. It was obvious that unless powerful forces could be brought in behind the 112th Regiment no further advance could be made, and yet there was no road sufficient for such forces, nor did they appear to be available.

It was impossible for the enemy to grasp the purpose of the 3rd Battalion, isolated in Schmidt, without armor, with a line of communications that was at best precarious in the extreme. Indeed, if things were as they seemed, the enemy did not doubt his ability to cut the Kall trail, annihilate the engineer groups working there, and deal with the forces in Schmidt and Kommerscheidt at will.

Even if the Germans had realized the failure of the U.S. command to grasp the obvious importance of the Roer dams, it would still have been difficult to understand the tactics of the 28th Division. General Cota himself, commanding the 28th Division, knew that he could not possibly move his battalions out of Schmidt and Kom-

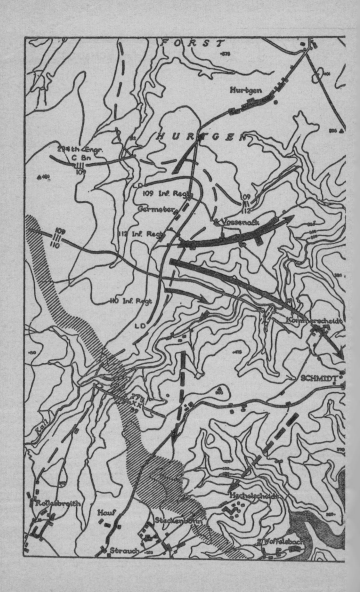

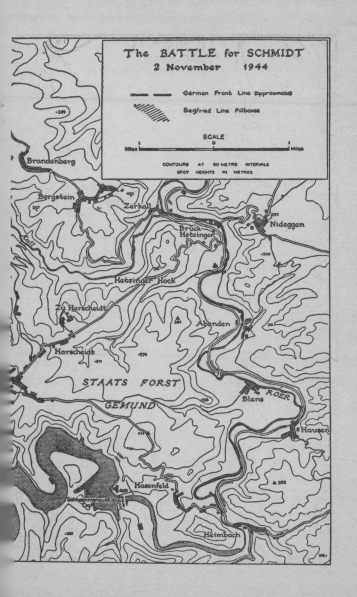

The BATTLE for SCHMIDT
2 November 1944

German Front Line (approximate)

Siegfried Line Pillboxes

SCALE

Miles   0   Miles

CONTOURS AT 50 METRE INTERVALS
SPOT HEIGHTS IN METRES

Brandenberg

Bergstein

Zerkall

Brück
Hetzingen

Nideggen

Hetzinger Hock

Zu Harscheidt

Abenden

Harscheidt

STAATS FORST

ROER

GEMUND

Blens

Hausen

Hasenfeld

Schwammenauel

Heimbach

merscheidt, either towards Strauch-Steckenborn, or anywhere else, without strong support. If he moved forward,
Schmidt and Kommerscheidt would be empty, the rear
would be wide open. Of his ability to remain in Schmidt
and Kommerscheidt he was soon in little doubt.

But in the German mind many possibilities could not
be too swiftly discarded. The development of a powerful
U.S. attack against the Brandenburg-Bergstein ridge
must be expected; and whatever the appearances, the
Roer dams must be the target. It was enough, therefore,
in the early stages to hold the flank attacks of the 109th
and 110th Regiments, to watch and wait, and to harass
incessantly with shell fire.

The forward companies of the 2nd Battalion on the exposed Vossenach ridge were a sitting target, whose least
movement might be observed. German patrols in the Kall
gorge woods watched constantly alert for any development
of a major threat, while their artillery and mortars made
the narrow trail deadly. The lack of defensive developments in the Kall gorge was bewildering, for unless the Kall
trail was secured there could be no hope for the battalions
in Schmidt and Kommerscheidt. Indeed, even in terms of
a reconnaissance in strength, an attempt to probe the
dam defenses prior to a major attack, or a feint to mask
an alternative approach, it was impossible in enemy eyes
to see any sane meaning in the remarkable situation.

But the presence of U.S. troops in Schmidt, even if it
could not be understood, could not be tolerated. The rest,
even Kommerscheidt, could wait.

ii.

It seemed to the men of the 3rd Battalion manning their
perimeter defensive positions at Schmidt that the enemy
shellfire burst upon them from all sides and from all
angles with less warning than the fall of an avalanche. In
fact, the shelling came in from three sides. As the sky
slowly lightened to the dirty brown of a new day, the men
forward, covering the Hasenfeld, Harscheidt and Strauch
roads with bazookas, felt as naked and exposed as their
mines, outcropping on the roads in full view.

As the morning barrage lifted, small groups of enemy
infantry burst from cover and raced across open ground
to gain the shelter of houses. A machine gun suddenly
opened fire from a building less than fifty yards from the

orward foxholes on the southeast, and at that Sergeant Ripperdam charged with two other men.

The enemy attack developed slowly, almost tentatively. A small group of infantry were seen advancing from the direction of Harscheidt, a large group appeared from the direction of Hasenfeld. The forward platoons of the 3rd Battalion met them with bursts of automatic fire, but all at once enemy infantry, gray in the gray-brown light, oozed towards Schmidt like an enveloping blanket, coming in from all sides save only the north, the road back to Kommerscheidt.

For nearly an hour the harsh din of machine guns, small arms, and mortars emptied out of the smoking ruins of Schmidt, and into it, so that all the high open ground held within the dark belt of woods had become a chaos of smoke and flame through which men moved, stumbled, screamed, cursed, and died like shadows under a lowering crimson lid of sky.

At ten minutes to nine o'clock corps and divisional artillery answered the urgent calls for fire from the hard pressed battalion, and for nearly half an hour the gray, encroaching blanket of enemy was held. Then suddenly a new and ominous note came to the ears of those still manning the foxholes forward on the road verges. From Hasenfeld and from Harscheidt the rumbling of armor grew to a dull roar as enemy Mark IV and Mark V tanks led columns of infantry. The armor came on steadily, five tanks leading from Harscheidt and five from Hasenfeld, raking the American defenses with fire, moving off the roads to avoid the mines so hastily and uselessly laid.

A direct hit on the lead tank from a bazooka on the Hasenfeld road made the tank swerve momentarily at the shock, but it came on. Those forward were unnerved. The 3rd Battalion began to break, slowly at first round the edges. Here and there men began to run, infecting others. Officers and N.C.O.'s roared orders, striving at first to halt the men, and then, when that was hopeless, to direct orderly withdrawal into Schmidt. Many ran for the woods and into the arms of the enemy. Those who were holding saw others breaking on their flanks.

Captain Rokey, a company commander, one of the first to sight the enemy, Sergeant Ripperdam, who had charged the enemy machine gun position, and others fought to rally men to their sides, but the tide was rising to the flood. In the northern outskirts of Schmidt the 81-mm. mortars were still firing. Machine gunners still manned their weapons. But there was nothing now to halt the enemy infiltrating into Schmidt in the wake of their armor.

Two company headquarter groups formed a line at the heart of the smoking wilderness of Schmidt, but nothing could stand against the confusion of fear that had gripped the 3rd Battalion. A single cry of withdraw from any mouth was enough to send those who faltered streaming back. The cries passed from mouth to mouth, withdraw, withdraw! "The word spread quickly, and none questioned its source."*

By ten o'clock Schmidt "with or without orders" was being abandoned. Only a handful of medical men remained, striving to ease the wounded. The dead lay where they had fallen.

At that hour a junior staff officer reached Kommerscheidt on his way to Schmidt with a regimental order to the 3rd Battalion to hold temporarily in Schmidt while the 110th Infantry Regiment continued its assault on the flanks. The staff officer was in time to see the first stragglers running back with shouts of "They're throwing everything they've got at us."

iii.

From the moment of Lieutenant Fleig's arrival in his Sherman tank the 1st Battalion in Kommerscheidt had been under light artillery and mortar fire. The din of war enveloping Schmidt was ominous, warning of danger imminent. Urgently the officers of the 1st Battalion looked to their defenses, and prayed for more armor. By midmorning the frightened stragglers coming back from Schmidt in ones and twos had grown to the proportions of "a demoralized mob," impervious to orders, appeals, threats.

Here and there in that disorderly stream officers and N.C.O.'s, tossed about like driftwood, fought to halt the flight, to find men steady enough to form groups to strengthen the 1st Battalion for the impending ordeal.

Sergeant Ripperdam had built a group of twenty-six men round his own indomitable figure, and with these he

*Quotes are from *Objective: Schmidt*, U.S. Army in World War II. Dept. of the Army, Washington, D.C.

took up a position to the northwest of Kommerscheidt, there to be joined by a small group from 3rd Battalion headquarters. Two company commanders had salvaged each a handful of men and three machine guns. In the woods a platoon commander organized two under strength platoons from the remnants of a company. If it would not go forward, at least it might rally to fight on the Kall trail.

The Kall trail was thick with men, each one carrying his burden of fear, resolved only on getting back along the trail through Vossenach and into Germeter. In the final count, less than one hundred men out of a battalion rallied to fight with the 1st Battalion.

All of this was no more than a confused blur in regimental headquarters and division remained totally unaware of impending disaster. Only communications with artillery seemed to be effective, for the American guns were giving more and better support as the day progressed, harassing the Germans regrouping in Schmidt almost as much as the enemy was harassing the 1st Battalion and the remnant of the 3rd in Kommerscheidt.

To Lieutenant Fleig, joined by mid-morning by two of his sergeants with their tanks, and maneuvering carefully to discover points of vantage for his small armored force, things looked very dirty, but the feel of battle stimulated him. Schmidt lay on a ridge commanding Kommerscheidt, and the enemy armor could dominate the American positions. It did not daunt Fleig.

At half past twelve o'clock P-47's swooped down upon Schmidt and came in bombing so close to Kommerscheidt that the defenders put out identification symbols. It was not until two o'clock in the afternoon that five German Panther tanks* led a group of infantry in not more than company strength from a bulge of the woods to the east. At once the American field artillery answered the radio calls of the 1st Battalion with accurate fire. Forward, Fleig led his three Shermans to a slight rise in the ground and opened fire, stopping two enemy tanks with his opening rounds. A few minutes later, maneuvering his tank to a new position to give heart to the defenders on the flank, Fleig saw a Panther approaching obliquely at a dis-

*Survivors state definitely that Tiger tanks came against them, but there were no Tiger tanks on the strength of *116 Panzer Division* at that time.

tance of two hundred yards. Opening fire at once he hit
the enemy twice with high explosive, but without notice-
able effect. He realized than that all his armor-piercing
ammunition was in the sponson rack. Scoring another
direct hit with high explosive, Fleig saw the German crew
leaving their tank, probably fearing a blow-up. Taking his
chance he leapt out of his Sherman with his gunner, re-
trieved the armor-piercing shells under heavy fire, and
regained his tank almost at the same moment as the enemy
regained theirs. Fleig's first round cut the barrel of the
Panther's gun, and his next tore through the hull. Two
more rounds sent up a great billow of black smoke to
mark the end.

Through all that day of November 4th, and again
through repeated attacks on the 5th and 6th, the 1st Battalion held on desperately in Kommerscheidt. Engineers,
tanks, tank destroyers, medical men, and supply columns
battled incessantly along the Kall trail, constantly infiltrated by enemy, incessantly harassed by mortars, shell
fire, and machine guns. By nightfall on November 6th
the Kall trail was virtually in enemy control, and at least
one company of combat engineers had been annihilated.

The almost total lack of security precautions caused
anxiety to the enemy, just as an open door might cause a
burglar to feel suspicion and to proceed warily. Constantly ambushed—at times whole squads of men were wiped
out by bursts of fire—the Americans simply continued
doggedly to try to force their way through and back. The
medical men worked on, Lieutenant Muglia among
them, organizing, tending, and evacuating the wounded
from the log-cabin dug-out, ignoring the enemy, heedless
of everything except their mission. Even when Muglia
found German sentries guarding his dug-out he paid no
heed, for at times they were there, and at times they
were not, in that strange confused struggle on the Kall
Gorge trail.

Among those who knew exactly what they were doing
and why was Lieutenant George, fighting his way
through with supply trains alongside others who pressed
grimly forward through the tattered ranks of those who
floundered back.

iv.

On the morning of November 5th it was clear to com-many commanders and N.C.O.'s in Vossenach that their position was critical. The men had stood up badly to the enemy shelling. One company commander stated that all his men should be evacuated as unfit to carry on. The battalion commander was himself a virtual casualty with "combat exhaustion." Indeed, combat exhaustion was spreading through the battalion, a blight, a canker, gnawing away at the human spirit.

On the morning of the 5th platoon commanders and N.C.O.'s tried to force many of their men to eat, to take notice. But for the shelling there was no visible enemy movement, no signs of attack.

By that time the 112th Regiment had become little more than a collection of isolated groups without cohesion and almost entirely lacking in effective communications. Even the 2nd Battalion in Vossenach was out of touch with its regimental headquarters.

At dusk on the evening of November 5th, a sudden burst of enemy shelling killed six men of G Company in their foxholes on the ridge, and at once set off a reaction that grew, slowly at first, to become an enveloping wave of fear. Ignoring the orders, and all the efforts of their officers, men got up, many weeping, and stumbled from their positions back to the shelter of the houses of Vossenach.

Company commanders urgently reported the situation to battalion, battalion reported to regiment, but there was no relief. The situation report of the 112th Regiment for that day reported the "combat condition" of its entire command as "excellent." Yet a colonel of engineers, returning from a mission on the Kall trail, was "so concerned" at the state of affairs in Vossenach that he reported it personally to regimental rear headquarters.*

On that day the commanders of the U.S. 1st Army and the 5th Corps visited General Cota at 28th Division Headquarters. Their ignorance of the true position remained profound. It was the eve of the last phase of the hopeless ordeal.

Through the night of the 5th-6th the men crouched in their foxholes, many digging down like moles in their efforts to find some warmth against the bitter cold of the night. Many were without overcoats or adequate clothing

*Letter from Col. Daley to Hist. division. U.S. Army.

for winter. At Vossenach and Kommerscheidt the 112th
Regiment awaited the dawn with a mixture of hope and
fear.

After three days and nights of effort that would not be
denied, five more tanks and nine tank destroyers had finally crawled over the Kall trail, many of them literally
yard by yard, shedding their tracks, bull-dozed, towed,
winched, and constantly under fire. Crews, repair units
and engineers all suffered heavy casualties in the task.
A machine-gun platoon and a rifle platoon had also
struggled up through from Richelskaul, and "a decimated
battalion" of the 110th Infantry Regiment, hastily organized and supported by light tanks and tank destroyers,
was on its way forward with the mission of retaking
Schmidt. No such wild illusion presented itself to the
weary and harassed men who still clung to their Kommerscheidt positions and knew themselves to be nearing
the end.

By the morning of the 6th, the Germans had again
mined the Kall trail and regained control of the bridge
and the main crossing points of the river. Yet serious as
were the prospects of the new day in Kommerscheidt, the
situation in Vossenach was more dangerous. A platoon of tanks and a platoon of tank destroyers patrolled
Vossenach ridge, and as the night paled slowly to dawn a
third platoon of tanks moved forward to join them. Two
platoons of engineers and three 57-mm anti-tank guns
strengthened the forces in the town. The two rifle companies still manned their original positions on the ridge,
and outwardly the position of the 2nd Battalion remained
as strong as on that morning, three days and four nights
earlier, when it had moved out behind its tanks to take
possession. Only the officers and N.C.O's in constant contact with their men knew the subtle and deadly sickness
in the blood and nerves that was steadily sapping the
strength of the battalion.*

The official record reads: "As daylight came the men
of Company G, in the most exposed positions of all on
the northern portion of the ridge became suspicious of
a strange silence."† This silence seemed more ominous
to the men than the usual barrage of the morning, and in
that silence men were the more acutely aware of the gaps

---

*It did not occur to anyone to rotate the battalion companies.
†*Objective: Schmidt*, U.S. Dept. of the Army.

in their ranks, and the wide gap in the center deserted by their comrades. Through the night in ones and twos others had crawled back into Vossenach.

A short burst of small-arms fire from an unknown source broke the silence. There was a "piercing scream," and again silence. When the enemy shelling began half an hour after daylight, panic gripped the men forward. Grabbing wildly at their equipment they began to run for the rear, and those few who might have held, finding themselves abandoned, joined in the flight. For a few minutes it seemed that the second company forward on the right of the ridge might hold. Platoon leaders tried desperately to force their men to orderly withdrawal, "but there was no control."

Back in the center of the town command groups strove to halt the tide of men surging in wild confusion, trampling upon those who fell, but nothing could stand in the face of the panic-stricken mob, believing itself attacked, and coherent only in its resolve to go back.

Forward on the ridge the armor waited, alert for the least sign of enemy movement in the woods beyond, but there was no attack, nor were enemy observed.* In Vossenach officers and N.C.O's stood firm with a remnant of the battalion to form a line of defense forward of the church to hold the eastern approaches. It was at this stage that a colonel of engineers resolved that his men should fight as infantry, and while the two engineer platoons held fast, more were swiftly armed with infantry weapons. Slow to realize the situation the enemy did not begin to infiltrate into Vossenach until noon. By that time the engineers were ready.

v.

In Kommerscheidt and along the northern fringe of the woods line the 3rd Battalion with the remnant of the 1st suffered the ordeal of November 6th sustained by the best artillery and armored support they had known. From their commanding positions on the higher Schmidt ridge enemy tanks brought down accurate fire pinning the men to their foxholes and raking the shattered buildings of the township. Utterly weary and bitterly cold, unable to move in daylight, the forward troops were forced to

*It has been established that there was no attack.

foul their foxholes, while some used K-ration tins for their excrement. The incessant din of fire from the Kall trail in the rear could mean only that they were surrounded. The strength of the 1st Battalion was slowly but steadily ebbing as men began to desert their posts.

At about noon the relief force designed for the task of retaking Schmidt had fought its way through the Kall trail to reach the northern woods line. There they dug in to give some security to the rear of Kommerscheidt. Two officers and fifteen men had been lost at the river crossing. Again the enemy tanks opened fire from Schmidt, and by this time even the sound of a tank engine roaring was enough to send men running for the rear.*

In an effort to give heart to the men, Lieutenant Fleig led out his tanks to draw the enemy fire while the tank destroyers attempted to work round on the opposite flank. Fleig fought his tanks, giving as good as he got, but the destroyers bellied down on the stumps of a hedgerow and were ineffective.

Before dawn on the 6th, Lieutenant George had again got through to Kommerscheidt with supplies, and at three o'clock on the morning of the 7th three weasels out of a convoy of nine fought through, led by Captain Rumbaugh in a jeep. An hour later, at four o'clock on the morning of the 7th, Lieutenant George formed a convoy of two two-and-a-half ton trucks and five weasels, loaded up the big trucks with wounded, and led off in driving heavy rain in his jeep down the Kall trail. The darkness was almost opaque. A shell burst killed George's driver, but he pressed on. In the heavy trucks, lumbering blind over the battered trail, severely wounded men groaned in agony.

The situation all along the trail was one of utter confusion. American and German medical men had negotiated truces between themselves to evacuate wounded. A column of obvious wounded was reasonably safe from direct attack, but tree bursts and mortar fire were deadly in the shambles of the forest.

Almost within sight of the end of the trail Lieutenant George was forced to abandon the heavy trucks at a blocked point. At the same time his convoy came under fire from small arms. Transferring the wounded to the weasels, George ordered every man who could hold a gun

*Three Battles. p. 350.

to fire like hell," and with that the Lieutenant raced his
onvoy over the ridge, skirting Vossenach, skidding over
he slippery ground to reach Richelskaul in safety.

That was the last convoy out of Kommerscheidt, and
t first light on the 7th, a terrific enemy barrage came
lown upon the last defenders of the town. With their
rmor reduced to a single tank and three tank destroyers,
he position was beyond hope. Colonel Ripple, command-
ng the relief force, tried to get a company to move for-
vard from the woods line to strengthen those who still
eld on precariously forward, but the company would not
nove. Forward the commander of the 3rd Battalion,
Major Hazlett, went constantly among his men, exhorting,
triving to give heart by his example. Long before noon
he remnants of two battalions with their reinforcements
nd supporting groups, less than four hundred men in
ll, withdrew into the northern woods line, while all along
he trail men staggered back, dazed and dying, mumbling,
mpervious to pain.

On the Kommerscheidt woods line the few officers left
live held the men together, resolved somehow to achieve
n orderly withdrawal, or to die where they were. But
or the fine artillery support we shouldn't have held the
voods line for twenty minutes, said a colonel.

Unknown to these men almost at the end of their
ether, looking out from the bleak fringes of the woods
ver the smoking blackened ruin of Kommerscheidt, a
vhole battalion had lost its way in an attempt to reach
hem. On the morning of November 8th the 3rd Battalion
f the 109th Regiment was advancing to give flank protec-
ion, to open up a line of withdrawal and to lead the way
ut. At dusk the survivors called for a last barrage to
nask their movements. The colonel commanding the re-
ief column had taken command. The crippled tanks and
lestroyers were rendered useless to the enemy, and every
nan stripped himself down to essentials. Litters were improvised from saplings and clothing, and soon after dusk
a column of wounded set off down the trail, unarmed and
rusting to luck to get them through. On the trail and in
ll the woods about, colonels and G.I.'s, unrecognizable in
heir filth, and crippled with wounds, crawled and fought,
nd in the gorge small groups of engineers fought on.

Under cover of the darkness, the last defenders of
Kommerscheidt began their withdrawal. Each man had a

hand on the shoulder of the man in front, and thus in the pitch darkness, through the shattered, shell-holed forest, without even a compass, the weary men struggled on, many losing contact before the bitter, icy rain turned to snow in the dawn. Between three hundred and three hundred and fifty men of all those who had gone forward so hopefully came back into Germeter and Richelskaul.

vi.

On November 8th, 515 replacements joined the 2nd Battalion, but numbers alone do not fit a battalion for battle, and the 112th Regiment was at once relieved.

The enemy meanwhile, having dealt the 112th Regiment a decisive blow, held the 109th Regiment in its attempts to strengthen the flank of the U.S. 7th Corps, and having inflicted heavy casualties on the 110th Regiment in its abortive efforts to advance on Strauch, at once regrouped and renewed his attacks designed to cut off the Americans along the base line of the Hürtgen-Germeter road.

The battle of Schmidt had not only been lost in the field, it had been lost also from the records, and might never be assessed in its context. U.S. 1st Army and 5th Corps, had maintained constant contact with 28th Division headquarters through all phases of the battle, and were at all times unaware of the true situation. Even had the G-3 reports* of the 28th Division been available for study by visitors, little could have been gleaned.

Charles B. Macdonald quotes the 28th Division G-3 journal, November 6th, 1944, as follows: "2d Battalion received very heavy and concentrated artillery fire, withdrew to reorganize and then regained their original position."

This was the day of the disaster at Vossenach, and Macdonald comments: "Actually the 2d Battalion had been routed, recovered none of the ground it had lost, and had been destroyed as a fighting unit."*

By November 19th the 28th Division had been relieved of further responsibility in the sector and moved into the quiet 8th Corps area of the Ardennes to recover. It had failed to achieve any of its objectives, including the movement of enemy reserves away from the 7th Corps

*Operations.
*Three Battles. U.S. Army in World War II.

front. Its losses had been severe, and in their nature, startling. The Division had suffered an estimated 6,184 casualties in this one assault, and of these the 112th Regiment had lost 2,093 officers and men. A distressing feature of the casualties was the very high proportion of 544 officers and men listed as "non-battle casualties." Combat exhaustion was becoming endemic in the U.S. Army, and General Cota, commanding the 28th Division, although assured that the situation was as bad in other units, expressed some alarm.

William Bradford Huie stated, particularly in regard to this front in November, 1944: "A commander could go up at night expecting to find two hundred men in the line and be lucky to find seventy. There was an epidemic of "combat fatigue," and division commanders swore at psychiatrists."*

Material losses were also heavy, including thirty-one out of fifty medium tanks, sixteen out of twenty-four tank destroyers, and large numbers of weasels, trucks, bulldozers, and weapons.

Author's note:
    These facts had a profound effect on American tactics and strategy and may be considered as one of the principal factors in changing the nature of war. The massive base in manpower needed to sustain one man in the front line was also growing with the weight of organization.

Students of war may be grateful for the meticulous and brave post mortem carried out on Schmidt. The post mortem examined all the organs of the division to discover the why and wherefore, but it did not put the battle of Schmidt into its context in the struggle for the Rhine-

---

*In an analysis of American manpower William Bradford Huie states: ". . . one youth out of every eight was excused from military service for reasons other than physical . . . their number was 1,532,500—the temperamentally unstable, the maladjusted, the sexually perverted, and the overly nervous . . . Of the 10,110,103 who were inducted only 2,670,000 were trained for actual ground combat; and of these a very large number, believed to be as high as a million men, soon managed to escape combat by such devices as bad-conduct discharges, or self-inflicted wounds, or by being excused by psychiatrists for some form of mental insufficiency . . . Among those who evaded combat were about forty thousand who were believed to have 'taken off' or 'bugged off' or 'deserted before the enemy'."
    See: *The Execution of Private Slovik.*

land. That was not the function of the researchers. The result is that no historian striving to pick up the strands from the war diaries of army groups, armies, corps, divisions, regiments, and brigades could hope to discover it. It is not there.

If I have labored the point, I hope I may be forgiven, for properly to have appreciated the importance of Schmidt in October-November, 1944, to have planned and mounted an attack to take and to hold that vital area and its menacing dams, would have changed the course of the campaign. But that attack was never conceived, never planned, and never mounted, and in the final upshot the irresponsible attack on and brief occupation of Schmidt in November, 1944, should not be assessed as "a chance lost," and which took three and a half months of bitter fighting to regain. The chance was never understood.

The vital significance of Schmidt is that it is one of the missing pieces in the puzzle of the Rhineland battle.

PART TWO: THE STRATEGIC REVERSE

5: THE NOVEMBER REALITIES

i.

FIELD MARSHAL MONTGOMERY was quick to grasp the November realities. The vision of a major thrust through to the heart of Germany, which had haunted him since mid-August, was at last killed.

When General Bradley took advantage of the German counterattack out of the Maas pocket to throw his weight behind Patton in his ill-timed, ill-judged, and abortive Saar offensive, Montgomery realized that the planned November offensive of the 1st and 9th Armies to burst out through the Aachen Gap into the Cologne plain was gravely prejudiced. The 21st Army Group must rely on its own unaided efforts to put its house in order. The hopes of the autumn were in ruins.

On the evening of November 1st the news of the successful assaults against the fortress of Walcheren guarding the mouth of the Scheldt, promised the port of Antwerp by the end of the month, and finally released the Canadian 1st Army, with the British 1st Corps, from the long and dreary struggle to free the estuary. With that the Field Marshal could regroup to face east and begin the operations which he referred to as "Preparations for the Battle of the Rhineland."*

By November 9th the Canadian Army with the British 1st Corps had taken over in the Nijmegen bridgehead from the 30th Corps and released also the two U.S. airborne divisions which had supported the 30th Corps since Arnhem. These two divisions together with the U.S. 7th Armored Division and the 104th Infantry Division, which had supported the 2nd Army, returned to United States command.

The Canadians with 1st Corps would guard the whole

*Normandy to the Baltic, by F. M. Montgomery.

left flank from Oss to the sea, and prepare for their major role in the great battle which lay ahead. They had exchanged one water-logged landscape for another, and the patient Dutch in their great cities north of the Maas, in Amsterdam, Rotterdam, Utrecht, and The Hague, resigned themselves to a diet of tulip bulbs throughout the long winter, their last hopes of liberation indefinitely postponed.

The 21st Army Group lined up along the Maas with the 30th Corps on the right flank, the 12th Corps in the center, and the 8th Corps in the north, at long last facing east.

The main task facing the 2nd Army was the elimination of the strong enemy bridgehead west of the Maas, and based solidly on Venlo and Roermond. The operations in mid-October against Overloon and Venraij, and the fierce enemy counterattack of October 27th, had revealed the strength of the pocket and the importance attached to it by the Germans. Nevertheless the Battle-of-the-Maas pocket was regarded as a matter of routine clearance. But it was far more than that. It should have been clear not later than the middle of October that there were only three sectors of major threat to the enemy over the whole northern front in the depths of winter, and these were the Nijmegen bridgehead, the Maas pocket, with its deep hard roots east of the river in the Heinsberg triangle, and the Roer and Urft river dams. These were all interdependent if a major offensive into the Rhineland was contemplated. The Maas pocket and the Heinsberg triangle was, therefore, the "Schmidt-Hürtgen" on the 2nd Army front.

On November 14th General Dempsey launched his attack with the 8th Corps on the left and the 12th Corps on the right, and men and machines began to move over that nightmare landscape of the Peel country, which no man wishes to revisit or to remember. Even in a normal winter this "land" embraced by the Wessem and Deurne canals and innumerable lesser cuttings and waterways, is flooded. In that November of 1944 hail, sleet, snow, and ice had added abundant miseries.

On the opening day of the Battle of the Pocket, Field Marshal Montgomery visited his old division, the 3rd British Infantry Division, at Oploo, a tiny Dutch village at the northern end of the enemy salient. The division had fought the unpleasant battle of Overloon, and had been engaged on the perimeter of the enemy defenses ever since, fighting at Venraij and down through Deurne to contain the counterattack on the Leisel-Meijel road. For a month the infantry had dug themselves in, while the tank men, with an immense distaste for this impossible country, had been even more uncomfortable above ground. In that month, from mid-October to mid-November, the enemy shelling and mortaring at close range had been regular and accurate. The only reasonably safe place to be through certain hours of each day, and particularly of each evening, was in a deep hole, or in a house with a tank drawn close up alongside as a bulwark.

November 14th would not have differed greatly from any other day for the 3rd British Infantry Division but for the Field Marshal's visit. The purpose was to pin up some medals, but the visit is notable because of a speech the Field Marshal made to junior officers and men. He stood, shoulders well back, thighs forward, so that his body described a gentle backwards arc, yet well balanced on his heels. His face, lean and bird-like, bright-eyed under the beret which drew a straight line across his forehead.

In a silence, unbroken by so much as the faintest clearance of a throat even in the depths of winter, he talked to men as if they were generals, and to generals as if they were men. His mind seemed muscular, grasping issues as though they were steel strands, and weaving them with a sure touch into his pattern, so that if he were wrong the pattern might be difficult to undo.

The Field Marshal's speech on that November 14th is memorable in this context for one passage in particular. He was speaking of the German mistake in counterattacking in Normandy instead of retreating to fight behind the Seine. He said:

"Why did the Germans make that big mistake? They have the same general in charge of the battle now as they had in Normandy, Field-Marshal von Runstedt. The reason was that von Runstedt was not allowed to do what he wanted to do because Hitler was running the war. It is very interesting to note what is happening now. A general gets the feel of what the other chap is doing when he is fighting a battle, can tell whether he has got a good grip

on the battle or not. It is my view that the German battle
to-day is being fought very well by the same man who
fought badly in Normandy, by von Runstedt, so I think
it's obvious that the German generals, having seen Hitler
off, are running the war in the way they want, and they
are running it very well."

That was the cardinal mistake not only of Montgomery, but of all the generals, and it led the Allies to terrible errors. In the light of it Field Marshal Montgomery's
final passage is interesting.

"You want to know," he said, "how long the war is going
to last. I have some money on it myself. The Germans
fought the battle for France on our side of the Seine.
Will the battle for Germany be fought on our side of
the Rhine? If the answer to that question is 'Yes,' then I
say 'That's easy.' "

The Field Marshal did not commit himself, but I think
it is clear from all his actions that he did think that the
battle for Germany would be fought on "our" side of the
Rhine. If that is so, he must have believed that von
Runstedt would make the same mistake as Hitler, for
surely if the "generals are running the show," as Montgomery said, the battle will be fought east of the Rhine,
not west.

ii.

On the morning of November 14th the enemy-held
pocket west of the Maas described an arc from the
Wessem canal north of Maeseyck in the south to Mashees
in the north, through a point slightly east of Weert and
embracing Meijel. The whole area within this "bubble"
was flat and water-logged, a maze of canals, cuttings,
dikes, and flooded fields, and through it three roads converged on Venlo. It was more like an elaborately mined
water system than a battlefield, and without the remarkable array of armored fighting vehicles provided by the
79th Armored Division progress must have been next
to impossible and casualties severe.

With its right flank on the Maas above Maeseyck the
12th Corps crossed the Wessem canal, the 7th Armored
Division seizing the lock gates at Panheel while the 51st
Highland Division from its watery positions round Weert
crossed the Noorer canal which traverses the Wessem at

right angles at Nederweert. On the right the 53rd Division pressed on towards Roermond. From the north the 8th Corps attacked south towards Horst and Sevenum from Venraij, and east across the Deurne canal on Meijel. It was tedious in the extreme. A great engineering effort had been necessary to make the only three available roads possible for traffic. The weather was a bitter enemy, washing out all possible features from a featureless landscape, and never had junior officers studied their 1:25,000 maps with more dismay. It was a battle for navigators.

Slowly and steadily the right flank of the 12th Corps crawled along the west bank of the Maas, and the compression bore in upon the enemy crushing him back across the river foot by foot. The whole tempo of the campaign had changed. The advances were over, and the long winter of attrition was setting in. Not only the troops and the generals, but the vast audience hungry for news and "spectacle," must adapt to it.

There was no doubt that Field Marshal Montgomery had adapted to it, and it may be that he watched the opening of the offensive of the U.S. 1st and 9th Armies on his right flank with a somber satisfaction.

On November the 16th, two days after the opening of the modest offensive to close the Maas, General Bradley launched the 1st and 9th Armies into the attack with the intention of advancing across the Cologne plain to the Rhine. To make up for a shortage of ammunition, bombers of the U.S. 8th Air Force and the R.A.F. dropped 9,700 tons of high explosive in the greatest "air-ground cooperative effort yet undertaken by the Allied air forces," tearing the heart out of the ancient town of Düren, and reducing Eschweiler, Julich and Linnich, and scores of lesser places to heaps of rubble.

In the wake of that ferocious effort eight U.S. divisions began to advance into the waste land of the Roer valley through driving rain, sleet, and snow. It was early afternoon. The enemy, dazed, but undaunted, retreated from his outposts to his main defenses, confident in the barrier of the Roer river. From the Hürtgen forest to Geilenkirchen the Germans met the United States divisions head on. Complex minefields covered the most powerful defensive system of strong points on the whole western front, and the Americans quickly learned that even the terrific bombardment the enemy had sustained from the air was no substitute for the ground artillery support they lacked.

But even had sufficient ammunition been available to the 1st and 9th Armies, it is unlikely that the results would have been substantially improved, and there was no hope that Bradley could "bulldoze" his way through. The attack had been foredoomed to failure. At best it could hope to do no more than close the Roer from Düren to Linnich in the same tedious fashion as Montgomery was closing the Maas. Cologne was never more than a hopeless dream, and indeed, with the Roer dams still in enemy hands, invulnerable to the heavy air attacks of the R.A.F., which now concentrated upon them, it is difficult to believe that Cologne was the object.

Above all the attack lacked imagination. The enemy was ready for it in strength with five infantry and two panzer divisions prepared to fight yard by yard through a maze of linked strong points in an industrial wilderness in depth. Every minefield was covered by mortar and artillery fire.

"The enemy, knowing how the attack must come, had only to block it head-on and inflict the maximum casualties," wrote the historian of the U.S. 9th Army.

Bogged down in mud, water, and snow and faced by an uncrossable river, the U.S. 1st and 9th Armies paid the bitter price of Bradley's folly, irresponsibility, and shocking generalship. With that one counterattack of October 27th against the right flank of the 2nd Army the enemy had reaped this rich reward, postponing indefinitely the battle of the Rhineland, and bringing about a stalemate which only the capture of Schmidt and the Roer dams could have prevented.

iii.

There was very little sugar on the bitter pill of the November operations, but what little there was the 30th Corps, with the U.S. 84th Infantry Division under command, provided. Preceded by an artillery barrage which poured twenty thousand shells into the little German town of Geilenkirchen, and with sustained and accurate artillery support, the 30th Corps attacked into Germany on the left flank of the U.S. 9th Army.

The U.S. 9th Army, supporting the main drive of the 1st Army, made slow but steady progress in the first few lays, but it had no illusions that it could do more than reach the Roer. On the morning of November 18th, when the 30th Corps went in on the flank, an American staff colonel said: "We are pushing slowly, but there is a lot in front of us to push."

The purpose of the British attack was limited to the protection of the flank, but there were new names to attempt to conjure with and new vistas. Within two miles of the pretty Dutch village of Sittard the armor rumbled into Germany through a deserted, but rich, countryside, through the empty villages of Wehr and Gengelt, knowing these villages, these fields, these shattered homes and stricken beasts, not Dutch, nor French, nor Belgian, but at last the homeland of the enemy. And the enemy was very close, pressing in from the left, hidden in the bronze belts of woodland and in the folds of the hills, as solid as a rock, for this was the outer bastion of that Heinsberg triangle destined to be a thorn in the flesh of the 2nd Army and to live in many memories for many weeks.

The intention of the 30th Corps was to take the town of Geilenkirchen, and to thrust northeast along the valley of the river Wurm to the ever elusive Roer. At the outset the going was deceptively easy, save for the ever-present menace on the left. On the 20th, the 43rd Division enveloped the smoking ruin of Geilenkirchen and battered on with the Petard tanks [tanks mounting heavy mortars] and flame-throwers of the 79th Armored Division into a harsh wilderness of strong points, of stone dwellings seeming to outcrop from the hillsides, of slag heaps, and tall chimneys, some blackened stumps, others like wilting candles pointing obscene fingers to the brown sky. This was the beginning of industrial Germany and the massive defenses of the Siegfried line.

In Geilenkirchen not one citizen of the 9,000 inhabitants could be found. The shop fronts had burst open, their wares strewn over the cobbles down to the Wurm, which raged in flood like some subterranean torrent amidst the smoke and rubble and ruin.

There was something deeply impressive about the dead dusk of this first German town to be entered by British troops; it was utterly abandoned. An old top hat sat on a child's mattress, reams of paper and pots and pans littered the narrow ways. It was a mark of the grim struggle ahead. Immediately in the wake of the troops the military government and civil affairs officers came in. Finding nothing to administer, no citizens to instruct, they asked themselves, would this be the way of it? To the bitter end.

But to the infantryman plodding steadily on, it was not only Germany but the first dry land they had known for weeks, a land of hills and valleys and dark sky lines, of fir plantations and everlasting menace. But that it was "dry" even though the unrelenting rain poured out of the November sky, was a compensation. There were no friendly people to enliven a brief halt, but there were no inhibitions in the way of roasting a goose or eating the masses of bottled fruits that seemed to furnish every larder.

For three days armor and infantry, Flail tanks [equipped with a rotating drum in front to which were attached lengths of flailing chains to explode land mines in the path of progress] Petards, and the flame-throwing Crocodiles [Churchill VII tanks with powerful flame-throwers in place of machine-gun turrets] churned the ground to mud as they strove to carve a path along the Wurm valley, enfiladed at every point, unable to gain a yard to the eastward. In that inferno of shot and shell around Suggerath and Beeck and Tripsrapth the walls of houses seemed to go in and out like concertinas to the unending concussion. A signpost at a crossroads pointed to "Düsseldorf 70 km" and "Koln 65 km," but even one kilometer through that maze of concrete and guns was a long way. Remorselessly the armor strove to break a way through, and remorselessly the enemy counterattacked. Every strong point had to be assaulted, blasted with petards, seared with flame, only to add its rubble and stone to the confusion. And as the rain teemed down unabated it became impossible for armor to maneuver.

On November 24th, the brief sortie into the enemy homeland had to be abandoned, and it would have been necessary to travel south to Alsace before finding a gain of more than the odd mile or two over the whole Allied front. The U.S. 84th Division returned to U.S. 9th Army command, and the northern armies of the U.S. 12th Army Group hung on in their impossible task, resolved at the worst to close the Roer river.

On the 2nd Army front, the pocket had become a series of small bubbles of enemy, forced out of base-ments to the second floors of houses by the rising floods, and retreating doggedly behind the broad Maas. By the end of the month all that remained to the enemy on the west bank of the river was a small but powerful bridgehead at Blerick, opposite Venlo.

From the Hürtgen forest to the Nijmegen bridgehead the whole land had reached saturation point, and the weather, almost as much as the enemy, called a halt. Thus had the high hopes of autumn vanished in the November slush. It was a situation demanding a re-appraisal, and arousing forebodings not alone in the mind of Montgomery, but in the minds of the Combined Chiefs of Staff, and of Churchill.

6: BEFORE THE STORM

i.

THE EVENTS of November revived the command crisis of the early autumn and revealed differences not only between the commanders in the field, but on the highest levels in Britain and the United States.

Throughout November, Field Marshal Montgomery had viewed the developing situation over the whole battlefield north of the Ardennes with a growing unease. He saw—and I think, absolutely rightly—the battlefield north of the Ardennes as one battlefield, and believed that it should have one ground force commander. But the events of November revealed the bankruptcy of Allied strategy.

In the south the French had smashed a hole through at Saverne to open the way to Strasbourg and the Rhine. The Allies could look out across the river to the Black Forest, tantalized by the apparent imminence of victory. But the enemy had reacted violently against French advances to the Rhine further south, and Hitler had ordered Himmler to take command and hold a bridgehead in the Colmar pocket at all costs. The U.S. 7th Army was engaged in fierce fighting in the difficult country north of Strasbourg on the right of Patton and steadily closing up to the Saar river. Metz had fallen, but the strongest of the forts still held out, and by the end of

November, Patton was bogged down. ". . . the Allied operations south of the Ardennes had failed by that time to relieve the *impasse* to the north." wrote John Ehrman.[*]

On the 25th of November, Churchill cabled a report of all these things to Stalin and referred to the northern front as follows: "In a week or ten days it should be possible to estimate whether the German armies will be beaten decisively west of the Rhine. If they are we can go on in spite of the weather. Otherwise there may be some lull during the severity of the winter, after which one more major onslaught should break the organized German resistance in the west."[†]

The succeeding days had failed to provide an answer, and as the month ended, it was clear that the Allied armies had bogged down completely all along the line.

In early autumn when Montgomery had expressed himself constantly and strongly against Allied strategy, his own alternative strategy had not been realistic. But on November 28th the news of the first convoy sailing up the Scheldt to dock safely in Antwerp promised the sinews of war, at last, behind the armies in the north. In addition, but for a small set-piece battle to clear the enemy from their last small bridgehead west of the Maas at Blerick, his own front was "tidy," as he expressed it. It was, therefore, on November 28th that Montgomery visited the Supreme Commander to express his views and his grave uneasiness.

General Eisenhower, patient and attentive, as always, was unsympathetic, and it is likely that Montgomery was too sweeping in his criticisms to appeal to the Supreme Commander. In Montgomery's opinion Eisenhower's failure to "implement his directive of 28th October was responsible for the situation."[§] The directive had ordered the main effort to be made in the north to bring about the decisive defeat of the enemy west of the Rhine, and the establishment of bridgeheads over the Rhine and Ijssel rivers. "We have achieved none of this," the Field Marshal said, "and we have no hope of doing so. We have therefore failed; and we have suffered a strategic reverse."[§]

This statement fails to take into account that the Oc-

[*]*Grand Strategy*. Vol. vi. by John Ehrman. p. 34.
[†]*Triumph and Tragedy*, Vol. vi. Churchill Memoirs. p. 223.
[§]*The Supreme Command*, by Forrest Pogue. p. 312.

ober directive was impossible and could not have been
chieved even had Bradley played his part. Nevertheless,
much of Montgomery's statement was justified, and on
November 30th he put his views in writing to the Supreme Commander,* stating categorically:

"We now require a new plan. And this time *we must
not fail*. The need to get the German war finished early
s vital, in view of other factors. The new plan *must not
fail*.

"In the new plan we must get away from the doctrine
of attacking in so many places that nowhere are we
strong enough to get decisive results. We must concen-
rate such strength on the main selected thrust that success will be certain. It is in this respect that we failed
badly in the present operations."

In the next paragraph Montgomery renewed his appeal for a change in command: "The theatre divides itself naturally into two fronts; one north of the Ardennes
and one south of the Ardennes. We want one commander
in full operational control north of the Ardennes, and one
south."

The Field Marshal ended with the remark: ". . . and
if you decide that I should do that work—that is O.K. by
me."

The Supreme Commander reacted with indignation and
flatly contradicted the Field Marshal. In his reply he embarked upon a defense of the Allied total achievement
since Normandy, but the real point at issue was Montgomery's fear that the emphasis of attack was shifting
away from the north. The British Chiefs of Staff shared
his view that this was the fundamental of Allied strategy,
to which SHAEF was fully committed. "To get involved in
operations which led away from that direction he [Mont-
gomery] considered faulty strategy," wrote Forrest
Pogue, "and to drive in the wrong direction, particularly
without reaching the Rhine, was 'a strategic reverse'."

Eisenhower's full reply is very long, but perhaps ex-
racts will not be out of place here. "I am not quite sure
I know exactly what you mean by strategic reverse; cer-
ainly to date we have failed to achieve all that we had
hoped to by this time, which hopes and plans were based
upon conditions as we knew them or estimated them

*Diary Office C in C. Italics in original.

when the plans were made. The Ruhr is an important place, but let us never forget for one second that our primary objective is to defeat the Germans who are barring our way into Germany. The Ruhr itself was always given as a geographical objective, not only for its importance to Germany, but because it was believed that in that region the *German forces* would be largely concentrated to meet our attacks."

The Supreme Commander then agreed that:

"a. We must determine how much profit there is in the continuation of our current attacks in the 12th Army Group area, and whether they give real promise of reaching the Rhine.

b. We must recast our future general plans in the light of the conditions as they now exist.

c. We must choose the best line of attack to assure success, including the maintenance of deception lines."

General Eisenhower then wrote: "I do not agree that things have gone badly since Normandy, merely because we have not gained all we had hoped to gain. Our line as late as D-plus-60 was not greatly different than what we had hoped to hold in the first week, but I never looked upon the situation then existing as a strategic reverse, even though out of the circumstances of our long confinement in the narrow beach head have developed some of our greatest difficulties . . .

"Moreover, I do not agree that more strength could have been thrown to the North than was actually maintained there during early September. Lines of communication in the north were so stretched that even delivery of five hundred tons to you at Brussels cost Bradley three divisions, the possession of which might have easily placed him on the Rhine in the Wurms area.

". . . I have no intention of stopping Devers' and Patton's operations as long as they are cleaning up our right flank and giving us *capability of concentration*. On the other hand I do not intend to push these attacks senselessly."

This message did nothing to relieve Montgomery's disquiet, and served only to emphasize his fears. It confirmed also the growing fears of the Chiefs of Staff and the Prime Minister, for in this message the fundamental difference between American and British aims may be seen. In a word, the Americans were fighting to destroy

he German army, and the British were fighting to gain
political victory. The northern route, to give control of
3remen and Hamburg, and finally Berlin, was, therefore,
ital in British thinking. To the British, geography was of
aramount importance; to the Americans, it was not.

In his immediate reply to the Supreme Commander,
Field Marshal Montgomery pointed out that he had not
ntended to suggest for one moment that the campaign
had been a failure since Normandy, but had intended to
tate that the directive of October 28th had not been
carried out. To this General Eisenhower sent his "prompt
and abject apologies" for misunderstanding. A meeting
was arranged at Maastricht for December 7th at which
Air Marshal Tedder and General Bradley would be present. Meanwhile the Germans again reminded the generals,
as they had reminded them on October 27th, that they
also had a say in the matter.

ii.

On December 2nd the Germans breached the dikes of
the Lower Rhine south of Arnhem, and relieved the 1st
Canadian Army of all further preoccupation with the task
of planning an attack to the north. At the same time
they emphasized the third of the three major sensitive
points of the northern battlefield and produced a huge
inland lake north of the Nijmegen-Cleves road to Emmerich. The Canadians had not been without expectation
of some such move, and the British 49th Division was
ready for the heavy attack by German paratroops, which
came on the 4th with the intention of driving them back
across the Waal. But the 49th stood firm, and the reduced
Nijmegen bridgehead, essential in the battle of the Rhineland, was swiftly consolidated. On the "island" south of
Elst, the troops looked forward, dubiously, to a watery
Christmas, patrolling in small boats, and regarding the
local geese with hungry eyes.

The German move, admirably timed, underlined the
"strategic reverse," and might have drawn attention to
the possibility that the still powerful German army might
still seek to impose a pattern upon the future. Montgomery was not perturbed. On December 3rd the 15th Scottish, aided by flails, bridging tanks, and troop-carrying
Kangaroos [converted Sherman tanks, capable of carrying infantry sections into battle] of the 79th Ar-

mored Division, put in a set-piece attack against Blerick, the last enemy strong point west of the Maas, and
enabled the Field Marshal to record that "we were now
tidy along the line of the rivers Roer and Meuse except
for an enemy salient in the Heinsberg area."* All that
now stood between the Field Marshal and his battle was
the clearance of that difficult pocket.

The difficult pocket was, in fact, the central linchpin between Schmidt and Nijemegen, and almost as important
to the enemy as Schmidt itself. Unyielding defense, coupled with an appalling saturation of the ground, compelled the postponement of operations, and the deep ab-
scess between the flanks of the 2nd and 9th Armies continued to fester. Along the base of that Heinsberg triangle, our troops had the doubtful pleasure of observing
the enemy in Venlo and Roermond across the broad Maas.

In the first week of December the U.S. 9th Army,
aided by British artillery support, had closed up to the
Roer to look across the unpromising brown swirling
flood upon the rubble of Linnich and Julich. The slow
dismal action had cost nearly 10,000 casualties, and the
U.S. 1st Army on their right was suffering at least twice
as heavily and moving half as fast in their bitter fight
through the Hürtgen Forest. The village of Hürtgen
which had changed hands a score of times, was at last behind them, and from Eschweiler and down the Grosshau
road they drew in steadily upon Düren. The Roer was
at last in sight, but beyond it, in a wide arc covering Cologne, the enemy had drawn up an impressive array backed
by the *6th Panzer Army*.

It was a sober outlook when the commanders met at
Maastricht on December 7th. Eisenhower travelled
through the Ardennes on his way to the meeting and was
disturbed at the absence of troops, transport, installations,
and indeed almost a sign that the area was defended. He
recalled the defeat of American armor in Tunisia. It
might be a "nasty little Kasserine," he remarked to Bradley, but General Bradley, somewhat irritably aware of
this broad gap in his long front, and minimizing it whenever his attention was drawn to it, had other things on
his mind. He had gravely weakened the 1st Army to give
Patton priority, and the total achievement after nearly

Normandy to the Baltic.

ix weeks of bitter fighting could not have given him
uch cause for pleasure. Attrition all along the line had
n unpleasant two-way meaning. Three divisions of the
st Army had been mauled in the Hürtgen forest to the
xtent of suffering 21,000 casualties, and at last he was
ully aware of Schmidt, the Roer dams, and all that they
neant. He could not cross the Roer without them.

Even in the air the outlook was gloomy. In mid-
November General Doolittle had said that the Eighth
Air Force might have to give priority to the task of re-
onquering the German Air Force instead of strategic
»ombing.

The Maastricht conference was conducted amicably, in
pite of the very strong feelings, but it served only to ac-
entuate the differences, not only between General Eisen-
ower and Field Marshal Montgomery, but also in the
American and British approaches to war. Only General
Bradley in all these exchanges seems to have shown bit-
erness, but Eisenhower and Montgomery were devoid
of malice, sharing a quality of innocence, which was
heir strength. Old ideas were reaffirmed, but it was
greed—as it had been agreed at Brussels—that the
najor attack should be in the north early in the new
rear. Ten U.S. divisions would be made available under
21st Army Group command for the right hook northeast
rom the Roer. But the secondary attacks would also be
nounted in the south. Eisenhower stated flatly that he
vould not check Patton while he could make progress,
and revealed his long liking for the Frankfurt area.

None of this suited Montgomery. He wanted the full
available strength of the Allies to attack north of the
Ruhr and all the rest to hold. He felt sure that two attacks would rob each other of the vital punch, and sus-
pected Eisenhower of continuing to pursue a policy of
opportunism. The Field Marshal pressed his strong argument for one ground force commander north of the Ardennes, but Eisenhower argued that the Ruhr was the
natural dividing line.

The profound disagreement underlying these issues
was masked by the Supreme Commander's insistence that
there was no real disagreement. "Believing that he had
sufficient forces to support the northern thrust adequately
and still mount a subsidiary attack," wrote Forrest
Pogue, "he saw no difference between his concept and

that of the 21st Army Group commander. But to Fiel
Marshal Montgomery, who believed that experiences o
the past few months demonstrated the lack of sufficien
resources for both attacks, the difference was betwee
success and failure—and therefore fundamental."*

The differences are mainly a matter of emphasis, an
to understand them fully it is necessary to follow and t
digest the whole long argument, waged often with acr
mony, henceforth to the war's end.

It was an argument the Americans were bound to win
on whatever level, for Eisenhower, as Pogue remark
"was in a position to make his view prevail. For this rea
son, if for no other, there was never a deadlock betwee
the two commanders-in-chief." The same applied betwee
Roosevelt and Churchill, between the British Chiefs o
Staff and the U.S. Joint Chiefs of Staff. Britain was—b
now overwhelmingly—the weak partner.

Nevertheless Field Marshal Montgomery left th
Maastricht Conference in high spirits to set about th
immediate task of regrouping his forces for the Rhinelan
battle. He had passed on his "differences of opinion" t
a higher level, and was ready to face up to the task i
hand with characteristic thoroughness and fervor, an
with no thought of failure. Such was his resilience tha
he now appeared to view the whole situation with grea
optimism. The U.S. 9th Army agreed to take over th
30th Corps commitment in the Heinsberg salient, an
with that Montgomery ordered the 30th Corps to mov
north into the Nijmegen bridgehead to mount the mai
attack under command of the 1st Canadian Army, whil
the 2nd Army headquarters got down to the intricat
task of planning the final crossing of the Rhine.

The way, it seemed, was as clear ahead as it could be
As soon as the Roer dams were taken, the U.S. 9t
Army would prepare for its role across the Roer, an
deliver the right hook up through Krefeld. The Cana
dians and 30th Corps with the bulk of the 2nd Arm
would navigate the northern floods to sail round th
flank of the Siegfried Line and smash through the defense
of the Reichswald forest. In the 2nd Army headquarter
they had begun, tentatively, to hum a little tune, 'Po
goes the *Wesel*', for Wesel was the target for the begin
ning of the end.

*The Supreme Command

iii.

The British Chiefs of Staff and the Prime Minister
ared Field Marshal Montgomery's fears in regard to
e future offensive on the northern front and felt uneasy
the "apparent disappearance of a master plan."
hurchill had at once cabled his friend, Field Marshal
nuts, a full account of the situation:

"In spite of Metz and Strasbourg and other successes,
e have of course sustained a strategic reverse on the
/estern Front. . . . I imagine some readjustments will
e made giving back Montgomery some of the scope
ken from him after the victory he gained in Normandy.
ou must remember however that our armies are only
out one-half the size of the American and will soon be
ttle more than one-third . . . it is not so easy as it used
 be for me to get things done."

This message was dated December 3rd and there was
ill room to hope for some successful outcome of the
laastricht conference. On the 6th December, without
aiting for a further report from Montgomery, the Prime
linister cabled Roosevelt:*

"As we are unable to meet, I feel that the time has
ome for me to place before you the serious and disap-
ointing war situation which faces us at the close of this
ear. Although many fine tactical victories have been
ained on the Western Front and Metz and Strasbourg
re trophies, the fact remains that we have definitely
ailed to achieve the strategic object which we gave our
rmies five weeks ago. We have not yet reached the
hine in the northern part and most important sector of
ie front, and we shall have to continue the great battle
or many weeks before we can hope to reach the Rhine
nd establish our bridgeheads. After that, again, we have
 advance through Germany."

The President's reply was unsatisfactory in the ex-
·eme. He had "bicycled over the terrain in the old
ays," and had formed the impression that it would be
a very stiff job" to close up to the left bank of the
·hine. "However our agreed broad strategy is develop-
1g according to plan . . ."

This was the kind of message to make the British tear
heir hair. Nothing could have been more disturbing, and
n December 12th General Eisenhower and his Deputy,

Triumph and Tragedy, vol. vi. Churchill Memoirs.

Air Marshal Tedder, met the British Chiefs of Staff a the Prime Minister in London. There was very lit headway. The Supreme Commander was prepared concede that an advance on Frankfurt should be secor ary to the thrust in the north, but he was looking at t whole strategical picture from a different angle than British. Summing up Eisenhower's views at that conf ence, John Ehrman wrote: *

"While admitting that the current operations in sectors would not prove immediately decisive, he (Eise hower) claimed that they were fulfilling his ultimate p pose by wearing down the Germans continuously alo an extended line—a process which, thanks to their la of mobility, they could not hope to check. To halt the operations in favor of those suggested by Montgome might on the other hand allow them to reinforce one se tor and to reorganize in others . . ."

British fears were gravely enhanced, and the Chiefs Staff prepared an immediate memorandum for the Pri Minister. In the spring, they estimated, Allied streng would be 80 to 85 divisions, and felt that this would r suffice for the two offensives contemplated by the S preme Commander. They proposed to press their view The situation was beginning to have unpleasant und tones, for if these differences were pressed to the limi it would amount to setting up one commander agair the other, and there would be a "showdown." Nothi would have been more disastrous, for each man po sessed unique and valuable qualities, and the loss of ther one of them would have been far more grave than continued disagreement. For it has not been sufficier ly understood that, despite all his protests, Fie Marshal Montgomery always carried out Eisenhowe orders not only with thoroughness and integrity, but wi enthusiasm.

General Bradley, on the other hand, seldom argue for he had a different method. Immediately following t Maastricht conference, he had ordered General Patto to prepare to mount an offensive against the Saar on D cember 19th to reach the Rhine by Christmas. Eise hower warned Bradley that, unless the offensive was su cessful beyond a doubt in the first week, it would hav to be called off. SHAEF also emphasized that the inter

*Grand Strategy, vol. vi. John Ehrman.

on of Patton's offensive was to aid the main effort in the
orth, "and that any crossing of the Rhine south of the
Ioselle was to be restricted until the success of opera-
ons in the north was assured."

Nothing could have underlined British fears more
rcefully or revealed more strongly Eisenhower's liking
r the south. Moreover, there were few illusions now
bout Patton's technique of "Rock Soup," as he called
, his method of committing his troops in such a way
iat they would have to be reinforced. The order to "Go"
as good enough for him. At this time also it began to
e feared that Bradley's influence with the Supreme Com-
iander was very great, and that he and Patton had
amed up to win the war their way. The British in the
eld certainly believed that "Bradley had the inside track
o Eisenhower."

On Patton's right flank the U.S. 7th Army was driv-
ig northward between the Saar and the Rhine, and had
lements of all its divisions on the German frontier. Noth-
ig succeeds like success, and on the face of it, the whole
ront north of the Ardennes looked far less promising.
Jevertheless, I believe that to risk compromising the of-
ensive in the north in favor of the south was a strategical
lunder of the first magnitude, and it was fortunate that
he Germans had decided to call the tune, and to lose the
ar on a battlefield of their own choosing.

iv.

The tactical burden of General Bradley's uncompro-
iising support of General Patton's 3rd Army fell con-
tantly upon the unfortunate shoulders of General
Iodges, and the U.S. 1st Army. From the end of Octo-
er, Hodges had been forced to fight the battles of Hürt-
en forest and the Roer in piecemeal fashion, under-
ianned, under-supplied, and denied artillery support
bove a minimum scale. No army faced a more powerful
nd determined enemy backed by a greater weight of re-
erves. No sector of the whole Allied front from Switzer-
and to Arnhem held the terrors and difficulties of terrain
f the Hürtgen area, and I would argue that no sector
ad a greater tactical importance than this key region to
he Cologne plain and the northern Rhineland. The enemy
eld that view.

By mid-December when Bradley ordered Hodges to

mount an offensive to take the Roer dams, the 1st Arm
and its commander were showing signs of strain. The 7t
Corps had been heavily battered in its struggle to reac
Düren; the 5th Corps on the right of the 7th had had
scarcely less severe strain, and in the Ardennes the wea
8th Corps was strung out over a very wide front, count
ing the battered 28th Division among its effectives.

First Army intelligence reports had been disturbin
since mid-November, revealing movement of enemy re
serves threatening the army front, apparently aimed a
first north of Aachen, but with a marked tendency to shif
the balance southward. As a result Hodges had askec
Bradley for two more divisions, and had been refused.

On December 10th the 1st Army chief of intelligenc
said: "The restoration of the West Wall is still a prob
able strategic objective . . . The enemy has let his situa
tion in both the upper Rhine and south of the Mosell
deteriorate while still conserving reserves between Düs
seldorf and Köln. Von Runstedt apparently is accept
ing defeats in the south rather than compromise his hop
of a decisive success in the north. This would appear t
be the keynote of his strategy in the defense of the Reic
west of the Rhine. During the past month there has bee
a definite pattern for the seasoning of newly-formed di
visions in the comparatively quiet sector opposite VII
Corps prior to their dispatch to more active fronts. Th
enemy is well aware of the tactical 'ace' which he hold
in the Roer River dams. Our recent attempts to breac
the dam walls by air bombardment, as yet unsuccessfu
have served to emphasize our own concern with th
flooding of the Roer valley. The enemy has reacted b
building up his forces on the route of approach to th
Schwammenauel and the Urfttalsperre, the key dams i
this system of barrages. Besides the divisions in the *Sixt.
Panzer Army,* the enemy has *2Pz* and *116Pz Divs* con
ditionally available for local counterattacks in the de
fense of the dams, in addition to at least two Volks
grenadier divisions which are available from the VII
Corps sector."

This intelligence report seems immensely revealing, an
it is not surprising that the 1st Army G-2 should be in
clined to concentrate on the Roer dams. Forrest Pogu
comments: "The importance of the Roer dams to bot
the Allies and the enemy seems to have outweighed othe

factors when the First Army intelligence chief drew his conclusions as to possible enemy capabilities."

For more than a month the enemy had not yielded a foot of ground without fighting stubbornly along the whole 1st Army front. The morale of prisoners was very high, and there were many other indications of danger ahead. 12th Army Group, however, was not impressed, and there is no doubt that relations between the two staffs were not good.*

On December 13th General Hodges had to order General Gerow, commanding the 5th Corps, to take Schmidt and the Roer dams, and 5th Corps began to move.

In the light of these events it seems clear that either General Bradley was incapable of commanding an army group operating on such an extended front both north and south of the Ardennes, or that Field Marshal Montgomery was quite right in insisting that the Ardennes made the natural division of ground-force command. Bradley often complained of the length of his front, and said that he had no time to examine essential reports.

It is inevitable, also, that the relationships existing between Generals Bradley, Patton and Hodges, should have been remembered. Patton had been Bradley's senior until the "slap in the face" incident had caused Eisenhower to judge Bradley to be more "emotionally stable." Bradley was deputy commander of the 2nd Corps under Patton, and had later commanded that corps in Patton's 7th Army. Hodges had served as Bradley's deputy commander of the 1st Army and had moved up to command when Bradley had been promoted to 12th Army Group. It seems at least possible that Bradley may have been conscious of Patton's former superiority, not only to Hodges, but to himself. But, in fact, Hodges was the veteran of them all, a soldier of World War I, an infantryman, aware of battle, and one of the very few American generals with any war experience. Yet, as Chester Wilmot has noted: "Bradley was forever con-

---

*Forrest Pogue discussed this question with all concerned after the war. He wrote: "While some effort was made by the principals to discount the effect of personalities involved, there seems little doubt that some personality conflicts, and sometimes a tendency to question the validity of predictions, existed between the 12th Army Group and First Army G-2's."

scious that Patton was not only his senior in rank, but also his superior in tactical skill and experience."

But with the exception of the strong currents of uneasiness in the 1st Army Headquarters there was a general sense of well-being all along the line in mid-December. On the 21st Army Group front the advance units of the 30th Corps were already moving to take up their new positions in the Nijmegen bridgehead to prepare for the Rhineland battle. On December 15th General de Guingand, the 21st Army Group Chief of Staff, went on leave to England, and Field Marshal Montgomery asked Eisenhower if he could be spared to visit home the following week. The Field Marshal expressed himself as optimistic about the whole front, and his directive of December 16th said so categorically. On December 12th the 12th Army Group had published a summary in similar terms.

At that time the Supreme Commander was giving special attention to the situation in the Colmar pocket. The enemy were keeping eight Allied divisions fully engaged, and Eisenhower ordered Devers to postpone "Operation Independence" against the enemy garrisons still holding out on the Atlantic coast of France and put all the force he could muster in against Colmar.

Strangest of all, on the morning of December 15th the SHAEF G-3 (Operations) briefing officer stated that there was nothing to report on the Ardennes sector. This could only mean that SHAEF operations and intelligence were out of contact.

All, in fact, was far from quiet on the western front.

7: "ES GEHT UMS GANZE"

i.

LONG BEFORE the dawn of December 16th enemy storm troops, moving rapidly out of the Eifel forest under the "artificial moonlight" of searchlights played against the overcast sky, had infiltrated the loosely held American forward positions in the Ardennes. Behind them in the south and center three army corps of the *5th Panzer Army* under General Von Manteuffel advanced on a thirty-mile front from Prum to Wilz, imminently to threaten St. Vith and Bastogne. Advancing from Echternach the German *7th Army* covered the southern flank.

At the same hour, the *6th Panzer Army* under General Dietrich began to advance on a fifteen-mile front upon Monschau and Malmédy.

When the Americans awoke that morning it was to the thunder of two thousand guns laying the heaviest barrage the Germans had fired in the campaign, while overhead shoals of V.1's, speeding upon Liége and Antwerp, laid their fiery trails across the heavy sky. In the upper air, unseen and unheard, V.2's carried their cargoes of high explosive to Antwerp.

In the north it had been snowing for a week, and soon it would be snowing in the Ardennes. It was bitter cold, and the enemy came like wraiths out of the morning mist, exultant, believing in victory. The men in the thinly held forward line had no chance.

The intention of the Germans was to seize crossings over the Meuse between Liége and Huy, and to sweep through to Antwerp with the *6th Panzer Army* on the right, while on the left the *5th Panzer Army,* matching its speed to the main thrust, took Liége and went through to Brussels. Thus, in one last great effort, Hitler hoped, he might split the Allied armies in two and force a Dutch Dunkirk upon the British.

As the 69-year-old Field Marshal von Runstedt had said—a man by all his training and experience not given to the loose or extravagant use of words—*"Es geht ums ganze,"* the German equivalent of "all or nothing."

Perhaps not least among the fundamental weaknesses of this last all-out offensive effort of the enemy on the Western Front was the lack of faith of its commanders in it. Von Runstedt himself thought it madness. Field Marshal Model and the young General von Manteuffel, the only two men who dared to argue with the Führer, strove to dissuade him from the venture. The corps and divisional commanders did not learn of their tasks more than three days in advance, too late to plan properly. Dietrich, the "Butcher Boy" protegé of Hitler, commander designate of the *6th Panzer Army* with the major role of the right-hand punch through to Antwerp, was equally ignorant. Such security precautions may have been necessary, but they weighed heavily against success.

Junior officers and troops had been led to believe the offensive would be aimed at Aachen, and this certainly had helped to mislead the Allies.

The Battle of the Ardennes still awaits a full assessment,* but that it was doomed to failure there can be little doubt. The very conditions essential to its possibility; the bad weather to prevent Allied air observation and attack; mitigated against success, hampering the swift movement of the armored columns and holding them to a slow tempo in the steep, muddied defiles that would soon be deep in snow. To succeed, the Meuse had to be reached and crossed by the third day at the latest. Even faced with the most meagre token resistance that task, in the mid-winter conditions, would have been severe. Above all, fuel was short; captured Allied fuel dumps would have to make good the shortage.

The Germans knew well the forces against them, but their appreciation of the American resistance was faulty. They relied on complete disruption and confusion and the precipitate evacuation of the key road centers of Bastogne and St. Vith, the overwhelming of Monschau, and the opening of the way through to Eupen and Verviers. Disruption and confusion there were; but as the early fog of battle began to clear, hard cores of resolute resistance became evident. The battered and unlucky 28th Division, with the wounds of the Hürtgen Forest scarcely healed and with many raw replacements in their ranks, streamed back through Bastogne warning 8th Corps Headquarters of disaster. But one regiment of that division stood and fought, barring the road long enough for the reinforcements rushing up from Luxembourg and from Reims.

Long before the shape of the battle was clear to commanders in the field, reinforcements were moving to key points. The U.S. 7th Armored Division speeding down from north of Aachen, picking up stragglers on its way, reached St. Vith, and brilliantly commanded by Brigadier General Hasbrouck, revealed qualities rare in the United States Army. For not only could it advance at lightning speed, it could also fight a withdrawing action, disciplined and tight as a drum.

On the enemy right flank Dietrich's Panzer army

*The Ardennes, Hugh M. Cole. U.S. Dept. of the Army, Washington.

blunted its nose on two divisions of Gerow's 5th Corps as they moved against the Roer dams on a line Butgenbach-Monschau. Thus at the outset vital impetus had been lost.

Nevertheless the confusion in the field was alarming. The lack of rear organization, the almost total absence of the apparatus of withdrawal, made of the rear areas a no-man's-land in which disorderly groups floundered, pursued by ghosts conjured often by their imaginations.

Meanwhile the enemy had organized a special American-speaking force in jeeps and tanks to rush through like a Trojan horse, and this force, coupled with rumors of large parachute drops in the rear, added to the confusion. In fact, the enemy planned air drop of 1,000 picked men under Colonel von der Heydte with the role of sitting astride the Eupen-Verviers road junction, had failed dismally.* Dropping by night from aircraft manned by unskilled crews, many were killed and injured in the drop and far from the target area. In the end von der Heydte collected 200 men, and with these he did his best, until he was captured, to disrupt communications and hamper troop movements.

Before dusk on the dark day of December 16th the Germans had cut the communications of the 12th Army Group and isolated General Bradley's headquarters in Luxembourg from effective control of his 1st and 9th Armies in the north. That night neither General Bradley, nor General Hodges commanding the U.S. 1st Army, knew very much about the battle, and were gravely under-estimating its potential. Only General Gerow, commanding the 5th Corps, appreciated the drive of the German *6th Panzer Army,* but his urgent request to Hodges to be permitted to call off his attack against the Roer dams was refused.

Through the night the German armor was rumbling over the battered roads, forced to by-pass Bastogne and to take Houffalize and Wilz in the south, split into twin streams by the defense of St. Vith in the center, and forced south of Malmédy in the north by Gerow, encrouching upon Stavelot, and soon to alarm 1st Army headquarters in Spa.

It took General Bradley two days to awaken to the full threat, while in the extreme north Field Marshal

*The Other Side of The Hill, B. H. Liddell Hart.

Montgomery reacted swiftly, halting the northward movement of the 30th Corps, and moving to cover his southern flank. By the night of December 19th British units were covering the road to Brussels, and the Meuse line was secured.

It is not my purpose here to describe, beyond this brief survey, the course of the Battle of the Ardennes, but to attempt to consider it in the context of my story, primarily its effects on the higher command and on the Battle of the Rhineland. Its effects on the Battle of the Rhineland were, of course, profound, and Field Marshal Montgomery showed himself a master of "maintenance of the objective." Not for one moment did he lose sight of the battle he was resolved to fight, and which must be fought, in the Rhineland in the furtherance of Allied strategy.

In the last count, it may be that Hitler's offensive in the Ardennes was lost not so much in the west as on the Vistula, for at the outset the renewed threat of Russian pressure compelled Hitler to call off complementary thrusts in the north.

The main thing wrong with the Ardennes offensive was expressed in von Runstedt's words, "all or nothing," and Hitler's point-blank refusal, as in Normandy, to withdraw, to adopt alternative and secondary objectives when the main targers were clearly beyond reach. Indeed, it may be argued that in the Ardennes the war in the West was finally lost militarily by the Germans and politically by the Western Allies. There was the graveyard of great hopes.

ii.

On December 21st while the Battle of the Ardennes was still in its early stages, the Supreme Commander recommended General Bradley's promotion to General Marshall. The 12th Army Group Commander, Eisenhower stated, "kept his head magnificently and . . . proceeded methodically and energetically to meet the situation. In no quarter is there any tendency to place any blame upon Bradley."*

It was too early to apportion blame; nevertheless, in defending Bradley in advance the Supreme Commander

*Eisenhower to Marshall. 21 Dec. in personal file.

revealed, perhaps, an expectation for the future. It was, in fact, a bad moment in the Allied camp, and with passions fully aroused by the appointment on December 19th of Field Marshal Montgomery to command the U.S. 1st and 9th Armies in the battle.

A full assessment of the intelligence reports and summaries, followed by interviews and correspondence with the heads of intelligence concerned induced Forrest Pogue to write: . . . "one may well ask what additional information the Allies would have needed to predict the 16 December attack. In many ways their information was highly accurate. Most of the units which made up the panzer armies had been spotted days and even weeks before the attack. Air reconnaissance, while hampered at times by bad weather, had marked the steady stream of men and supplies westward across the Rhine. Despite the clever deceptive measures of the enemy, the Allied intelligence experts had correctly analyzed most of the German dispositions and, in the closing hours before the counteroffensive, were aware of shifts toward the Ardennes area and of the arrival of new units in the zone of VIII corps."*

General Bradley was the principal man concerned with this "accurate information," and by his preoccupation with the Saar offensives of General Patton's 3rd Army he had starved the whole Ardennes front, even in the face of many warnings.

Major General K.W.D. Strong, the SHAEF Chief of Intelligence, consistently expressed his uneasiness and drew attention daily to the possibilities open to the enemy "for at least a fortnight before the attack."† In his appreciation of the uses the Germans might make of the panzer army, General Strong emphasized three main courses, (a) to go to Russia; (b) to counterattack an Allied penetration; (c) to stage a relieving attack through the Ardennes.

General Strong went further. He stated that the German attack through the Ardennes would come whenever the enemy had a prediction of six days of bad weather. General Walter Bedell Smith, the SHAEF Chief of Staff,

*The Supreme Command.

†Letters addressed to Forrest Pogue, office of Chief of Military History, Washington, from Generals Strong and Bedell Smith, and dated Aug. 31 and Nov. 1, 1951.

confirmed these views, and was so greatly impressed
with the possibility of course (c) that he asked General
Strong if he was sure General Bradley was aware of the
possibility. "I replied in the affirmative," wrote General
Strong, "but nevertheless General Smith instructed me to
go to 12 A.G. [Army Group] and see General Bradley
personally and warn him. This would be about the first
week in December. I saw General Bradley personally for
about ¾ hour and he told me he was aware of the danger but 'that he had earmarked certain divisions to move
into the Ardennes area should the enemy attack
there' . . ."

To General Bedell Smith, Bradley said "Let them
come."

Right up to the eve of the attack Colonel Dickson,
U.S. 1st Army Chief of Intelligence, continued to report
enemy troop movements of an ominous nature, particularly in the Bitburg-Wittlich area. This was one of the
principal points from which the offensive was mounted
and Colonel Dickson also reported the presence of engineers with bridging equipment. In addition, a German
order was captured calling for speakers of the "American dialect" to report to *Waffen S S* Colonel Otto Skor-
zeny's headquarters for special training. This pointed
clearly to some kind of plan for sabotage behind the
American lines.

Two days before the German offensive Colonel Dickson's warnings grew more urgent, and on December 15th
the 1st Army estimate read (in part): "Reinforcements
for the West Wall between Düren and Trier continue to
arrive. The identification of at least three or four newly
re-formed divisions along the army front must be reck-
oned with during the next few days. . . . it is possible
that a limited scale offensive will be launched for purpose
of achieving a Christmas morale victory for civilian con-
sumption. Many PW's now speak of the coming attack
between 17th and 25th December."

None of this, the generals complain, was sufficiently
definite to induce them to take action, and one wonders
what they could have expected from their intelligence
advisers. It is the role of intelligence to discover as many
facts as possible, to keep track of enemy troop movements, and to evaluate the courses open to the enemy.
This they did with remarkable accuracy.

In his book General Bradley wrote: "No one came to me with a warning on the danger of counterattack there (the Ardennes)." This ignores or denies the categorical testimony of Generals Bedell Smith and Strong. In the same passage General Bradley remarks that he was commanding nearly three quarters of a million men spread out over a front of 230 miles. "It was impossible for me even to scan the intelligence estimates of subordinate units."*

The clear inference does not need to be labored further.

The fact is that not one of the generals was prepared to consider the possibility of enemy offensive action. They had made up their minds that the enemy was incapable of more than counterattack, and that this would come in the Roer front.

The intelligence chief of the 1st Airborne Army came nearer than anyone else in an accurate forecast, according to Lt. General Brereton in *The Brereton Diaries,* but these warnings were ignored because airborne units were not in the line at that time.

The 21st Army Group Headquarters had also followed with interest the German build-up, and had plotted the course of the *6th Panzer Army* with the restlessness of an old lady searching for a pea in her bed. But their conclusions were colored entirely by Field Marshal Montgomery's certainty that "von Runstedt was running the show." An enemy offensive was ruled out because it must lead to the more speedy defeat of the Germans. Thinking on those lines they were accurate about what von Runstedt would have done, but Hitler was running the show, and for him it was "All or nothing." He achieved complete tactical surprise.

iii.

The news of the German offensive reached General Bradley during the afternoon of December 16th while he was in conference with the Supreme Commander and senior Staff officers at SHAEF. "You've been asking for a counterattack," General Strong remarked. "Now it looks as if you've got it."

"A counterattack, yes," said Bradley, "but I'll be damned if I wanted one this big."

*A Soldier's Story

Nevertheless it was three days before Bradley confided to Patton that it was a good deal bigger than he had thought, and nearly a week before the full extent of the offensive was realized. Characteristically, Patton had taken steps to commit one of his armored divisions in order to avoid any interference with his own planned offensive. Equally characteristically he disengaged his whole Army from the Saar on Bradley's orders three days later, and moved north with tremendous drive and speed. Patton's disengagement and subsequent move with six divisions was a masterpiece of generalship, for with very great skill he swung north at right angles to his original line of attack, and compelled the attention of the weak German *7th Army,* and made Manteuffel nervous about his left flank.

At the same time Devers 6th Army Group moved to fill the breach left by the 3rd Army, and in so doing dangerously uncovered Strasbourg and the Alsatian plain.

Immediately upon hearing the news of the attack at SHAEF, Bradley had ordered the 7th Armored division to St. Vith, and the 10th Armored to race up from Luxembourg to Bastogne. Generals Bedell Smith, Whiteley, and Strong had at once appreciated the vital importance of holding the road centers of St. Vith and Bastogne, thereby squeezing the German armor into the defiles. The 18th Airborne Corps, refitting at Reims after its long spell in the north since Arnhem, was ordered at once into the fight, and by the 18th the 101st and 82nd Airborne Divisions were racing overland to the rescue of the hard pressed units holding out at the nodal points in the south and center.

Already Hitler had been forced to cancel his plans for an attack by the *15th Army* against Aachen, and had alerted *Army Group H* to prepare to assault across the Waal and the Maas. SHAEF, aware of these possibilities urgently scraped the bottom of the Allied barrel for reserves, grateful that Antwerp was at last open. But the port was under heavy pressure from the torrent of V-2's demanding immense efforts to keep the port functioning while fire fighting and attending to the needs of the population. In these weeks the Belgians were called upon to display all the fortitude they could muster. At the same time the problem of feeding the liberated peoples of Belgium and the Netherlands became acute, putting an added strain on Allied resources, not only in supplies, but in ships and aircraft. Without Antwerp it would have been impossible for the Allies to have met their obligations or to have replaced and reinforced their own losses. And Antwerp was gravely threatened.*

Meanwhile Montgomery's swift action in halting the movement to the north of the 30th Corps, and almost at once ordering the Guards Armored, three Armored Brigades, and the 43rd, 51st and 53rd Divisions, to the area Louvain-St. Troud, had not only provided effective screening of the Meuse and the roads through to Brussels and Antwerp, but had also freed Hodges to put the whole weight of the U.S. 1st Army into the battle.

By the night of December the 19th, although it was becoming clear that enemy hopes of seizing crossings of the Meuse and of exploiting bridgeheads for any further advances, had virtually disappeared, there were still many alternative courses the enemy might pursue with great profit to himself, and massive loss to the Allies. Already he had driven a wedge through the heart of the 12th Army Group, isolating Bradley from effective control of his armies in the north.

On the evening of December 19th, while the generals in the field still considered the enemy attack as an attempt to divert Patton from his drive against the Saar, and Hodges from his offensive to seize the Roer dams, General Strong appreciated the true situation, and at once suggested to General Whiteley that Field Marshal Montgomery should be ordered to take command of the U.S. 1st and 9th Armies without delay. Whiteley agreed. Indeed such a move had become unavoidable, not only because Montgomery was the only possible man capable of the task, but also because he controlled the essential reserve of the 30th Corps. The two generals put their proposition to General Bedell Smith. A quick check discovered that the 1st Army had been virtually out of contact with 12th Army Group headquarters for two days, and General Smith telephoned Bradley.

Bradley's reaction on the telephone was far less heated

*Two-thirds of the houses of Antwerp were hit, and one fifth destroyed. Liége suffered even more severely. In the six months. October-March, 8,000 Belgians were killed and 23,584 wounded by bombing, the worst of it coinciding with the German offensive. In January there was a dock strike in Antwerp.

than his subsequent reaction to the definite decision o. General Eisenhower to give the command to Montgomery.*

"Certainly, if Monty's were an American command, I would agree with you entirely," he said to Bedell Smith "It would be the logical thing to do."

In that sentence all the difficulties between the Allies are expressed: they were of two races; they had to attempt to fight as one.

It was in fact the "logical thing to do." The north o: the Ardennes had become "one battle front needing one ground force commander." The enemy had prevailed when all Montgomery's arguments had been in vain Awakened during the night of the 19th with the news o. his appointment, the Field Marshal at once called a conference at 1st Army Headquarters with Generals Hodge. and Simpson, commanding the 9th Army, for the morning of the 20th.

The descriptions of the meeting on that morning in U.S. 1st Army Headquarters emphasize a situation which but for the integrity and simplicity of the two principal: in the long command controversy, Eisenhower and Montgomery, might well have bedeviled and even disrupted the working of the Alliance. Chester Wilmot quotes a staf officer as saying: "The Field Marshal strode into Hodges H.Q. like Christ come to cleanse the temple." Montgomery's chief of staff, confirms the Field Marshal's remarkable resilience, and perkiness. It was, wrote de Guingand, just his "cup of tea."

Montgomery's whole mien and high spirits were in sharp contrast to the American generals. Hodges in particular showed signs of anxiety and strain. Both general: were weary men. They had been the rounds trying to gather precise information, and it must have been the more galling to find Montgomery with the situation, apparently, at his finger tips. His personal team of liaison officers, operating in scout cars, had brought him all possible news of the latest developments, and with masterly efficiency he unfolded his plan to the American commanders. The U.S. 9th Army would take over the commitment of the U.S. 1st Army on the Roer. The U.S. 7th Corp: would disengage and begin to form a reserve under General Collins to await the precise moment of necessity

---

*Eisenhower's last words to Bradley were: "Well, Brad, that' an order."

No man was better equipped militarily to deal with the situation than Field Marshal Montgomery; few men could have been less fitted to deal with Americans in their particular humor at that time, in that place. Already for weeks the intense bitterness evident in 12th Army Group Headquarters had been a source of worry to SHAEF, and nothing less than sheer necessity would have persuaded the General Staff and the Supreme Commander to appoint Montgomery to command American troops at such a time.

Montgomery's great problem from the outset was to restrain the Americans, and to build reserves. At a time when they wanted to throw everything they had into the battle the Field Marshal knew that it was vital to withdraw troops. He doubted the ability of the 3rd Army to halt Manteuffel's drive through to the Meuse on Givet and Dinant and believed that he must face the probability that he would have to halt, and finally destroy, the *5th Panzer Army* as well as the *6th*. He was alarmed about the strained condition of General Hodges, uncertain for several days whether the General would be up to his job and worried about what might happen if Hodges had to be replaced. Eisenhower quickly took that responsibility squarely upon his own shoulders, and Hodges settled the problem by recovering. In addition the Field Marshal found many American divisions below strength in infantry, some of them by as much as 7,000 men. In the rear areas the absolute confusion, the lack of any clearly defined lines of communication, the remarkable absence of security precautions in signals which were feeding information to Dietrich and Manteuffel as fast as to their own units and formations, must have offended his military sense. Yet he acted with great restraint, austere, uncritical, supremely confident, doing the job with an absolute certainty of touch, and unyielding in his resolution.

It was not easy. It required as much force of character as military skill. He had to force men to withdraw, to take up rear positions, to organize and prepare in patience—men whose whole attitude to war was "amateur." His insistence that the 7th Corps must disengage filled the corps commander and Hodges with "dismay."

Decisions of extreme urgency were also called for at the heart of the battle, particularly in the fight raging for St. Vith. With great skill and courage Hasbrouck's 7th Armored Division had checked and held the enemy, forcing the enemy armor into narrow channels to the north and south, but on December 22nd Hasbrouck was outflanked holding a 25-mile crescent front round St. Vith, and under tremendous pressure. Knowing that he must be overwhelmed, Hasbrouck sought permission to withdraw to strong positions west of the Salm. Permission was refused. Hasbrouck had no illusions but that this meant "the end of the 7th Armored Division," but Montgomery, hearing of this astounding refusal, indefensible on any grounds, insisted upon withdrawal in the face of fierce and bitter opposition from Generals Ridgeway and Hodges. The brave defenders of St. Vith were saved.

Almost at once a similar decision had to be taken in regard to Major General Gavin's 82nd Airborne Division. In this case the situation was complicated by Gavin's desire to be destroyed rather than withdraw. He realized fully that tactics, strategy, and reason, demanded his withdrawal, yet he supported his senior commanders. His cry, that his division had never withdrawn in "it's combat history," held in it the whole tragic problem of the United States Army in war.*

While Montgomery was fighting with Ridgeway and Hodges to save Gavin's division from itself, the enemy moved with speed to force Ridgeway's entire reserve into the battle, and gain a local tactical victory. Only then was Montgomery able to insist on withdrawal, and to save something from the wreck.

The period of crisis reached the peak on December 23rd when Manteuffel had an armored spearhead within its supplies, and was virtually impotent against the Allied four miles of the Meuse. The spearhead had overrun attack. It was the first and last brief look the enemy had of the broad river, and the end of his hopes. On that day also the fog lifted from the Ardennes, and the Allied Air Forces swooped down upon the enemy supply lines, and the columns trapped in the narrow defiles. In four days more than 10,000 sorties were flown, and all that remained to the enemy was withdrawal. But Hitler was

---

*Chester Wilmot wrote: "The stubborn determination to stand their ground was a source of great defensive strength to the Americans." Yet he admits that it deprived them of "tactical flexibility and strategic balance." I hold the view that the American inability to withdraw deprives them of defensive strength. In many battles, not least in Korea, this view has been reinforced.

adamant, compelling his armies inexorably to their destruction, as he had done in Normandy. From that point forward it is probable that the Americans had a clearer idea of the German intentions than was possible for Montgomery. Hitler's strategy was in fact very like their own, while Montgomery's military mind had to consider the probable moves of other military minds, such as Von Runstedt's and Manteuffel's.

Through these early days of anxiety Montgomery steadily held the northern jaws of the vice that must inevitably close upon the enemy, awaiting the precise moment to strike, holding back the Americans from premature counterattack, while Bradley fumed in his headquarters, writing bitterly to Hodges, but unable to command him, or to divert Montgomery from his plan. The enemy, Montgomery knew, was defeating himself. In good time he would move to destroy the Germans, and ensure that few should escape to confront him in his final drive to the Rhine.

iv.

The Supreme Commander and Field Marshal Montgomery met in conference at Hasselt on December 28th. Earlier on that morning snow had begun to fall heavily over the whole battlefield to mask the scars of war, and to slow the enemy armor as it sought to maneuver over the difficult ground.

On December 26th Patton's armored column had reached Bastogne at a moment when the enemy had begun to shift the weight of his attack to the south and southwest, and so to intensify the struggle for the key road center. Already the American defenders of Bastogne had written an indelible page in the story of war. Now the long epilogue, which was to involve ten German divisions in a vain effort to its defeat, was about to begin.

All along the salient from Bastogne through St. Hubert and Marche to Malmédy and Elsenborn, the German offensive was firmly held. All roads to the Meuse were blocked. The tide of battle was on the turn.

None would deny that when Field Marshal Montgomery met General Eisenhower at Hasselt on the morning of December 28th, the British Commander had brought order out of chaos. He had taken over command of the U.S. 1st and 9th Armies to find the 1st Army off balance, under heavy attack, and in a state of confusion. In less than a week he had restored the Army to equilibrium, while at the same time contriving a tactical reserve and holding the most powerful offensive the enemy was capable of mounting.

The task of regaining the lost ground and of destroying the enemy in the Ardennes now faced the Allies, and for this task the Americans considered the British Commander entirely unsuitable. Bradley had expressed himself strongly on this point to General Bedell Smith on December 26th, and Patton endorsed his chief's views. Bradley wrote: "Although I had hoped Montgomery would soon join our counterattack with one from the north, I found him waiting expectantly for one last enemy blow on the flank. Not until he was certain that the enemy had exhausted himself, would Montgomery plunge in for the kill. Disappointed at the prospect of further delay, I headed back to St. Trond."*

Already Bradley was urging upon SHAEF and the Supreme Commander that the time had come for the return of his armies and the complete restoration of his 12th Army Group Command.

Montgomery, for his party, was uneasy lest Bradley and Patton should seek to drive through from the south prematurely, and force the commitment of reserves "piecemeal."

Meanwhile, far from the battle front, dangerous rumblings had begun to stir the fires of discontent. Criticism of the Supreme Commander had been given some prominence in the British press, and with that, support had grown for "one ground force commander." To the commanders in the field this was an old and bitter story, but to the press it seemed brand new, and arising out of the Ardennes situation. All moments would have been bad for such criticisms, but there could not have been a worse moment than this, with passions rising high in the American camp. Reaction in the United States was swift, definite, and uncompromising.

It was with this unfortunate situation nearing a climax that Field Marshal Montgomery logically, as he saw it, pressed his old arguments for a single ground force commander north of the Ardennes and for confirmation of the British view of strategy that the full force of the

*A Soldier's Story.

Allied offensive must be in the north. Nothing seemed more reasonable to Montgomery than to press his claims at a time when his views seemed to have been vindicated by events; never had the time seemed more ripe than at this meeting with General Eisenhower at Hasselt.

It was ironical that at this moment when Montgomery held the command he had argued for for so long, it had become impossible for him to retain it. General Marshall had cabled Eisenhower at once in reaction to British press reports:

"My feeling is this: under no circumstances make any concessions of any kind whatsoever. You not only have our complete confidence but there would be terrific resentment in this country following such action. I am not assuming that you had in mind such a concession. I just wish you to be certain of our attitude on this side. You are doing a fine job and go on and give them hell."*

General Eisenhower, aware of the powerful undercurrents, remained, as always, restrained, patient, and eminently fair. Montgomery, as a mark of the Supreme Commander's confidence, would retain the U.S. 9th Army for his attack in the north, and this would give the Field Marshal as many divisions as he could hope to deploy on that front. The U.S. 1st Army would return to Bradley. The old pattern of command, and of strategy, would be maintained. It had paid magnificent dividends.

But Montgomery, undismayed, and with the British Chiefs of Staff behind him, continued to press his point, and on December 31st Eisenhower, after thanking the Field Marshal for his "frank and friendly counsels," uttered a warning. He would deplore "the development of such an unbridgeable gulf of convictions between us that we would have to present our differences to the combined chiefs of staff. The confusion and debate that would follow would certainly damage the good will and devotion to a common cause that have made this Allied Force unique in history."*

The situation had reached the boil, and de Guingand, Montgomery's Chief of Staff, fearing the worst after a talk with General Bedell Smith, warned his chief that if

*Eisenhower personal file.
*Eisenhower personal file, dated 31 Dec. '44.

it came to a showdown "someone would have to go and it would not be the Supreme Commander."*

Montgomery was astonished. The storm of controversy raging round him had passed him by. Without wasting a moment he wrote at once to assure Eisenhower of his devoted loyalty. Between the two men it could not have been in doubt. The long command crisis in the field was almost at an end. At the conference table between the Chiefs of Staff it was only at its beginning.

v.

The main purpose of the Hasselt meeting had been to reach agreement on the timing of the counterattack in the Ardennes. Montgomery stated that he would be ready to move over to the offensive about the 2nd or 3rd of January. Eisenhower appears to have understood him to say the 1st of January. Actually, New Year's Day itself belonged to the Germans, reminding the Allies that it was unwise to take chances with their terrible enemy even in the air. On that day the Luftwaffe, mustering all its strength, struck in low-level attacks against Allied airfields throughout Belgium and the Netherlands. It was the heaviest enemy use of air power in the campaign and something of a shock. The losses of aircraft on the ground were severe, but far from crippling, and it was small consolation that the enemy had also paid a heavy price. For the enemy it had been a desperate throw.

Nevertheless it gave warning that it was time to press home the counterattack, and on January 3rd the U.S. 7th Corps went into the attack against the northern shoulder of the enemy salient. The snow was thick upon the ground. Guns and men moved with difficulty over a white wilderness that hid mines without trace and against an enemy resolved upon a controlled fighting withdrawal, an enemy moreover still capable of offensive action. The cold was intense.

Slowly from that day forward the jaws of the vise closed, and on January 7th, knowing the battle won and the final result beyond doubt, Field Marshal Montgom-

*The Supreme Commander's advisers at SHAEF urged him to force a showdown, see "The Supreme Command," p. 386.
Operation Victory, p. 434, by Major-General Sir Francis de Guingand.

ry gave a press conference which was doomed to set he seal upon the crisis of command.

Members of Montgomery's staff, fearing that their chief would almost certainly say the wrong things, or the right hings in the wrong way, strove to prevent the conference. The Field Marshal was adamant. He owed it, he believed, o the Supreme Commander and to the Americans to ut the record straight and to correct some of the mis-understandings which had arisen from British press crit-cisms of General Eisenhower. Few doubted that he would achieve the reverse.

Yet Field Marshal Montgomery's statement earned him the warm praise of *The New York Times* in an edi-torial: "No handsomer tribute was ever paid to the American soldier than that of Field Marshal Montgomery in the midst of the combat."*

His analysis of the battle was, as always, masterly. His tributes to U.S. commanders and men unequivocal; his sentiments, unexceptionable. Nevertheless General Brad-ley and the U.S. commanders were "outraged" and ut-terly "exasperated." From that moment it became hope-less for the British Chiefs of Staff to press their views on strategy or to pursue their suggestion for a new dep-uty supreme commander to replace Air Marshal Tedder, and to act as a "Ground Force Commander."†

When General Eisenhower tentatively broached the subject of a ground-force commander to General Brad-ley, the 12th Army Group Commander stated flatly that he would ask to be relieved of his command rather than serve under Montgomery. Moreover, the next offensive must be under American command. The American pub-lic would not stand for a secondary role.

*New York Times, Jan. 9, 1945

†At the Malta conference of the Combined Chiefs of Staff 30th January-2nd February, the British pressed their strategic view-point and also pursued the subject of a "Ground Force Com-mander." Alexander was designed for the role. The Americans would not consider it, nor would they budge from Eisenhower's "two-attack" strategy. See: *Grand Strategy*, vol. vi. "It (the dis-cussion) was indeed vehement as well as prolonged." It pro-voked "the most acrimonious dispute between the CC of S dur-ing the war." See also: *The White House Papers of Harry Hopkins*, vol. ii. "One can read the official minutes of these meetings without suspecting that a single harsh word had been exchanged. But they were very angry men."

It seemed then that Montgomery's battle of the Rhineland was in jeopardy, for it was becoming difficult for the Supreme Commander to hold to his intention that the main drive should be in the north. It had become politically essential that a secondary drive should take place and that, if possible, it should steal the thunder. With Bradley and Patton out for blood it was not unlikely that, secondary or not, it would do just that.

Doctor Goebbels was quick to turn the controversy to German advantage. A broadcast in English, giving a skillfully distorted view, purporting to be British, was readily believed, notably by General Bradley, despite the denials of Mr. Brendan Bracken. Churchill weighed in with handsome tributes to the Americans, emphasizing the Ardennes as an almost total American battle and followed a statement in the House of Commons with a grave warning: "Let no one," he said, "lend himself to the chatter of mischief-makers when issues of this momentous consequence are being successfully decided by the sword."* It was, at least, a reminder that the price was being paid in flesh and blood.

The reaction continued to plague General Eisenhower for many weeks. It had bitten deeply into the minds of many American senior officers and was not soon forgotten. In a letter to General Marshall, Eisenhower wrote that it was the most difficult incident with which he had ever had to deal.

It must be clear that Field Marshal Montgomery's statement to the press of January 7th, harmless though it was in content, and intended to clear the air, served to spark a situation that was already primed and ready for explosion. It would be wrong, I think, to leave the matter there. The passage singled out by General Bradley, and which roused his bitter and lasting anger, reads as follows:

"When Runstedt attacked on December 16, he obtained a tactical surprise. He drove a deep wedge into the center of the United States 1st Army and the split might have become awkward; the Germans had broken through a weak spot, and were heading for the Meuse.

"As soon as I saw what was happening, I took certain steps myself to ensure that if the Germans got to the Meuse

*Hansard 1944-45, 407 H. C. Deb.

they would certainly not get over that river. And I carried out certain movements so as to provide balanced dispositions to meet the threatened danger; these were, at the time, merely precautions, i.e. I was thinking ahead.

"Then the situation began to deteriorate. But the whole Allied team rallied to meet the danger; national considerations were thrown overboard; General Eisenhower placed me in command of the whole northern front.

"I employed the whole available power of the British Group of Armies; this power was brought into play very gradually and in such a way that it would not interfere with the American lines of communications. Finally it was put into the battle with a bang and today British divisions are fighting hard on the right flank of the United States 1st Army.

"You have thus the picture of British troops fighting on both sides of American forces who have suffered a hard blow. This is a fine Allied picture.

"The battle has some similarity to the battle that began on 31 August 1942 when Rommel made his last bid to capture Egypt and was "seen off" by the Eighth Army."*

Taken out of their context, these words and this mode of expression might be irritating to highly susceptible men, but it was not so much Montgomery's words as his manner, his "what a good boy am I" attitude, that so infuriated the Americans in the field and induced General Bradley to strip himself of the dignity becoming to the commander of a Group of Armies—or, indeed, of a platoon. His was the "calculated risk" that had brought these results and was costing an average of more than 2,000 American casualties each day of the battle. He was the man responsible for dragging the whole weight to the south in constant support of Patton at the expense of the 1st Army. Perhaps, indeed, his anger sprang out as a result of some such inner awareness.

"There was a danger that Bradley's high prestige *vis-à-vis* his troops might become undermined," wrote de Guingand,† referring to the Field Marshal's statement, but Bradley's high prestige with his troops could not be undermined by any words of Montgomery's.

*See: *The Supreme Command*, and for comment.
†*Operation Victory*, By Major General Sir Francis de Guingand.

Throughout this storm the two men most concerned, Eisenhower and Montgomery, maintained their dignity and their balance. Montgomery, for his part, seemed almost unaware even that General Bradley bore him anything but good will and the warmest regard.

8: *THE MOMENT OF TRUTH*

i.

AT NO time in the whole war was the enormous extent of the Nazi military power more apparent—and, in a way, more awe inspiring—than in this January of 1945, when, assaulted from east, south, and west, the vast military machine moved into its dance of death, and strategy into its last phase. It is possible to fix the moment of truth with some precision.

In the north, while the Battle of the Ardennes was at its height, it had been a time of vigilance, of incessant patrolling, of many severe, but limited, encounters, and constant menace. All along the line of the Maas and the Roer Rivers the enemy had a resurgence of hope and energy, even borrowing from the Chinese some of the violent noises of battle. Amplifiers dinned the rumble of armored columns into the ears of the men manning their brens in the forward positions. Men of 47 Royal Marine Commando fought a tremendous battle with a German parachute division on the island of Kapelsche Veer in the middle of the Maas northeast of Breda. A small but powerful force of enemy crossed the Maas at Wessem. All along the right flank of the 2nd Army from Sittard to Geilenkirchen the activity was intense, and it was clear that a major battle would have to be fought to clear the Heinsberg triangle and open up the last stretch of the Roer from Linnich to Roermond. That battle, postponed under the name "Operation Shears," because of the assault in the Ardennes, was ready to go in in mid-January under the code name "Operation Blackcock." The 12th Corps had earmarked the 7th Armored Division, the 30th Armored Brigade, the 43rd (Wessex) Infantry Division, and the 52nd (Mountain) Infantry Division for the job. The men lay there in the snow, keyed up and ready, their outposts in Germany and their supply lines in Holland, their ears assaulted by the new Nazi "music of battle."

At the southern end of the Roer the great dams remained securely in enemy hands and would demand a major effort from the U.S. 1st Army if they were to be taken and Schmidt revenged. Fierce enemy attacks came in against Düren, and the threat to Aachen was at times severe.

But it was in the south that Hitler chose to strike a major blow at the very climax of the Ardennes battle. Taking advantage of Patton's move to the north the enemy had mounted an offensive driving south and west of Bitche, while at the same time a strong force crossed the Rhine north of Strasbourg to link up east of the Vosges with an attack planned to strike north and west out of the Colmar pocket. The plan was bold and extremely dangerous, threatening Strasbourg and precipitating a crisis with the French. For an agonizing twenty-four hours it seemed that Strasbourg might fall again into German hands, and with appalling results. The whole Alsatian Plain was threatened at a moment when the U.S. 6th Army Group, maneuvering to shorten its lines, had left Strasbourg uncovered and would have been prepared to yield the city to the enemy had such a course proved as politically possible as it seemed militarily expedient.

General Schwartz, the French Commander of the Strasbourg Garrison, strongly supported by Generals Juin and de Gaulle, reacted with horror. The thought of the reprisals the Nazis might wreak upon the people would have been alone sufficient to deny Strasbourg to the enemy at all costs. Three hundred thousand people in Alsace were in fear of their lives. Churchill flew anxiously from London in response to a plea from de Gaulle to sit in at a conference with Eisenhower and the SHAEF Chiefs of Staff while the French generals disabused the Americans of any notions of expediency. There was no need for the Prime Minister to do more than sit there with his head thrust forward, his jaws set hard, saying nothing at all. President Roosevelt had refused to interfere.

The enemy offensive, under the code name NORDWIND, had opened on the last night of the old year to reach its maximum intensity in the bridgeheads north and south of Strasbourg between the 5th and 7th of January. At that point the French took over responsibility for the defense of the city.

In the Colmar pocket the enemy continued to hold, and on January 23rd, with an enemy threat to the Saverne Gap still a menace, a very outspoken meeting took place between the Supreme Commander and General Juin. The French had been starved of reinforcements, waging a bitter war in the Vosges for months, and now in January, with their front doubled in extent, they could make little headway. When Eisenhower expressed the hope that the French would be inspired "to excel their own former records,"* General Juin reacted with a sharp note on the following day, pointing out the extent of the French effort and criticizing "the goings-on in the neighboring Army further to the North."†

"The important thing to-day," General Juin's letter ended, "is that you win the battle of Alsace as you have won the battle of the Ardennes. That, in my opinion, as I told you yesterday, should be your sole preoccupation of the moment."§

It was, however, a moment of many grave preoccupations for the Supreme Commander, a moment when great prospects were opening ahead.

But by January 25th the Germans had fought themselves virtually to a standstill in their bid for Alsace. They had fought themselves to a standstill everywhere. Now in the west they stood with their backs to the Rhine as, in the east, they had their backs to the Oder. The stage was being set for the last battle.

ii.

The worst of the Allied troubles in the Ardennes were over at the time of the enemy offensive in the south. On January 10th, while the enemy threat to Alsace was still being furiously maintained, although in fact past its climax, Field Marshal Montgomery and General Bradley issued their joint orders for a combined counterattack by the U.S. 1st and 3rd Armies. This would strike the enemy a knock-out blow, and regain all the lost territory.

*The Supreme Command
†U.S. 7th Army.
§Letter, Juin to Eisenhower, 24 Jan., 1945.

Feeling that his work in the Ardennes was virtually at an end, Montgomery wrote generously to Bradley on the 12th, the eve of the combined attack:

"My dear Brad,
"It does seem as if the battle of the 'salient' will shortly be drawing to a close, and when it is all clean and tidy I imagine that your armies will be returning to your operational command.

"I would like to say two things:

"*First*: What a great honor it has been for me to command such fine troops.

"*Second*: How well they have all done.

"It has been a great pleasure to work with Hodges and Simpson: both have done very well.

"And the Corps Commanders in the First Army (Gerow, Collins, Ridgeway) have been quite magnificent; it must be most exceptional to find such a good lot of Corps Commanders gathered together in one army.

"All of us in the northern side of the salient would like to say how much we have admired the operations that have been conducted on the southern side; if you had not held on firmly to Bastogne the whole situation might have become very awkward.

"My kind regard to you and to George Patton.

"Yrs very sincerely,
B. L. Montgomery."

A copy of this letter was sent also to General Eisenhower with a covering note stating: "It has been a very great honor for me to command two American armies."

While there is every reason to believe that these notes express Montgomery's genuine sentiments, there is equally every reason to believe that anything Montgomery could say added only gall to General Bradley's load.

In the dawn of January 13th the 1st and 3rd Armies moved from north and south to crush the enemy out of the salient. Already the *6th Panzer Army* had been ordered out of the line by Hitler and was about to rush east to add its remaining strength to the troops fighting desperately to halt the Russian avalanche.

On the 16th of January, units of the 1st and 3rd Armies joined hands across the stream of the Ourthe where it runs deep in the gorge through the little township of Houffalize. The heavy snow lying in deep drifts in the narrow defiles blanketed the offal and debris of war, but could not conceal the desolation of the little towns and villages, reduced to blackened skeletons in the ebb tide of war, in the wake of "Les sales Boches," 1914-1918, 1940-1944. In the villages women buried their dead, and old men searched in the ruins of homes for some treasure. Rochefort, Champlon, Bure, and Houffalize itself were in complete ruin, but Houffalize on the morning of January 17th was the symbol of the American victory. Powdered snow drove fiercely in the bitter wind, so that the ground had a virgin look, unmarked by wheel or footprint, as infantry patrols moved forward soon after dawn. Within an hour the snow had erased all signs of their passing. A man approaching from the south saw no signs of life, and knew only a loneliness as of the grave, a strange calm within the distant noises of battle. Shattered tree stumps stood up in grotesque shapes on the slopes of the steep gorge, and icicles veiled the outcropping rocks. Houffalize was no longer a place of human habitation. A cat ran startled out of a heap of rubble, wavered, uncertain which way to turn, and crouched in terror under what had been a road block. Presently a very old man leaning on a tall stick came slowly up the hill. There were no other signs of life.

At the foot of the hill a handful of American troops straddled the timbers of the blown bridge, clambering across to shake hands with a patrol from the north. Engineers moved about like housewives with heavy floor polishers looking for mines.

"Beat, ain't it?" said a soldier.

The battle of the Ardennes was to rage on into the fourth week of the month as the enemy fought to extricate something from the wreck of his last hopes, but Houffalize on that morning meant the end. The enemy had inflicted a tactical reverse upon the Allies, compelling the postponement of their planned offensive, but the cost had been far greater than he could afford to pay. The wreckage of at least 600 tanks, and of countless rucks, lay over the roads, and in the rear beyond the Rhine immense quantities of rolling stock had been smashed to ruin by Allied air attack. Above all, the drain on the last remaining German manhood had been severe. At the lowest estimate the enemy had suffered 80,000 casualties in the battle. It was probably nearer 100,000. It had cost the Americans very little less. It had been their battle. They had lost 75,482 men against the British total of 1,408. That is the measure of it.

Again, as in Normandy, Hitler had imposed catastrophe upon his armies, refusing to permit withdrawal while withdrawal was possible, refusing to agree to alternative objectives until it was too late. Yet, although Hitler may be said to have lost the Battle of the Ardennes, Field Marshal Montgomery deserves very great credit for his part in the victory. Beset by Bradley, and to a lesser extent by Hodges and Ridgeway, his whole plan and tactics loathed and condemned, and even at times compromised by impulsive action, Montgomery kept the battle firmly under control from beginning to end.

I would say that he saved the American 1st Army 20,000 casualties, including the U.S. 7th Armored Division. The blood was American; the brains and the moral courage were his.

Moreover his handling of the British 30th Corps was consistently masterly. Unless he had concentrated his mind upon the "maintenance of the objective" in the north, the Battle of the Ardennes might well have cost him the Battle of the Rhineland, taking the campaign out of British hands, and condemning the 21st Army Group to a minor role.

Nothing would have been easier—or brought him higher praise from the Americans—than to commit the 30th Corps to the battle. Instead, he most carefully avoided entanglement with the U.S. lines of communications while using his troops to the best advantage. Their role was to guarantee the line of the Meuse through the time of crisis, to provide security and a vital reserve, and at the last by strengthening the right flank of the U.S. 1st Army to lend it maneuverability.

On the day of Houffalize the 30th Corps divisions were pinched out of the battle, having served their purpose admirably. On that evening of January 17th the U.S. 1st Army returned to the operational command of the U.S.

12th Army Group. It behooved Field Marshal Montgomery to withdraw his troops, to regroup with all speed
and to move north.

iii.

January 12th is perhaps the most easily recognizable of
the decisive dates in the history of war, for on that day
vast forces were set in motion which were to change the
face of Europe, and to mark a decisive turning point in
the story of European civilization. Of those few who were
aware of these things at the time it is unlikely that any,
apart from Stalin and Churchill, saw the portent. For
Stalin it was enough to observe with satisfaction. For
Churchill no action was possible.

Yet the promise of these things had stirred Churchill
and Eisenhower to something like exaltation. From early
December Eisenhower had been anxious to have some
news of Russian offensive plans for the Winter. No news
had been forthcoming. Early in January Air Marshal Tedder had set out by air for Moscow to see Marshal Stalin,
but on the night of January 5th his aircraft was grounded
in Cairo. Impatient at the delay, Churchill sent a personal cable to Stalin on the 6th, and had a reply the
next day promising "large-scale offensive operations
against the Germans along the whole Central Front not
later than the second half of January." Churchill at once
cabled his grateful thanks for the "thrilling message.*

At dawn on January 12th Marshal Koniev advanced
from his bridgeheads on the Vistula, and two days later
the armies of Marshal Zhukov, crossing on his right flank,
swung north over the Pilica, while on his left General
Petrov's Army threatened Jaslo. On the extreme right of
this violent assault, which swiftly enveloped Warsaw and
Cracow, Marshals Rokossovsky and Chernyakhosky advanced upon Tilsit, obliterated East Prussia, and gained
bridgeheads over the Vistula in the north to join with the
right wing of Zhukov's armies. In the south, stiffening
the pressure which they had never relaxed throughout
the winter, Malinovsky and Tolbukhin enveloped Buda-
pest, and the roads to Vienna and Berlin opened ahead.

In three weeks, moving at an average rate of 14 miles
a day as the crow flies, the Russians were on the river
Oder 280 miles from their start point. From north to south

*Churchill Memoirs. Vol. vi. Triumph and Tragedy.

300 Russian divisions backed by 25 tank armies and hordes of Cossacks, rolled back the Germans with an irresistible force. East Prussia and Poland were engulfed; Bulgaria plucked like a rotten fruit; Hungary doomed in violent struggle; Roumania shattered, while the fate of Czechoslovakia could not be long in doubt.

Such was the significance of January 12th, 1945, in human affairs. By the time Field Marshal Montgomery was ready to mount his offensive in the Rhineland, the Russians were within 40 miles of Berlin with their center, and their right flank on the Baltic, and their left ready to sweep on Vienna.

It may be unfair to say that the Western Allies "fiddled while Rome burned," but at this moment, as the great tragedy—which was world tragedy—unfolded, moving into its final phase, the U.S. 1st Army was still trying to take the Roer dams, and undo the Battle of Schmidt. The U.S. 9th Army, under Montgomery's command, was not only immobilized behind the Roer river awaiting the taking of the dams, but was also awaiting the return of its divisions involved with the 12th Army Group.

The rivalries and petty jealousies stemming from the Ardennes prohibited the launching of the main offensive in the north, for this would not only offend Generals Bradley and Patton, but would not be tolerated by the American people. Yet, it would have been possible for the Western Allies, welded in an absolute loyalty of interests, in political and military faith, to grasp the nettle danger, and to strike a blow for the future of Western Europe. That they failed to do so was implicit in the split in their military and political thinking. The gulf, which seemed to many little more than a matter of emphasis, was in reality a chasm. And it could not be bridged.

There might have been a chance not only to win the war, but to win the peace. All the arguments for "broad fronts" and "narrow fronts," bandied back and forth since August, dwindle to insignificance in the face of this huge challenge. This was the moment of truth. This was the moment when Montgomery's brave, but hopeless, cry of August, 1944, had it been uttered again, might have sounded down the centuries:

"Give me forty divisions. Give me a force so strong as to fear nothing, and I will drive through to the heart —to Berlin, and so end the German war!"

In mid-August, 1944, it had been militarily and logistically impossible. Now, at the end of January, 1945, with the Germans defeated, with the freight trains from Antwerp pouring in troops and the sinews of war behind the armies, it was militarily and logistically possible, and politically utterly without hope.

Thus, at the end of January Allied strategy was in chains, and German strategy had ceased to exist. For the Germans there was no tomorrow. The war had moved beyond the point when all previous wars have ended, and this, I believe, was inevitable. The Allied policy of "Unconditional Surrender" has often been blamed as perhaps the principal reason why the war did not end at that point. But this cannot be true. Unconditional surrender is, in any case, a meaningless form of words, for there are always terms or conditions, and millions of Germans did surrender on those "terms."

Hitler, and Hitler alone, bears the whole weight of responsibility for the beginning and for the end. His were the terms, and the terms were these: he would bring down the Reich in chaos, and divide Europe with his last strength, demented and steeped in evil, eyeless in the bunker.

Eighty-five divisions faced eighty-five divisions west of the Rhine, on the last battlefield, and in its death throes the German Army in the west was still a most terrible and potent force.

PART THREE: BATTLE OF THE RHINELAND

9: MAINTENANCE OF THE OBJECTIVE

i.

THROUGH ALL the delays and emergencies of the autumn and winter Field Marshal Montgomery had not for one moment permitted himself to lose sight of the major role his armies must play in the north. In the late December conferences with the Supreme Commander, the decisions of the Brussels Conference of October 18th had been re-affirmed. The Battle of the Rhineland as originally conceived would be launched in its original pattern. The U.S. 9th Army, under 21st Army Group command, would undertake the right hook, "Operation Grenade," crossing the River Roer at Julich, and swinging northeastward on Düsseldorf with its right flank, and in the center through München Gladbach and Krefeld to meet the British thrusting down southeastward from the Nijmegen bridgehead upon the central target of Wesel.

On the right of the U.S. 9th Army, the U.S. 1st Army would secure the Roer dams and press on across the Cologne plain.

Yet the months since mid-October had wrought great changes for the enemy and for the Allies. The lack of emphasis on the northern battle, and the fear that Eisenhower's "Broad front" strategy would permit two major offensives to develop at the same time, had always worried the Field Marshal and the British Chiefs of Staff. Now that lack of emphasis was even more marked, and the uneasiness had increased. As a result of the Ardennes, it seemed likely that the southern thrust of the U.S. 12th Army Group aimed on Bonn on the left, through Prüm in the center, to close the Rhine from Cologne to Mainz, for all the insistence on its secondary nature, might develop into a major offensive and gravely prejudice the final advance in the north. The American public wanted to hear of its commanders and troops in the major roles, and it was certain that General Patton, abetted by General Bradley, would do his best to fulfil their hopes.

In mid-January, as Field Marshal Montgomery turned north, and the British 30th Corps disengaged rapidly from the Ardennes, the U.S. 9th Army was down to a strength of five divisions as a result of Bradley's demands upon it. Those demands might increase rather than diminish, and Montgomery had pressed Eisenhower to make up the 9th Army to sixteen divisions. He had been promised twelve divisions. In addition Montgomery felt some doubts as to the urgency and awareness with which the U.S. 1st Army approached the difficult task of seizing the Roer dams before it was too late. The task had been gravely bungled, and the dams had withstood all attempts upon them from the air. The time for instant and decisive action had arrived. Failure would immobilize the U.S. 9th Army and literally "wash out" the planned right hook of "Operation Grenade."

Nevertheless, convinced that he had achieved all that was possible, Montgomery agreed with the Supreme Commander on a target date for the Rhineland battle, "Operation Veritable," to open on February 8th, with "Operation Grenade" to follow two days later. With that the Field Marshal became wholly absorbed with his great tasks in the north and left the British Chiefs of Staff to pursue their strategic arguments to the bitter end.

On January 14th the 30th Corps Headquarters moved north to join the Canadian 1st Army Headquarters in the detailed planning for "Operation Veritable." The intention was to destroy all enemy forces between the Rhine and the Maas from Nijmegen to the general line Julich-Düsseldorf. On January 21st, 21st Army Group issued its final orders for the battle. The stage was fast being set, and the task was immense. It would be, almost certainly, the last great battle paving the way for the final assault across the Rhine.

It would be difficult to overstate the diabolical feats of planning and organization to be crammed into the final three weeks before "Operation Veritable" opened.

An immense weight and variety of equipment and stores, ammunition, bridging, fuel, signal cables, and general supplies had to be brought in, assembled, and concealed. Roads were few, narrow, and constantly collaps-

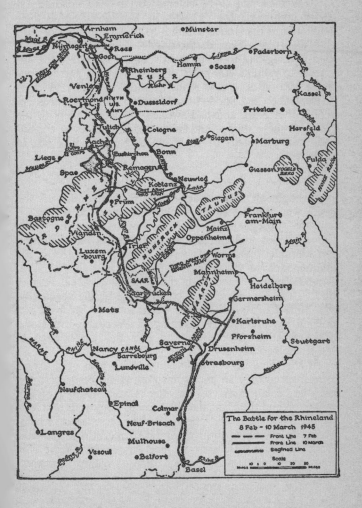

The Battle for the Rhineland
8 Feb – 10 March 1945

Front Line 7 Feb
Front Line 10 March
Siegfried Line

Scale
10 5 0   10   20   30   Miles

ing under the weight of traffic, and only the freight trains running constantly out of V-bombed Antwerp made possible the realization of the Rhineland battle. A total of 340,000 men had to be catered for under Canadian 1st Army command for "Operation Veritable," and their maintenance demanded a build-up of 10,000 tons of supplies each day. Tens of thousands of tons of rubble for road making had to be brought forward to enable the engineers to rebuild 400 miles of existing roads and to construct 100 miles of new road. In addition the heavy rains of December had flooded the Maas up to 1,000 yards beyond either bank and had swollen the River Niers to the east. All these things, and many more, had to be considered and provided for in advance. Nothing was left to chance.

ii.

Through all December, while the attention of the world was focused almost exclusively upon the Ardennes, and the subsequent developments round Strasbourg, the Canadian 1st and the British 2nd Armies had achieved considerable feats of organization and of arms in the maintenance of the offensive projects and the preparations to mount them with the smallest possible loss of time. These tasks had been complicated by the absence of the 30th Corps, which had been actively involved not only in the preliminary planning of "Veritable," but also of "Operation Blackcock," an essential preliminary to the Rhineland battle.

At the same time it had been necessary to hold a very long front against an enemy inspired with new hopes, and capable of launching severe attacks at a number of key points. While the Canadian 2nd Corps deployed its troops in the Nijmegen bridgehead, seeking constantly to improve its positions, the British 1st Corps held a 125-mile front on the Maas, alert to meet an enemy threat with four divisions aimed through Breda against Antwerp. This threat did not develop; but it had remained a very real and potent menace at the height of the Ardennes offensive.

The British 2nd Army had also been busy, its headquarters involved with the complex planning and massive preliminaries for the Rhine crossing, an amphibious operation envisaged as second only to the Normandy landings. 2nd Army troops also held the line of the Maas from Roermond to Cuijk, uneasily aware of the thinly held flank south to Aachen.

Above all in December urgent consideration had to be given to "Operation Blackcock," the clearance of the Heinsberg triangle to close the line of the River Roer from Linnich to Roermond and remove this awkward salient from the joint of the British and U.S. armies. The task was handed over to the 12th Corps, and on December 31st planning instructions were issued to all troops available for the battle. These consisted of one armored division, two armored brigades, elements of the 79th Armored Division, and two infantry divisions. Corps and divisional artillery would be greatly strengthened by two groups of British artillery. In addition the 8th Corps would give artillery support on the left while the U.S. 13th Corps performed a similar function on the right.

These were formidable forces, amply justified by the nature and urgency of the task confronting them. The enemy, deeply entrenched, shielded by wire, and with the powerful strong points of the Siegfried Line anchoring the flanks, must be expected to fight hard to hold this last piece of key territory west of the Roer. Allied success was as essential to the opening of "Operation Veritable" as the seizure of the Roer dams would be to the opening of "Operation Grenade" by the U.S. 9th Army.

On January 10th Field Marshal Montgomery issued his final orders for "Blackcock," and on the 15th the 1st/5th Battalion of the Queens Regiment moved to secure the start line. The weather was appalling, a sudden thaw turning the roads to slippery mud-traps to hold up the main assault of the armor. One of the main provisos of the plan was that the ground should be suitable for the use of flails and armor. But "Operation Blackcock" could not be delayed.

10: THE "BLACKCOCK" REHEARSAL

i.

THE WEATHER for Operation Blackcock provided all the possible variations on a theme of winter except sunshine,

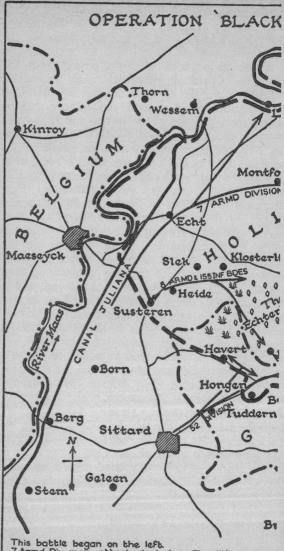

OPERATION `BLACK

This battle began on the left.
7 Armd Div. main attack started on Jan 16th
8 Armd Bde and 155 Inf Bde advanced on Jan 17th
52 Div. attacked on Jan 18th
43 Wessex Div. attacked on Jan 20th
8 Armd and 155 Inf Bdes rejoined 52 Div. on Jan 21st
HEINSBERG was assaulted on Jan 24th
POSTERHOLT fell on Jan 27th

COCK' XII CORPS

ROERMOND

inne

St. Odilenberg

rt

A N D

R. Roer

Posterholt

Kempen

lbosch

Echterbosch

Obspringen

bosch

Waldfeucht

Heinsberg

Bocket

Braunsrath

Coningbosch

Aphoven

Saeffelen

Laffeld

43 DIVISION

Schierwaldenrath

reberen

Waldenrath

E R

M

A

Gangelt

Tripsrath

N

Y

unssum

Geilenkirchen

Scale

Miles | 0   1   2   3   4   5 | Miles

| International Bdys |
| German Front Line |

bright, and cold. It thawed, froze, fogged, snowed, and rained, sometimes all five in a mushy mixture within twenty-four hours. It was always bitterly cold. The white snow suits provided for most of the forward troops, the careful white camouflage of armor, including flails, crocodiles, troop-carrying Kangaroos, and almost all vehicles, was not in vain. It was more often "whitish" with snow or dank and dim with fog than anything else, and the nights were long and dismal, lit in the hours of night attacks by searchlights reflecting down from the clouds in "artificial moonlight." It was a battle for infantry.

But the pattern of warfare was new. It was fought out on a small confined stage inside Germany, from river to river and brook to brook, from copse to copse, hamlet to hamlet, and house to house. Yet, in common with every major process of "mopping up" since the Normandy victory, it lacked the essential of a battle: the enemy could not win. At best the enemy could hope to slow down the momentum of losing while awaiting a political miracle. Only the Ardennes had borne the characteristics of a major battle, and even there the possibility of enemy victory had seemed unreal, even in the worst moments.

Operation Blackcock was a very unpleasant and important example of the long mopping-up process ahead. In that narrow triangle of difficult, deceptively undulating country, with Roermond at the apex, with the sides held in the west by the line of the Maas and the Juliana canal, and in the east by the intricacies of the rivers Wurm and Roer, the enemy had constructed three defensive trench systems protected by trip wires and minefields.

Every enemy village was a strong point, every stream a heavily defended obstacle, the crossing points covered by mortars and artillery. The numerous small copses of the central woodlands of the Echterbosch were ideal points from which to inflict heavy casualties upon the attacker. Civilians were very few. The whole area was a battlefield, and the heart of it was inside Germany. It had become a fortress held by two infantry divisions, and a first class regiment, *Regiment Hubner,* garrisoning Roermond. Some ninety field guns, including self-propelled guns of 7.5-cm caliber, were available to the enemy within the triangle, and some support might be expected from the heavy guns of the Roer. There would not be reserves. These men would fight, die, or be captured or retreat beyond the river barrier. Their counterattacks would be strictly local, and by their courage or cowardice nothing could be gained or lost, except time. Their army had suffered a ferocious purge of its officers, and behind them their country was disintegrating rapidly in physical, spiritual, and moral ruin.

Henceforth this in essence is the nature of the campaign in Northwest Europe, and in this it is unique in the history of war. It is endowed with a rare and terrible quality of tragedy, of wastage of life and courage, a vain, empty, suicidal self-inflicted total defeat growing worse with every hour, availing nothing, and nurturing the seeds of chaos.

The Allies had allotted ten days for the elimination of the Heinsberg triangle. A careful plan had been prepared, detailed yet flexible in the hands of good commanders. A skillful regrouping had been carried out calculated to deceive the enemy. Two brigades of the 43rd Division had relieved the 52nd Division on the extreme right. The 52nd Division had moved to the center to relieve the right flank of the 7th Armored Division, and it was hoped that these moves would encourage the enemy to expect a stalemate to continue, or that an attack would be aimed direct on Heinsberg from the Geilenkirchen sector.

Instead the 12th Corps plan was to strike on the extreme left, driving north to open the roads Sittard-Limbricht-Holtum-Dieteren-Echt-Maasbracht, and the main Sittard-Roermond road running with the railway some two thousand yards to the east.

It was intended to develop immediately two left hooks, using the 8th Armored Brigade, a brigade of the 52nd Division, and the 22nd Armored Brigade. These two forces would swing east to embrace the central woodland area bounded by Aardenburg, Waldfeucht, and Kooingsbosch. The 1st Commando Brigade would spearhead the attack on Maasbracht and Linne while the main force of the 7th Armored Division advanced northeastward on Montfort, Posterholt and the Roer river at St. Odillenberg.

At first light on D-plus-two the 52nd Division was timed to attack in the south center, assaulting across the

Saeffeler Beek, [beek is Dutch for stream or brook] seizing Hongen, clearing its left flank and swinging right handed on Bocket. It would then develop its attack eastward on Heinsberg.

On or about January 20th the 43rd Division would come into the action on the extreme right, moving east from Waldenrath to reach the river Wurm south of Heinsberg and join the U.S. 102nd Infantry Division thrusting north from Linnich.

Artillery support was on a massive scale, designed to blast the enemy out of the ground. Typhoons, fighters, and fighter bombers were ready to take advantage of all breaks in the weather. The enemy had already suffered a great weight of bombs and was harassed constantly at all salient points.

The British troops were acutely aware that they would be fighting inside Germany for the first time, and that their initial assault would heave the Germans from one of their last holds on eastern Holland south of the Waal. Doubtless the enemy was also aware. Operation Blackcock had a special savor.

ii.

At first light on the morning of January 15th a company of the 1st/5th Queens moved silently out of its forward positions escorted by three flail tanks. From its size it might have been little more than a powerful fighting patrol to probe the enemy defenses. Its purpose was to take the village of Bakenhoven, one mile to the northwest of Susteren, seize a good crossing point of the Vloed Beek, and secure a good start line for an attack against Dieteren.

Preliminary work had already been done on the approaches to the Beek. At nine o'clock on the night of the 15th the Royal Engineers, covered by the 9th Durham Light Infantry, a machine-gun platoon, an anti-tank battery, and a squadron of flail tanks of the Lothians, would move to the crossing point and bridge the Vloed Beek ready for the armor to surge into the triangle.

It was a grim morning, grayish white, the snow beginning to mush with the sudden thaws. The thin coating of ice on the roads was turning to a film of grease. The Queens reached Bakenhoven almost without incident. The Flails beat a way through the minefield to the south, finding the going difficult. Belts of woodland enclosed the village on the east and west. A copse came down to the water's edge of the Vloed Beek on its eastern bank and fringed the north side of the road which runs from Gebroecht to Susteren. Bakenhoven was strangely quiet. The weather got worse. The flails beat the mushy ground, and very soon the mortar bombs began to burst in confused fierce patterns, spattering the village and the approaches to the Beek. Gray shapes, running swiftly from cover to cover in the fringes of the woods, drew the fire of the Queens. They had studied the ground with care, and the menace of the woods had not eluded them. All through that day of the 15th the company fought an isolated battle in the village, on the approaches to the Vloed Beek, and in the woods. The flail tanks revealed that they were not simply armor bearing revolving drums with chains to beat the ground, but fighting vehicles, not to be despised. The Queens held on, sections fighting hand to hand with bayonet and grenade. By afternoon they knew that they would have to hold on all night as well as all day.

By early afternoon the state of the ground and the uncertainty of the weather had decided the commander of the 7th Armored Division to postpone the follow-through until the morning. It was half past seven o'clock on the morning of the 16th before the Royal Engineers with their supporting troops moved up to the Beek under mortar fire. The 9th Battalion of the Durhams went through the Queens and took the village of Dieteren. Enemy mortars concentrating on the crossing point of the Vloed Beek took a steady toll of the engineers. Armor attempting to move up smashed the prepared approaches, the tanks slithering on the grease. Medium artillery added weight to the enemy mortaring. Two bulldozers were knocked out. It was a dreary, deadly, day without promise.

All through the night of the 16th-17th the engineers worked under heavy mortaring and shell fire. The infantry held on in the villages. An isolated Flail tank fought a brave action and beat off a counterattack coming in from the woods bordering the stream. By morning on the 17th the Vloed Beek was bridged, but it seemed as though the enemy merely waited for the light to bracket the position, and blow up the bridge with a direct hit. Grimly the R.E.'s [Royal Engineers] dragged their equipment two hundred yards down stream and began again. A day and a half of valuable time had gone. The plan of the swift armored thrusts to the north and east had faded. The pattern was becoming clear: it was, and would be, a battle for infantry all the way, of swift adaptation from hour to hour, from village to village, while the engineers fought to bridge the beeks and open the roads.

In the detailed plan of the battle, phase followed phase in sequence, and each phase was sub-divided in sequence. Thus the opening phase, code named ANGEL, was sub-divided into ANGEL I, II, III. At the outset a stodgy, timid, or unimaginative command would have bogged down the whole operation by sticking to the book. Such a course would have been disastrous, threatening the delicate and elaborate timetable of the Rhineland battle. Fortunately the two divisional commanders most closely concerned, Major General L. O. Lyne of the 7th Armored and Major General E. Hakewill Smith of the 52nd Lowland Division, were men of action, initiative, and moral courage. The commander of the 7th Armored Division swiftly appreciated the situation, and by the evening of the 16th had switched his opening sequences to meet the case. At dawn on the 17th the 1st/5th Queens crossed the Vloed Beek on foot to move on Susteren in ANGEL III, while ANGEL II formed up in the rear. Armor, Flails, flame-throwing Crocodiles and troop carrying Kangaroos would be fed through as and when possible. Meanwhile the infantry would press on. It was clear that an immense burden would fall upon the Royal Engineers, for without bridges and roads the armor would not be able to move in strength and would be held to a crawl.

Awaiting his moment of attack in the center the commander of the 52nd Division, keeping in close touch with the opening developments, realized that the success of "Blackcock" might depend upon the speed and ability of his troops. The armored thrusts designed to move eastward to embrace the central woodland area would undoubtedly move behind time, and a brigade of the 52nd was with the southern thrust. With his remaining brigades Hakewill Smith must move, therefore, with all speed on Waldfeucht, Koningsboch and Echterboch, possibly without support. The high ground at Bocket on the road to Waldfeucht must be taken without delay.

By the afternoon of the 17th, the Queens had gained Susteren, and the 2nd Devons, leading the advance of ANGEL II, had struggled up to their start line at Dieteren. The going was appalling, the combination of trip wires and mines deadly in the mess of ice, snow, and slush. Two troops of tanks had crossed the Vloed Beek at a bull-dozed crossing to join the hard pressed Queens in Susteren. A few tracked vehicles had got through to Dieteren with ANGEL II, only to bog down. It was half past three o'clock in the afternoon when the 2nd Devons struck off across country from Dieteren, a few tracked vehicles struggling along behind. The plan was for one column to move on the western route to the north through Ophoven on Echt, while the right-hand column opened up the main road from Susteren to Schilberg.

The left column made good time, fighting a stiff sharp action in Ophoven, and getting its forward companies in the outskirts of Echt by nightfall. It was necessary to press on, night and day.

On the right, the main column of the brigade—the 131st—struck trouble a mile and a half outside Susteren. At this point the railway crosses the road. The enemy had dug in on the embankment, and supported by self-propelled guns held solid. Without armor the infantry could not storm the strongly entrenched position. It was then dusk. Snow had begun to fall.

By five o'clock that afternoon the engineers had the main bridge in commission across the Vloed Beek, and the armor began to move across, the roar of tank engines bringing cheer to the infantry ahead. It was impossible for the tanks to maneuver off the road, but all through the night infantry and tanks battered at the enemy road block.

It was clear at this early stage of the battle that holdups could not be permitted. As fast as the engineers could bridge the beeks, men, armor and "Funnies" [unusual army vehicles adapted to difficult terrain] moved into the battle, the infantry lugging all that they could carry on their backs. A relief column moved up swiftly on the western route to find Echt occupied by midnight. There, joined by Crocodiles the relief column prepared to attack eastward on Schilberg to outflank the enemy and break the road block on the main road position north of Susteren.

At half past six o'clock in the morning the attack went in, and at that hour the 4th/5th Royal Scots Fusiliers of the 156th Brigade of the 52nd Division launched their assault northeastwards from the village of Tuddern across the Saeffelen Beek. Hakewill Smith had decided not to wait upon success on the left. The balance of power was moving his way, and he grasped it. Directly ahead of his troops lay the formidable obstacle of the Saeffelen Beek, twenty feet wide, with marshy approaches made worse by the mixture of thaw and freeze, and with a high bank shielding the north. In the opening phase the cluster of villages north of the beek had to be taken to gain a firm bridgehead, and the key town of Hongen must be won to establish the main route of advance.

Three hundred guns supporting the assault fired on the villages of Stein and Lind before the leading infantry had reached the Saeffelen Beek under concentrated enemy mortaring, small-arms, and Spandau [a German machine gun] fire. It was nearly nine o'clock before the engineers had the first of two assault bridges in place, and the infantry climbed up and over the northern bank. Nothing on wheels or tracks could follow, not even a Weasel. The forward observation officers of the gunners crossed with the infantry, but wireless links with the guns broke down.

By this time the congestion growing on the battlefield was reflected in the congestion of the artillery. An immense fire plan had been arranged, but the air was so filled with a confused pattern of signals, and the going was so slow and unpredictable, that the gunners had to adapt to conditions as best they could.

Nevertheless the 156th Brigade pressed on, the 6th Cameronians moving up under heavy mortaring over one thousand yards of open ground to cross the beek on the second assault bridge. Three tanks had managed to cross by the first of the bridges in early afternoon, only to bog down. Three Flails suffered direct hits at the approaches to the second bridge. The enemy in the villages of Stein and Lindt were fighting like demons, using communication tunnels from house to house, snap-shooting from all angles, and at one point heaving grenades into a group of wounded. It was a grave mistake. It inspired the Royal Scots Fusiliers to a burst of fury which wiped out the enemy before dusk. It was a costly day. Seventy-five men of the leading companies lay dead or wounded in and around the village of Stein. More than forty such villages lay ahead on the divisional road to the key town of Heinsberg.

iii.

The 18th of January was a day of desperate infantry fighting, and the key day in the battle of the Heinsberg triangle. By their determination to go forward regardless of support by armor or artillery, and without much hope of being served by anything larger than a jeep, the 4th/5th Royal Scots Fusiliers, the 5th Highland Light Infantry, and the 6th Cameronians of the 156th Brigade, broke through the main enemy defensive line at a crucial point and opened the way through to the whole area of the Echterboch.

In the early stages the Canadian Rocket battery had fired three salvoes in devastating support of the crossing of the beek and the gaining of footholds in the hamlets beyond. The battery, consisting of twelve rocket projectors each of thirty-two barrels, fired ripple salvoes at 5,000 to 7,000 yards, bringing down 350 rockets, each the equivalent of a 5.5-in. shell, into an area two hundred yards square. From the villages of Breberen and Havert the enemy emerged dazed, shocked, and speechless from the cellars to totter blindly into the hands of the attackers. Each salvo obliterated the area upon which it fell, but the battery swiftly shot its bolt.

The 6th Cameronians, following swiftly on the heels of the Royal Scots Fusiliers, went forward in the face of terrible mortaring, skirting Stein, where the fusiliers were fighting bitterly from house to house, and swooping on to Heilder. With Heilder taken the key point of Hongen could be assaulted from the rear, and the main divisional route opened across the Saeffelen beek. All day the mortar platoon of the 6th H.L.I. [Highland Light Infantry] blanketed Hongen in the smoke from 11,000 smoke bombs to mask the direction of the drive, and add confusion to the enemy.

The continuing thaw immobilized all vehicles and

forced the 52nd Division to organize eight hundred men as carriers while the 5th Highland Light Infantry crossed the beek and secured the left flank of the bridgehead, storming through Havert, assaulting Schalbruch, and securing the small lateral road network Nieuwsted, Schalbruch, Havert. Meanwhile in Stein the battle raged fiercely through the day and far into the night, its issue in the last resort depending on the personal valor and sacrifice of individuals. It was here on this day that Fusilier Donnini, charging in the face of machine-gun fire, regardless of grievous wounds, and pressing home his attack to the point of death, earned the Victoria Cross. It was a fitting symbol of that day of struggle.

By the dawn of the 19th the German town of Hongen was cleared by the Cameronians attacking down from the north, and the 52nd Division became the first to establish their headquarters on German soil. Swiftly the engineers put a Bailey bridge across the beek and opened the road from Sittard. With that the wheels and tracks, the Flails, the Crocodiles, the Kangeroos, the Weasels, and the whole array of battalion and brigade vehicles began to move steadily forward into the bridgehead to supply and sustain the forward troops on the lateral road network to the outskirts of the Echterboch.

It was as well that the 52nd had pressed home the attack with such energy, for it was clear by the evening of the 19th that the 8th Armored Brigade with the 155th could not get through on the southernmost of the hooks to embrace the Echterboch. There was no alternative but to withdraw the armor back through Sittard, and to put it through on the 52nd divisional axis. But this also had become impossible, and had to be abandoned. To the north the column of the 22nd Armored Brigade, striving to open up the way through to Montfort, and to swing right upon Aadenberg, fared little better. The enemy resistance in the north was proving of a more durable quality than that in the south. A tremendous fight had begun to gain the village of St. Joost on the direct line of advance. Backed by skillfully placed self-propelled guns, prepared to deny every yard of ground and to fight independently for every house and barn and strong point, the enemy held firm against the repeated attacks of the 1st Battalion, the Rifle Brigade. The tanks of the 8th Hussars, confined to the icy roads, could do little in support and for thirty-six hours the weary men of the Rifle Brigade, having fought and endured for five days and nights of the severest weather of a severe winter, battered themselves against an enemy amply reinforced by elements of the crack *Regiment Hubner* covering Roermond, and the extreme apex of the triangle. It was becoming apparent that the enemy regarded the north as the hard core to which he must hold.

Without delay the 52nd Division brought its artillery across the Saeffelen Beek, and with its infantry closely supported pressed on with all possible speed, clearing the villages to the east and north, and preparing to assault Waldfeucht, the central core of the enemy defenses. Searchlights played on low clouds made an "artificial moonlight," guiding the troops by night under its strange, sometimes greenish, pallor. The alternate thaw and freeze made the going treacherous for men and machines, but there was safety from Schumines (a deadly little mine that exploded when stepped on) in the tracks of the Flails, even though the Flails themselves were hampered in their beating by the snow. The news from all sides was of a struggle against blizzard, snow, fog, ice, and slush. One company of the 7th/9th Royal Scots, trying to get through to assault Heide from the west, rashly attempted to move on the ice through a tunnel under the railway embankment, only to find themselves neck deep in icy water. But the three brigades of the 52nd Division were all in the battle. Swarming over the bleak and broken countryside, assaulting villages, clearing coppices, and constantly crossing the narrow channels of the beeks, a score of platoon and company actions gradually formed a coherent picture of sustained assault. On the morning of the 19th the 4th K.O.S.B. [King's Own Scottish Borderers] had reached the woods to the west of Koningsboch and were ready to attack the straggling village. At the same time the 7th Cameronians attacked Saeffelen in the face of terrific enemy concentrations of mortars, spandaus, and small arms.

The pressure was maintained relentlessly by day and night. On the 20th, Bocket fell to the H.L.I. with very little trouble, and opened the way for the attack on Waldfeucht and the Echterboch. The recurrent blizzards seemed to confuse the enemy more than the mountain-trained British infantry, and it became clear that the enemy was off balance. An enemy counterattack in battalion strength and supported by Tiger tanks had been ready mounted against Bocket. It failed to come in. Because of this Waldfeucht was taken by the 5th K.O.S.B. in a night attack with three companies while the 4th company moved into Echterboch. It was in these two villages throughout the 21st of January that the 5th K.O.S.B. were to fight the stiffest action of Operation Blackcock.

The night of January 20th/21st was bitterly cold. The whole countryside lay under thick snow, and the village of Waldfeucht with its ancient gateways wore a peaceful look. Moving in almost soundlessly in the early hours of the morning the 5th K.O.S.B. swiftly moved into all round defensive positions in a silence that was uncanny. Before the dawn enemy shelling heralded an attack, and at half past six o'clock two Tiger tanks loomed out of the grey light followed by infantry in small groups. Four of our own tanks were swiftly knocked out by enemy shellfire, but the anti-tank gunners held on until the enemy Tigers were cruising in the village street and within one hundred yards. Only then did the men manning the 6-pounders open up to smash the two enemy tanks with direct hits. It was the beginning, not the end, a mere prelude to a major assault.

As the enemy shelling grew intense, six Tiger tanks with at least four Panthers, all draped with German infantry men, came swiftly out of the north. Fifteen self-propelled guns in close support began to rip buildings to rubble filling the narrow channels of the streets with flying fragments and insane din. Under this cover the enemy infantry infiltrated from the northeast cutting off one company. A solitary Tiger tank, penetrating to the heart of the village, roared like some berserk and invulnerable beast up and down the main street, rotating its gun turret, blasting houses point-blank with its 88-mm. gun. German civilians emerged from their cellars to shout warnings and directions to the tank crew, while infantry men stalked the invader with sticky grenades and P.I.A.T.'s. [Petard Infantry Anti-Tank, a type of mortar].

Two men manning a P.I.A.T. in a bedroom ducked under the long barrel of the Tiger's gun as it poked through the second-story window and blasted room and house to a chaos of rubble and plaster. The solid old brick gateways at each end of the street were too narrow for the Tiger tank to pass, and in the narrow confines within the gates the tank fought for three hours, seeming immune to the many grenades and bombs exploding against its armor. The regimental aid post was shot up, and many of the wounded were again wounded or killed. Finally the enemy tank battered a way through to its own troops in the northeast corner of the village, and for eighteen hours the three companies of the 5th K.O.S.B. held on until relieved by their sister battalion, the 4th. Even then the enemy fire was so accurate, and the battle so closely waged in the streets that one soldier received five bullets through his hand as he raised it from cover to signal to the relieving troops.

That day and night in Waldfeucht was an indication to the nature of the struggle ahead. Waldfeucht was one of the first of the larger German villages to fall to our troops, and the contrast to the fighting in the Dutch villages was striking. There would be no more safety, no more helpful civilians, no more welcomes in friendly and grateful homes, no more of that kind of relaxation. On that day, I think, on the northern front, a new sense of the grimness of the struggle was in many minds.

The German counterattack on Waldfeucht had been pressed with strength and determination, but an operation order captured from the 341st Army Assault Brigade revealed that the attack had been originally mounted against Bocket and had been hastily remounted against Waldfeucht. The speed of our advance had been well repaid. With the capture of Waldfeucht the way was open for the final assault against Heinsberg.

iv.

By January 22nd there was also good progress in the north. The 22nd Armored Brigade, battling on dourly with small groups of armor supporting infantry as best they could, helped the Devons into Aardenberg. The 1st Commando Brigade, moving north out of Echt and screening the left flank, was ready to assault Maasbracht. But it was not until the morning of the 24th that the 1st/5th Queens, having taken over in Aardenberg from the Devons, attacked Montfort.

The 131st Brigade were by now making good progress on the right flank of the northern attack, and advancing northeastward from Aardenberg upon Reutje. When on the night of the 23rd/24th January the 7/9th Royal Scots and the 4th K.O.S.B. moved out of Aphoven in two columns upon Heinsberg, only the last splinters remained of the thorn which had festered for so long in the right flank of the 21st Army Group.

The village of Aphoven lies some three or four miles to the southwest of Heinsberg. The countryside is open with trees lining many of the roadsides, and from the ridge of the valley the ground falls away in a gentle slope to the banks of the rivers Roer and Wurm and a skein of confusing waterways. The village of Aphoven was the start line for the final assault upon Heinsberg. Before midnight on January 23rd the troops for the assault began a long march from the Bocket area. At Laffeld the 7/9th Royal Scots split into two columns, each column with one company of the 4th K.O.S.B. The moon was well up, and the night sky was lurid with the crimson flashes of shells, and the slow parabolas of tracer. Yet the march was tedious. The roar of the tanks of the 8th Armored Brigade, and the rumble of the tracks of Crocodiles and Flails, made harsh patterns of sound, weaving in with the crunch of boots on the thin ice covering the road. At times the beams of the searchlights mixed a greenish tinge on the confused palette of the sky. There was little danger. The wild confusion of sound and color seemed divorced from the long column of marching men, borne steadily forward as though impelled by the monotonous rhythm of their boots.

It was two o'clock on the morning of the 24th when the columns passed through Aphoven on the last lap of the journey, one column moving to the left, the other to the right, to encircle Heinsberg before the dawn. The remaining two companies of the 4th K.O.S.B. with battalion headquarters and support troops would follow through and clear Heinsberg on the center line from south to north.

The flanks were well held. The 129th and 130th Brigades of the 43rd Division, coming into the battle on the 20th, had moved east to clear the road through Waldenrath to Dremmen. Opposition was slight. The U.S. 102nd Division moved north up the valley of the Wurm to close the last gap in the south.

Once over the eastern ridge of the valley, the twin

The Schwammenauel Dam located southeast of Schmidt controlled flood waters of the Roer. Most sensitive and vital point in German defenses, the dam was ignored in U. S. attack plan. (*U. S. Army photo*)

Heinsberg Steeple. Jumping-off point for the attack. Beyond lies Cologne and the Rhineland. (*Imperial War Museum photo*)

155-mm. self-propelled gun gives supporting fire. The 112th Infantry Regiment, leading attack on Schmidt, lost over 2,000 officers and men. (*U. S. Army photo*)

Near Vossenack a Weasel pulls a jeep out of the mire. Throughout the battles, Weasels proved invaluable, bringing up supplies and carrying out wounded. (*U. S. Army photo*)

German prisoners being carried out of Waldfeucht after two days of stiff fighting. (*Imperial War Museum*)

Kangaroos carrying troops through Kranenburg. Allies were now inside Germany to stay. (*Imperial War Museum*)

British Churchill tank batters its way through the Reichswald. (*Imperial War Museum*)

Red Cross jeeps push on through flooded streets of Kranenburg. (*Imperial War Museum*)

On the way to Cleve a British scout car finds the country completely submerged. (*Imperial War Museum*)

A Fascine (left) and a bridge-laying tank, A.V.R.E. (right) move up through the Reichswald forest. (*Imperial War Museum*)

Kangaroos plough through mud to bring reinforcements to Kervenheim. (*Imperial War Museum*)

Scots Guard troops setting up their sign at the gateway to Hitler's Reich. (*Imperial War Museum*)

The battle for Goch was a tempest of fire. Here troops entering the town. (*Imperial War Museum*)

British tanks pass through Cleve. (*Imperial War Museum*)

Before guns could be moved through Cleve, streets had to be cleared by bulldozers. (*Imperial War Museum*)

The gaunt wreckage of Udem can be seen behind advancing troops. (*Imperial War Museum*)

columns of encircling troops could see the roofs of Heinsberg luminous with frost, reflecting the macabre disorder
in the sky. It had been a town of 5,000 people, an ancient
town of tall, thin buildings with dormer windows in steep
roofs above narrow streets, and all huddled within the
massive gate houses. It was no longer a place of habitation, but a maze of cellars and rubble after constant
hammering from the air. Yet for a little while, in the night,
it held the illusion of a sleeping town, the roof tops belying
the reality.

All at once, it seemed, the shell fire, which through the
night had seemed remote, became personal, and a body of
some sixty enemy, clothed in white, materialized out of
the snow, to put in a fierce attack on the left flank. A
Tiger tank roared its challenge in close support, but the
column met the onslaught with controlled machine-gun
and anti-tank fire. The rhythm of the night was broken.
Moving swiftly the encircling columns drew a noose round
Heinsberg before the dawn and dug themselves in, watch-
ful and waiting.

It was almost exactly six o'clock in the gray half light
when the remaining two companies of the 4th K.O.S.B.
moved upon Heinsberg from the south under intense
mortar fire, and grateful for the partial cover afforded by
a sunken road. In the main the country was open. A mile
short of the town a massive wooden cross held the cruci-
fied Christ under the shelter of a tree stricken by shellfire,
and the tall thin spire of a church gave form to the misty
shape of Heinsberg, rising from the snow like the hummock of an island. A sense of aching desolation seemed
graven upon that place.

There was no great battle for Heinsberg, no great determination in the German rearguard of defenders. The
scorching bursts of flame from the Crocodiles brought
many up from the cellars with little stomach for a fight.
Grenades crashed in the dark, enclosed caverns of the
houses, and here and there pockets of men fought with terrible fury, while the mortar bombs and the scream of bullets held attackers and defenders alike in invisible cages
of death.

The two flanking companies of the K.O.S.B. swiftly
joined their fellows in Heinsberg's last moments of truth,
but an enemy strong point came suddenly to life on the
southern outskirts of the town to trap B Company on

open ground as it attempted to follow through. In the first
burst of mortar and machine-gun fire, the company commander and the company sergeant major were seriously
wounded, and the second in command killed. There was
no way forward or back, no conceivable cover beyond
the low shelving of a ditch or hummock. Alone in all that
remained of company headquarters Lance Corporal
Leitch of the Royal Corps of Signals lay with one leg
almost severed, and the other gravely wounded, striving
none the less to make contact with the guns. His voice,
"with the Lowland lilt in it," the gunners say, came to
them clearly through all the confusion and hubbub of
signals traffic, and calmly, yet in unconventional terms,
directed fire and smoke upon the enemy with such speed
and accuracy that the company was saved.

Long before evening Heinsberg was secured, and the
last of the villages had fallen to the 52nd Division on the
banks of the Roer. In the North the 1st/5th Queens, still
in the van, the Durham Light Infantry, the Devons, the 5th
Dragoons, the 11th Hussars, and the 5th Royal Tanks
combed the last pockets of woodland, secured Posterholt,
and took St. Odilienberg. From those points they could
look down upon the last remaining enemy bridgehead of
Vlodrop, secure for the time being under his own guns. It
was less than a grain of sand between the toes of the
advance, and could avail nothing. In the south, for thirty
hours the enemy heavy batteries east of the Roer poured
shells into the rubble of Heinsberg, and by the end of
the month the last bridge capable of bearing vehicles
across the Roer had been blown. Such was the nature of
the battle of the Heinsberg triangle—a battle of a hundred
villages, a battle made up of scores of fragments, and with
the attacker eating swiftly into the soft spots, surrounding
and reducing the hard cores. It revealed the need for the
swift regrouping of brigades, for rapid changes of plan,
for the constant leap-frogging of small groups of infantry,
tanks, Flails and Crocodiles. On a small scale this would
be the pattern of the last great battle.

11: VERITABLE—THE PREPARATION

i.

THE OPENING of the port of Antwerp had enabled General Crerar, commanding the 1st Canadian Army, to assemble a vast weight of materials in the Nijmegen bridgehead in preparation for Operation Veritable, the Battle of the Rhineland.

The final period of the build-up began on January 25th, and by the end of the month the whole region behind the northern front bore the unmistakable imprint of Field Marshal Montgomery. Seldom, if ever, has so much activity, so immense an expenditure of energy, taken place in so confined a space. It resembled the incessant toiling of ants. Seven divisions, two armored brigades, and an immense weight of artillery under command of General Horrocks' 30th Corps, moved steadily into the assembly area behind the battlefield. Two more divisions of the British 2nd Army were ready to move in as soon as there was room, finally to swell the ranks of the Canadian 1st Army to a total of thirteen divisions, three armored brigades, the 30th Brigade of the 79th Armored Division, five artillery groups, two anti-air craft brigades, and the Canadian rocket battery. The ration strength of the Canadian 1st Army, together with attached personnel, reached a peak of more than 470,000 men of which nearly 400,000 were fighting troops.

All these would funnel through the narrow space between Grave and Nijmegen to debouch into the Reichswald forest, and close the west bank of the Rhine from Emmerich to Wesel, from the Nijmegen-Cleve-Emmerich road on the left to the Geldern-Xanten road on the right.

It is essential for the layman, in considering such a battle, to lend his imagination to the meaning of such numbers of men and quantities of equipment, in terms of movement, food, ammunition, and the expenditure of the intricate paraphernalia of warfare as it was in the mid-Twentieth Century, for only by so doing is it possible to form judgments on matters of strategy. Thirty-five thousand vehicles and 1,300,000 gallons of gasoline were needed to move these troops and their equipment to their assembly points. Many hundreds of trains and thousands of vehicles in constant transit were essential to their supply and their continued movement. 1,880 tons of bridging equipment were used to bridge the River Maas at four points prior to the battle. Seven bridges would be needed, and because of flooding four hundred feet of folding-boat equipment were brought forward to meet the emergency.

A steady intake of 7,250 tons of supplies each day had enabled General Crerar to amass 250,000 tons in his stockpiles. In the last stages before the battle the daily maintenance reached 10,000 tons, which included 2,800 tons of ammunition. The variety of goods was very wide, from drugs and medical supplies, toilet rolls, and boots to shells for the super-heavy guns. A great array of buoys to mark channels in the flooded areas seemed grotesque, adding a whiff of the sea to the saturated inland scene, and this impression was enhanced by large numbers of amphibious vehicles constantly to be observed in the forward areas.

In addition to the immense road-building and repairing tasks of the engineers and pioneers, it was necessary to build 95 bridges, each 75 feet long, to span huge flooded craters 12 feet deep and up to 70 feet in diameter, blown by the enemy with 500-lb. bombs in the few existing roads. Traffic-control police in close collaboration with the engineers were forced to re-route traffic each day, and to add to these problems, essential traffic moved mainly by night, especially to the gun sites. The dumping program for ammunition began on January 25th and was completed on the night of the 1st/2nd of February. In that period 500,000 rounds of ammunition of 350 different kinds, and weighing 11,000 tons, were moved forward to the gun sites and camouflaged. At that time many of the batteries comprising a total of 1,034 guns of all calibers, including more than 300 mediums, heavies, and super-heavies, had not reached their positions. Errors in distribution would eliminate batteries. There were no errors.

Anticipation of extensive flooding had caused the assembly of more than half a million gallons of fog oil for burning in a probable 100,000 smoke generators in case it should be necessary to mask the whole of the left flank. These were in addition to the normal smoke supplies.

The Signal Corps also made heavy demands, and supplies included more than 8,000 miles of four different kinds of cable, 151,000 yards of assault cable, and 14 pairs of double-armored submarine cable to be laid across the Maas.

It would be possible to compile a dozen lists equally impressive, and all these materials had to move constantly under cover through Nijmegen and over the Maas-Waal Canal, through Grave to Mook, or over the few minor roads between these two points. On February 8th, it was estimated, trains would run into Nijmegen itself, right behind the battlefield, and in the month of February alone 350,000 tons of supplies would feed the stockpiles.

On January 31st a thaw added suddenly to the burdens of the army of road-maintenance personnel and served further to compress the great weight of transport moving in continuous streams into the area held within the loop of the Maas between Nijmegen and Grave. In every village and town the troops were assembling fast. Tilburg and s'Hertogenbosch were crammed with men and vehicles. Conferences were in constant session, and commanders from generals to second lieutenants studied the 800,000 special maps and 500,000 air photographs, together with massive sheaves of orders, which had been prepared for them.

ii.

Operation Instruction No. 47 issued on February 3rd announced simply: "30 Corps will destroy the enemy between the R. Maas and R. Rhine and break through in a southerly direction between the two rivers."

The simplicity of such instructions contrasts oddly with the immense complications of the tasks involved. On February 4th the troops detailed for the opening attack began to move forward into the six-mile-wide funnel between Nijmegen and Mook. They moved essentially on two roads, the one through Nijmegen itself to the left flanking positions, and through Grave to the right flank. In scores of towns and villages of southwest Holland the forward brigades of the 15th Scottish, the 53rd Wessex, and the 51st Highland Divisions, who, together with the 2nd and 3rd Canadian Divisions, would provide the spearhead, made ready for battle. The pipe band of the Camerons had marched through Breda to thrill even the

jaded inhabitants and to excite their own hearts in cel-
ebration of the birthday of Princess Beatrix. In every
town and hamlet there had been outbreaks of "spit and
polish," which often in the British Army presage rough
times ahead.

Reacting with remarkable patience and kindness to the
upheavals which for five months had been a part of life,
the Dutch wished the men Godspeed and even produced
in some villages concertina bands to cheer the marching
troops. Perhaps, at last, the end was in sight.

In scores of headquarters, commanders of battalions,
brigades, divisions, corps, and armies, focused their whole
attention upon the battlefield. To the west, along the line
of the Maas and facing north, the Canadian 1st Army
maintained responsibility, which included dummy positions and concentrations intended to mask the intention
of the Rhineland battle and to suggest to the enemy an
attack directed upon Utrecht. In the north center the 30th
Corps confronted the mass of the Reichswald forest and
the flooded complexities of its flanks. To the south the
greatly depleted forces of the 2nd Army maintained a
watch on the Maas. It would not take part in the battle.
Further to the south the U.S. 9th Army assumed responsibility for the still strongly held enemy positions at Venlo
and Roermond and prepared to cross the River Roer in
Operation Grenade. On the right flank, the U.S. 1st
Army at last moved against the Roer dams.

Thus on the morning of February 4th four armies from
the Nijmegen bridgehead to the Ardennes stirred to the
opening phases of mounting the greatest battle of the
campaign since Normandy. Here from the Ardennes to the
extreme north was one front, one battlefield, plain for all
to see, and beyond a shadow of doubt. Field Marshal
Montgomery had seen it for many months, and now his
long argument for one ground force commander north of
the Ardennes was underlined by topography, strategy, and
military necessity. It was underlined above all by the
Roer and Erft river dams.

But the argument was an argument no longer, thrown
out by the Supreme Commander, and so bitterly opposed
by General Bradley that its further pursuit would have
had grave consequences. Yet the broken strategy inher-
ent in the positions of the U.S. 12th Army Group was
never more apparent.

There was no longer any attempt on the part of General Bradley to veil his dislike for Field Marshal Montgomery. His dislike transcended strategy and the common purpose. Even at the end of January, with Montgomery committed to the battle of the Rhineland, Bradley continued to urge the Supreme Commander to permit his armies to drive through the Eifel to the Rhine and to relegate the northern battle to a secondary role.

Eisenhower, however, was adamant. He had always intended that the major thrust should be in the north, and all Bradley's eloquence failed to move him. On February 1st Bradley was ordered to halt his armies. It was time—past time—to move troops to strengthen the U.S. 9th Army. It was also past time for General Hodges' 1st Army to attack and to gain control of the Roer and Erft dams. This was a task Bradley had wished to avoid, for the control of the dams by the enemy strengthened his argument for the main thrust in the south center, and it is difficult (for this writer) to avoid the conclusion that the immense strategic importance of the dams in the northern battlefield colored General Bradley's thinking. Eisenhower, however, ordered Bradley to employ a ford of "two or three divisions" to do the job, and on February 4th Hodges attacked. Once again the key target was Schmidt.

At the same time General Bradley told Patton and Hodges to press on with their advances until the 10th. Patton, in any case, had no intention of halting, although he realized the need to keep his intentions quiet. Patton continued to advance in the Eifel north of the Moselle under the impression that he and General Bradley were "putting something over on SHAEF," and above all upon Field Marshal Montgomery. "The matter was kept quiet so as not to draw objections from Field Marshal Montgomery."*

But the Field Marshal, with his vision ranging over the whole northern battlefield, was well aware of these things and he maintained a stream of protests that "the operations in the north were not being properly backed."

Only Field Marshal Montgomery himself can say how much or how little he relied upon the opening on time of Operation Grenade as the right arm of the embrace he

*Pogue, *The Supreme Command*

had designed to crush the German armies in the northern Rhineland. It is certain that he viewed the slow progress of the attack upon the dams with grave misgiving and was resolved to fight with his strong left arm, even if his right remained tied behind his back. He knew that his forces would face the most powerful troops and defensive positions remaining to the enemy on the western front. He knew that if Hodges failed in his attack on the dams and the enemy succeeded in flooding the Roer valley, thereby immobilizing the U.S 9th Army, massive reinforcements would become available against the Canadian 1st Army. With memories of Caen and the great battle of the hinge in Normandy, such an eventuality may have seemed foreordained, an eventuality even to be wished for. Indeed, it is possible that such considerations played a part in the massive build-up of men and weapons.

Such then is a glimpse of the position on the front north of the Ardennes on the eve of "Veritable." It was a vision which did not greatly concern General Horrocks, commanding the British 30th Corps and the 2nd and 3rd Canadian Divisions in the opening phases of the coming battle. His immediate problem was one of constriction, the launching of more than 200,000 men and their armor "through the eye of a needle."

iii.

The Reichswald forest, a dark coniferous mass, some ten miles in depth from west to east and five miles wide, filled the center of the immediate battlefield facing the British 30th Corps. The forest is flanked on the north by the town of Cleve and to the south by the railway and road junction of Goch, the heart and main anchor of a powerful defensive system. In the northwest corner the gently undulating forest land rises to a height of 150 feet, and between the edge of the forest and the town of Cleve a narrow neck of high ground forms an escarpment to shelter the town from the south.

The Canadian 2nd and 3rd Divisions had maintained their forward defensive localities on the fringe of the forest proper in the area of Groesbeek immediately facing the forward defensive system of the Siegfried Line running from Wyler to anchor on the Maas south of Mook. Throughout all the long winter of preparation these troops alone had held the bridgehead, actively patrolling and denying information to the enemy. Up to the very eve of battle no enemy patrol could hope to gain the identification of any unit other than Canadian.

The Canadian positions round Groesbeek would be the starting line for the attack which would open the Battle of the Rhineland. It would be essential for the Canadians to secure the village of Den Heuvel, gain Wyler, and thus open the main road through from Nijmegen to Kranenberg.

The Reichswald was a state forest cut into rectangles by long tracks and trails, giving long fields of fire to the defenders. The forest was closely planted, and giving a visibility of no more than a dozen yards except in the clearings and along the paths. Old clearings had become thickly overgrown with low scrub, but the new clearings would give fields of vision up to two to three hundred yards. There were small groups of deciduous trees. Maps were unreliable, and air photographs had failed to add precise knowledge of the conditions on the ground. Many of the trails and tracks were overgrown; others were sandy. It was certain that the going would be hard or impossible for wheeled or tracked transport.

Two new roads of concrete ran through from north to south, from Cleve converging at Hekkens, the one curving through Kranenberg-Frasselt, the other through Bedberg. These roads enclosed roughly the central third of the forest area, including the neck of high ground known as "the Materborn feature," covering the town of Cleve.

From the Hekkens crossroads the road runs west to Gennep and southeast through Asperden to Goch. The main Cleve-Goch road bounds the forest to the east. Beyond it lies the railway and the small forest of Cleve, a tight square mile of trees in the center of the position.

The heavily fortified town of Goch, normally a considerable manufacturing center of some 15,000 inhabitants, was surrounded by a maze of concrete pill boxes anchored to the two main defensive systems of the Siegfried Line, the westernmost covering the Kranenberg-Frasselt-Hekkens-Goch road, the other anchored on the defenses of Cleve in the north, passing behind the forest of Cleve, sited east of the railway line to Goch. Beyond this lay a third main defensive system running from Rees forward of the Hochwald forest and continuing south to Geldern. This was known as the Hochwald lay-back, the last line of defense covering the Rhine and the Wesel road and rail bridges.

The immediate enemy defenses of the whole area consisted of continuous trenches along the east bank of the Maas, and an anti-tank ditch covering the western edge of the Reichswald forest. These first defensive positions were organized for 2,000 yards in depth. Roadblocks and anti-tank guns covered all roads, trails, and tracks. Trench systems had been dug to defend the Materborn feature, linking in with the main defenses of Cleve. Further trench systems and strongpoints had been developed at Nutterden and Donsbruggen on the road between Kranenberg and Cleve.

Isolated farms in the Reichswald, and small villages everywhere, were known to be strongpoints and self-contained "boxes of defense." Mine fields and wire had been laid on an elaborate scale. The whole area of the battlefield comprised the flood plains of the Rhine, Maas, and Niers rivers, low undulating forest alternating with marshes, backwaters, and flood channels. Tall poplars revealed the lines of many ditches, and orchards often surrounded the smaller villages.

The River Maas was flooded up to 1,000 yards beyond both banks, and the River Niers had overflowed to turn its water meadows into swamps. In the north the Rhine floods had converted the land north of the Nijmegen-Cleve road to a series of inland lakes.

This whole formidable area, with Cleve and Goch as the hinges of its powerful and narrow jaws, had to be forced against the finest troops remaining to the German army in the west, the *1st Parachute Army* under *Army Group H*. These troops, paratroops only in name, were nonetheless highly trained, young, and dedicated to the defense of their homeland. The *84th Division* defended the Reichswald forest, and with the *180th, 190th* and *606th Divisions* in close reserve, supported by a probable 114 guns.

It was clear that if the U.S. 1st Army's assault on the Roer dams should fail, and the U.S. 9th Army should be immobilized, the enemy would be able to move heavy reinforcements to the northern battlefield. There also remained the possibility of further extensive flooding on the northern flank, and the whole battlefield wore an aspect of isolation, an island in the midst of its rivers and floods, and without possibility of expansion.

A sense of excitement, of decisive events in the making, was inescapable. It seemed to imbue all ranks as they struggled forward, manhandling trucks, guns, equipment, brewing up by the roadsides, extraordinarily patient. Even the least observant among them could not fail to be aware of the immense weight of guns and armor building up, and few doubted that the story which had begun on D-day on the Normandy beaches was at last nearing its end.

iv.

The troops immediately available to General Sir Brian Horrocks, commanding the 30th Corps, were the 2nd and 3rd Canadian Infantry Divisions, the 15th (Scottish), the 43rd (Wessex), the 51st (Highland) and the 53rd (Welsh) Infantry Divisions, the Guards Armored Division, the 6th Guards Armored Brigade, the 8th and 34th Armored Brigades, and the 30th Armored Brigade of the 79th Armored Division. These were supported by the guns of the Canadian 2nd A.G.R.A. [Armored Group, Royal Artillery] and the British 3rd, 4th, 5th, and 9th Royal Artillery Groups, the 74th and 106th Anti-Aircraft Brigades, and the Canadian Rocket Battery. In the air the 2nd Tactical Air Force would provide close support, while on D-minus-1, 1,000 bombers of the R.A.F., supported by heavy and medium bombers of the U.S. 8th and 9th Air Forces, would attempt to blast the key towns of Cleve, Goch, and Emmerich from the face of the earth.

All this, together with the opening barrage of more than 1,000 guns, to which would be added the fire pattern of three machine-gun battalions and the 8th Armored Brigade's tanks, revealed Field Marshal Montgomery's intention to shoot his way in to the battlefield and to force the jaws closing the way to the Rhine.

But the tactical plan and the tactical battle on the ground belonged in the early stages to General Horrocks. He had decided to attack with five divisions up, to force the narrow Materborn gap, to open the road through Cleve, and to burst out into the more open country. It was a plan which would have been optimistic over hard ground, for it entailed the swift passage of two infantry and one armored division on a single main axis of doubtful capacity. Over the saturated and flooded ground ahead it loomed as a nightmare, a nightmare to be faced, nonetheless, with that sublime humor and courage which, although it may seem old-fashioned, has been one of the distinguishing characteristics of British troops at least since the Crimea.

The line-up, and the intention, was as follows:

Right:

> 51st Highland Division, to capture, clear, and hold the high ground north of the southwest corner of the Reichswald, to swing south and hold down enemy attempts to move troops to the north. To open route Mook-Gennep-Hekkens-Goch.

> Take over Goch from 43rd Wessex Division.

Inside right:

> 53rd Welsh Division, to seize the high ground on the northern edge of the forest, and move east through the northern half of the Reichswald.

Center:

> 15th Scottish Division, to capture Kranenberg; to breach the Siegfried Line north of the Reichswald, capture Nutterden and the Materborn feature. To attempt to capture Udem and Calcar with mobile columns, and clear Emmerich road to west bank of the Rhine. To clear and hold Cleve.

Inside left:

> 2ND Canadian Division, to capture Den Heuvel and Wyler, and open the main road to Berg-en-Dal.

Outside left:

> 3rd Canadian Division, to protect the left flank, to capture and clear the low ground between the main road Wyler-Kranenberg-Cleve and the Rhine up to the line of the railway Cleve-Griethausen.

> The 43rd Wessex Division to follow up and pass through the 15th Scottish Division, to capture Goch. Prepare to hand over to the 51st Highland Division, and exploit southeast to Weeze, Kevelaer, Geldern.

Guards Armored Division, to pass through Materborn behind the 43rd Division, and advance on axis Udem, Hammerbruch, Wesel. To capture and hold the high ground north of Sonsbeek. Push forward mobile columns to capture Wesel bridge (if intact). Capture Xanten.

In support:

22nd Dragoons
141st R.A.C.
6th Assault Regt. R. E.

At five o'clock on the morning of February 8th the barrage would open. At half past seven o'clock a smoke screen would be laid by the guns for ten minutes, to be followed by ten minutes of silence to give the Survey Regiment a chance to locate any enemy batteries which might be active. At twenty minutes past nine o'clock a barrage of high explosive and smoke would open to be followed by a complete barrage at ten o'clock, heralding H-hour at half past ten o'clock.

That was the bare bones of the program which would launch five divisions into the battle. The detail was immense. It was studied in the days before the battle by all the commanders concerned, and especially by the brigadiers of the 15th Scottish Division, for they were the spearhead. On them, on their ability to thrust through with speed, must depend the whole time table of events to follow. The heavy thaw had set in, and through the mud by night the brigades heaved themselves with great difficulty and determination into their forward positions.

v.

Each night of the first week of February, as soon as it was dusk, the armored brigades, the machine-gun battalions, the field regiments of Royal Artillery, the field companies of Royal Engineers, and all the strange and varied paraphernalia of warfare, moved forward on converging lines through Grave and Nijmegen to add their firepower to the opening barrage and to drench the forward positions of the enemy with steel and explosives. The field companies of the Royal Engineers would open the way.

Only two axial roads were available, the one from Eindhoven through Mook to Nijmegen, the other from

Tilburg through s'Hertogenbosch and Grave to Nijmegen. All movement by day, except for reconnaissance groups, was forbidden forward of the Eindhoven-s'Hertogenbosch road.

On the night of February 4th in pitch darkness and in relentless rain the leading brigades of the 15th Scottish, the 53rd Welsh, and the 51st Highland Divisions, began to move. All divisional insignia had been removed. Each truck, each Kangaroo with its load of men preserved an anonymity, and it was as though eyeless creatures felt their ways through a nightmare. The road Eindhoven-Mook-Nijmegen swiftly collapsed and became a ill-defined morass of liquid mud in which the provost companies, the engineers and the pioneers toiled with a desperate yet inspired fatalism, bulldozing, laying mattresses of logs, creating diversions where no diversions were reasonably possible, always saturated, yet always sustained by a relentless driving force, directing the tortured streams of men and vehicles through the hours of darkness. Only by efforts beyond all normal expectation were the roads cleared by daylight. There was no comfort, no possibility or expectation of comfort, no hope of reward, and no wish for anything other than to do whatever task there was to do. Such was the spirit animating this great body of men, an almost miraculous spirit which, making war possible, could, if it could be produced in peace, make peace possible also. It existed in all those who must fight, and in most of those who, directly in contact, aided them to fight.

The rain beat down in that incessant steady rhythm of permanence, and neither by day or night did the sky show a loophole of hope. An all-pervading blanket submerged men and vehicles in morasses of mud. Yet there were no signs of depression in those long columns, which were still as much as they moved. The suck and squelch of many boots, the roar of engines, muffled curses, and a multitude of metallic noises filled the nights. In the trucks many sat, lay, sprawled, according to their luck, invariably in silence, some few sheltering the glow of cigarettes in the cups of hands grown red and calloused.

No rewards of peace could have induced men to this patience, to this readiness for incessant effort, to labor until they dropped, to live in mud, and often to sleep in it, to feed upon biscuit and bully beef and mugs of "char"

[tea] of a more horrible milk-and-sugared kind than they had ever known. Above all to die, to crawl over wire and mines to drag back some person previously unknown, to share a last cigarette.

It was—it is—a miracle impossible for me to define, a platitude of war which must be stated, a phenomenon, perhaps of human perversity, perhaps a pointer to the possibility of human greatness. All men who have known this experience must hunger for it, a vision as unattainable as the Holy Grail, proving what might be.

But something had happened in that first week of February to renew drooping spirits. For months men had been lost, directionless in scores of bleak wildernesses, all different, all with a dreadful drab sameness, the dereliction and emptiness of war which must be filled with the human spirit to render it tolerable. Week after week men had filled recurring vacuums of mud, in barns, billets, dykes and dug-outs, unaware of where they were, or why —except in the larger sense that this was the madness of war, and its demands were infinite. As men arrived wet and weary at a journey's end, it might prove, as often as not, merely a beginning. They might be urged irritably to double back on their tracks. They would enter the first dry billet they had known for weeks only to about turn before their blankets were down. Always death might be in the midst of it. Few men of the 15th Scottish, the 53rd Welsh, the 51st Highland, were unaware of that; old Baldy, young Toby, Jenks—the lists were lengthening— had "bought it." These were their milestones.

In the course of a few weeks those who followed and tried to keep track would encounter the same battalions in a dozen different places, whether in Belgium or Holland very few knew or cared, one week in southwestern Holland watching the gray Maas, another in the snows of the Ardennes. Then back again. Some were often under fire, knowing an enemy, others almost never, alerted, taking cover, digging in, waiting, mortared, and shelled. Off again. It seemed purposeless, undoubtedly mad. It was war. Yet in all the frustration a response was evoked from every kind of man which no other human activity on a large scale has been able to approach. Men were at the same time individuals and a part of a great whole. All the petty irritations and stresses of life had been removed and replaced by fundamentals. There was always humor.

And then, suddenly, on February the 4th there was the sense of direction for which thousands had been waiting. It came down from the top, from the Field Marshal visiting his old division, through the corps commander inspiring the battalions of the 15th Scottish and setting off such a glow with his words, his controlled yet infectious enthusiasm, that it spread down through all ranks. In many diaries are the words, "This might be the end."

Everyone knew where he was going. It was eastward at last, east and always east, into Germany, to engage and defeat the enemy in his homeland.

Thus on the nights of the 4th, 5th, and 6th of February the three leading divisions forced their ways through morasses of mud over two roads, one of which was not a road, and through drenching rain in complete darkness. For a week the infantry had worked with the armor, the tank crews, the men of the Flails and Kangaroos, Petards, Crocodiles, and a host of strange devices. As they came into the bridgehead, the reconnaissance parties went forward into the Canadian front lines, into Nederijksche wood and Groesbeek, looking out over the flat land between them and the first line of enemy defenses and to the dark barrier of the Reichswald towering on the rising ground, formidable and forbidding. To the left there was nothing but flood water beyond the Nijmegen-Cleve road, the main axis, flood water of uncertain depths hiding the wire and mines of the ground defenses.

The enemy was aroused to mortar the road to Groesbeek as the field companies of Royal Engineers labored to make it possible for men and armor to reach their start lines. The mines were buried deep and difficult to locate. Bulldozers pushed trees off the road, and exploded mines. Many dikes were bridged and ditches filled while mattresses of logs were laid over the worst stretches. It was routine work, work which had been done again and again, work which was never done, but this time the engineers felt a new rhythm in it. They, too, knew where they were going.

Further back on the western edge of the forward area the crews of tanks, Flails and Kangaroos were "marrying" up with the infantry they would support and carry. On D-minus-one the guns were still coming up, finding their camouflaged sites and stocks of ammunition, digging in with not a minute to lose. By dusk the 46th Infantry Brigade was on its mark to the left, the 71st Infantry Brigade was in the center, the only Welsh voices in all the lilt of Scots, and on the right the 154th Infantry Brigade, the assault brigades of the 15th, the 53rd and 51st Divisions. From Groesbeek back through Nijmegen and Grave to Tilburg every square inch of sodden ground, road, and ditch was packed with men and vehicles and guns. It was the end of silence.

12: *VERITABLE—THE OPENING PHASE*

i.

THE DOWNPOUR abated in early afternoon, and towards evening on the 7th the rain ceased. The sky, which had been like mud for some days, had cleared to the pale color of oysters. In the waiting silence it seemed that some giant metronome measured off the minutes, soundless yet insistent. The spires of the churches of Cuick and Gennep rose above the sable belt of the Maas like steelgray spears, austerely beautiful, borrowing pale light from the pale sky. Yet the impression in that serenity of the swollen river, the flooded meadows, the dark forest, the villages, the spires piercing the sky, was one of menace.

It was impossible to believe that the enemy was ignorant of the huge force ready to burst upon him, of the stillness of fifty thousand men wedged into the narrow bridgehead. Between six o'clock and nine o'clock there was scarcely a sound in all the region of the Maas from Nijmegen to below the village of Cuick. Men lay or squatted or stood about in barns, houses, schools, vehicles, heads propped on hands, waiting, seeming thoughtful, some sleeping. The darkness came like a benison, and shortly before nine o'clock a muffled roar grew out of the western sky, rose to a crescendo overhead, and within seconds exploded in the opening deluge of the air bombardment. Nearly 2,000 tons of high explosive thundered down upon the ancient town of Cleve to heave it out by the roots in eruptions of dreadful violence. Most men knew the meaning of that shuddering impact of sound:

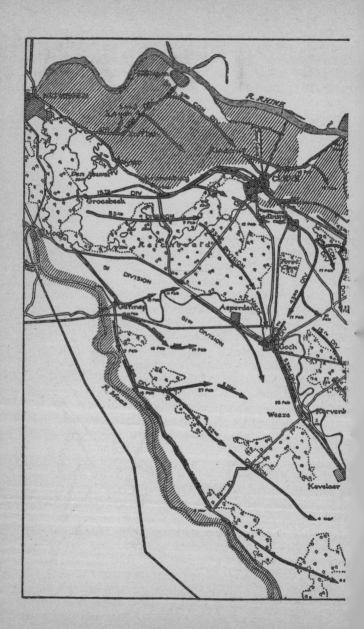

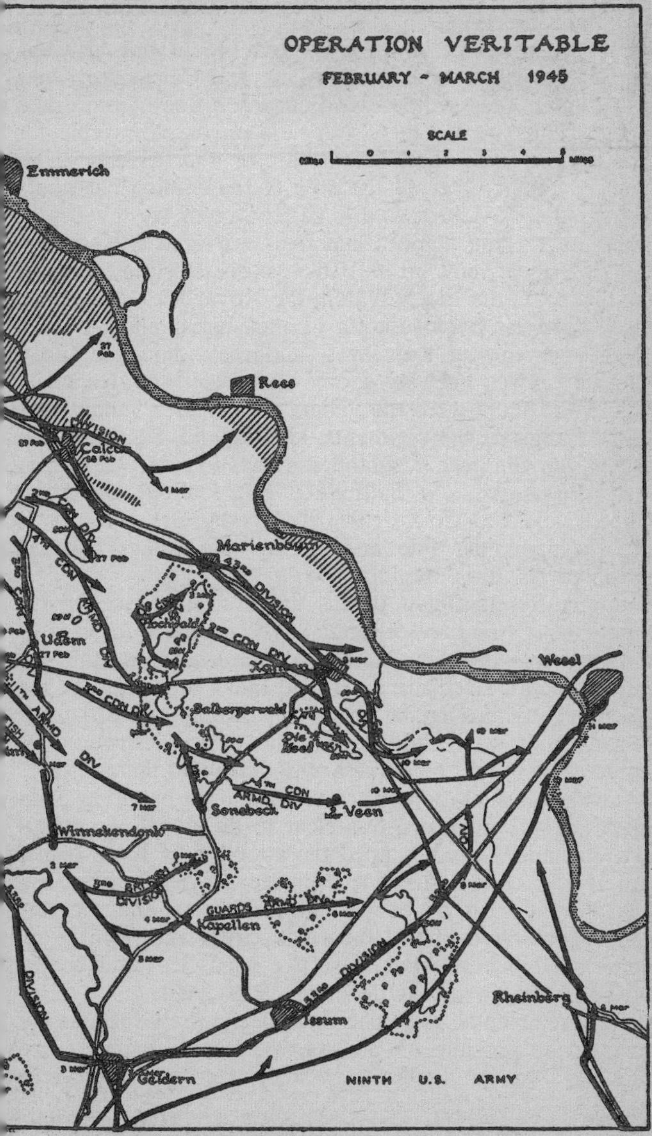

OPERATION VERITABLE

FEBRUARY - MARCH 1945

SCALE

Emmerich

Rees

DIVISION
Calcar

Marienbaum
43rd DIVISION

Wesel

Uedem
Hochwald

Xanten

Balbergerwald

Die
Reed

Sonsbeck

Veen

Winnekendonk

GUARDS
DIVISION
Kapellen

Rheinberg

Issum

Geldern

NINTH U.S. ARMY

D-minus-one. Heavy bombers will obliterate Emmerich, Cleve, Goch . . .

Not only Emmerich, Cleve, and Goch, but also the smaller townships of Weeze, Udem, and Calcar, key links in the main enemy defensive line. Each one of these was uprooted to subside in a shapeless chaos, admirable for defense and impassable for the armor and vehicles of attacking troops. Over all the area of the coming battlefield the sky flickered with gunfire, with a color wash reflected from the surging flames. The river mirrored the crimson trails of tracer, and on its banks scores of simple men of the Gordons, the Black Watch, the Royal Welsh Fusiliers, the Oxford and Bucks, the East Lancashires, reflected some of the meaning in their eyes, and their reddened faces, intensely alive. Forward from Groesbeek and Nederijksche wood there were the valiant echoes of a valiant past in the names of the regiments, all England, Scotland, and Wales, the Glasgow Highlanders in the van, the Cameronians, the Argyll and Sutherland Highlanders, the Scots Guards and the Coldstream, the Derbyshire Yeomanry, the Lothians, the Fife and Forfar, the names like the music of tradition sounding down the years.

Soon after midnight it was apparent that the narrow muddied axis of the 46th and 227th Brigades forward of the river would be of doubtful service even to sustain the initial assault. Even the Flails and tanks in support of the leading battalions might fail to get through, and to think beyond that was unprofitable. The difficulties would be immense; it would be necessary to surmount them.

These considerations were very clear to battalion commanders and engineers, less clear to divisional commanders, and might have escaped the attention of those higher up. It was certain that the Nijmegen-Wyler-Kranenberg-Cleve road must be opened without delay and that the road Mook-Gennep and thence to Goch must swiftly become available. Without these two roads it would be impossible to fight the battle of the Rhineland.

The regimental aid posts had been established as far forward as possible on the starting lines. Engineers and pioneers worked tirelessly to keep the muddied tracks open.

On the northern flank of the Reichswald the Regiment de Maisonneuve and the Calgary Highlanders of the 5th Canadian Brigade of the Canadian 2nd Division prepared to seize den Heuvel and Wyler and to open up the main axis. Until that was done the 44th Brigade of the 15th Scottish Division and the 43rd Division behind th. n would be immovable in Nijmegen. Already in the hours of darkness the waters were rising to threaten the road and to force the Canadian 3rd Division into the water over the whole northern flank.

All through the night the men of the infantry battalions were moving to their assembly areas over the deeply rutted tracks through the gun lines. Many spent the entire night in Kangaroos, jogging, jolting, slithering and slewing yard by yard. A few, mainly of the leading brigades of the 51st and 53rd Divisions, enjoyed some sleep, and the first entry in the war diary of the 1st Battalion of the Oxford and Bucks Light Infantry for February the 8th is a laconic comment on the opening of the heaviest barrage fired by British guns in the Second World War:

0500 hours. Reveille!

At that hour all those troops still passing through the gun lines felt the tremendous impact of one thousand guns bursting suddenly into action. Reveille may have been at an earlier hour for many that morning; it is certain that for none was it later. The effect on those who lay or moved under the guns was awe-inspiring, constraining a new awareness, a tentative appraisement of what might lie ahead. Impossible to imagine the effect upon the enemy as the air vibrated with incessant thunder to deaden the senses, and the earth shuddered.

It was some time before eyes and ears adjusted to the din and the gigantic panorama of the sky. At no point was the spectacle at once more splendid and awe-inspiring than on the banks of the Maas in that stretch of the river between the steeples of Cuick and Gennep. All the wild pattern of the sky kindled the gray water to the semblance of a boiling cauldron of fire and flame. Soon it was possible to distinguish the instruments in the vast uproar, the heavies and mediums in layers above the threshing and burning of the smaller weapons. Underneath the great weight of the barrage the Bofors were firing flat while the tanks of the armored brigades and the machine gunners of three battalions drenched the forward positions of the enemy.

Slowly the sky lightened, and at half past seven o'clock the barrage lifted for ten minutes of an eerie silence in which all normal movement seemed deadened and unreal. Tanks, Kangaroos and a host of vehicles lumbered forward, all lurid with cerise fluorescent panels, giving them a look of fury as though they had come up dripping with blood and fire from hell, or the depths of the Maas.

When the barrage lifted from its opening phases at half past ten o'clock, and the forward troops advanced on its heels through the minefields, it seemed that no man could have lived in the enemy positions, that no tree could still be left standing in all the Reichswald forest. The Glasgow Highlanders, leading the attack in the center, were within five hundred yards of the enemy. All but one of their Flails had bogged down on the starting line, and the infantry went on alone. Behind them the one remaining Flail cleared a path through the minefield for the tanks, and the tanks of the Coldstreams surged through to engage anti-tank guns and 88's before they, too, bogged down. But the Glasgow Highlanders had brushed aside the slight opposition from the dazed enemy in the forward trenches, and were on the German frontier with their right flank on Lubertsche Straat, and their center overwhelming the villages of Haus Kreuzfuhrt and Hettsteeg. The enemy had been called upon to endure a sustained weight of fire calculated to dull the senses, and it is astounding that he was able to react so well. On that small stretch of front the Glasgow Highlanders had the best of it, but on their left it was more difficult. The Canadians had swooped upon den Heuvel with scarcely a shot fired, but the Calgary Highlanders, fighting to clear the vital road point at the small town of Wyler met a resolute enemy behind a maze of mines, and as the day grew towards dusk, heavy artillery and bombers were called to their aid. It was night before Wyler was cleared, and the road was not yet open. The rain had begun again soon after dawn, and all through the day the 44th Brigade of the 15th Scottish had waited to go forward from Nijmegen to join the 46th and the 227th. But the 46th and the 227th looked to their fronts. The Argyll and Sutherland Highlanders, leading the attack on Kranenberg, rode the tanks of the Scots Guards through an old minefield left by the U.S. Airborne troops and were at once under heavy enemy fire. The Flails and all the carriers had bogged down in the sea of mud churned up by the Churchill tanks. A sergeant, striving to blaze a trail

through the minefield, lost a foot. Heavy mortaring began
to take a steady toll, killing off all the officers of the company on the left at a single blow. Rallied by the company
sergeant major the company went on, and within the hour
the Argylls were on the German frontier.

The light outer crust of the enemy defenses had crum-
bled without much difficulty. The Cameronians, going in
behind the Glasgow Highlanders soon after mid-day had
time to curse their own artillery for falling short, while
some said that the gunners seemed to have forgotten
about hill clearance after so much time in the flat lands of
Holland. Patrols of the Cameronians, probing into the
outskirts of Frasselt in the valley, found the village strongly held, and the battalion called for armor and Crocodiles
to aid in the main attack. On the fearsome shambles of
the brigade axis, pioneers and engineers worked like demons to help the armor into battle.

Before dusk the H.L.I. [Highland Light Infantry]
had got across the main enemy anti-tank ditch to join
with the Argylls in the assault on Kranenberg. One tank
of the Scots Guards had somehow churned its way
through with the Argylls only to bog down within sight of
Kranenberg railway station. It had done fine service.

In the late afternoon these troops on the high ground
round Kranenberg had been cheered by the sight of the
Cameronians searing their way into Frasselt behind the
flame throwing Crocodiles and fighting with grenades
from house to house. By nightfall the forward battalions,
in awful discomfort on the sodden earth, knew themselves inside Germany. For some of them there was that
night the miracle of a hot meal, for battalion and company cooks had caught the inspiration of the drive into
Germany, and men toiled forward on foot, in and out of
ditches, caked in mud, bearing the precious containers to
put warmth into the troops.

The two leading brigades of the 15th Scottish had done
well, but they were not alone. On their right the Cameronians could see the Royal Welsh Fusiliers going into the
forest with the Flails of the Westminster Dragoons and
the tanks of 147 Royal Armored Corps. It was heartening,
but on the mind of every battalion commander was the
acute awareness of the shambles of the axis, and the
knowledge that his men might be isolated and without
armor, to stick it out without much cover and less com-

fort, very thin on the ground. Each battalion was without its transport, and behind them A.V.'s R.E. [Assault Vehicles, Royal Engineers] of every kind, some bearing fascines and bridges for the anti-tank ditches, were fouling the trees at the sides of the narrow tracks. It seemed impossible that men and armor would be able to get it through. It was a fight against nature, against the already ominous rising floods, more than against the enemy.

On the right, the way to the forest for the 53rd and the 51st Divisions and the way to the Mook-Gennep road was easier in the early stages. The 1st Battalion the Black Watch with ten Churchills, Crocodiles, and Flails, had found the going comparatively easy at first. By 12:45 they were more than three hundred yards inside the Reichswald itself and on high ground inside Germany. On their left the 7th Battalion of the Black Watch was also making progress with one troop of tanks supporting each company, and with its A.V.'s R.E. and fascines churning along somehow.

On the extreme right the 2nd Derbyshire Yeomanry was performing miracles with the 5th/7th Gordons, and by midnight they too were established on the high ground to the southeast, having reached their objective in the midst of an enemy take-over. For more than an hour the Gordons, heavily outnumbered, had fought fiercely hand-to-hand in the forest in the pitch darkness before they beat off an enemy even more confused than themselves.

In the center the 71st Brigade of the 53rd had achieved its miracles. The H.L.I. had forced their way forward on the right of the Royal West Fusiliers, while on their left the Oxford and Bucks crossed the anti-tank ditch and were inside Germany by early afternoon.

Thus by midnight at the end of the first day four brigades of three divisions had reached their objectives with their assault battalions and odd fragments of their armor. The Gordons of the 227th Brigade had been forced to wait back in Nederijksche wood to come under command of the 44th Brigade when the 44th could get through.

By all reasonable measures the way in on the axis of the 46th and 227th Brigades was non-existent, and the main road was not open through Wyler and on to Kranenberg before nine o'clock at night. The Canadians had had a tremendous struggle to make good their opening role, and the mines were deadly. All through the day and far into the night of February 8th the troops of the 44th waited loaded into their Kangaroos on the outskirts of Nijmegen, exposed to the cold, incessant drizzle which had begun soon after dawn, and to the minor, but unpleasant, attentions of the Luftwaffe. The struggle of the Armored force supporting the 44th to force its way forward to join battle is itself an epic of the determination and endurance of men. All along that hopeless shambles of the brigade axis men labored to get the armor moving, many with tears of rage seaming faces thick with grime, others drawn and haggard beyond all normal measurements of exhaustion. The scene was nightmarish, wild with the stark monstrous patterns of massive vehicles, the huge outlines of the bridging tanks, cranes, fascines, bulldozers, standing out against the shapes of splintered trees—all these in a lurching, towering, roaring, heaving chaos of sound and movement. Deep ditches lined the narrow track on the 46th Brigade axis. There was no room to maneuver, and when at last the armored force had ploughed through over that diabolical route, its men worn out with the struggle, there was then forthcoming the leadership and the strength to press on. By that great effort the anti-tank ditch was reached and bridged, and the way cleared for the assault on the main defenses of the Siegfried Line.

In such conditions as these Brigadier Cumming Bruce commanding the 44th Brigade passed his brigade through to mount attacks on the vital twin hills of the Materborn protecting Cleve. That great effort to get through had finished the axes available to the 15th Scottish division.

Meanwhile the Canadian 3rd Division had embarked on its watery task of clearing and covering the whole northern flank to the Rhine bank at Emmerich. "Embarked" is the literal word. Already the rising floods had washed out the bridge on the Canadian 7th Brigade axis, and because of this, and the flood probabilities still to be considered, the division had exchanged its tanks for Buffaloes. In these lightly armed and lightly armored amphibious vehicles the Canadians sailed in the late afternoon of February 8th from Wainwright Beach, named after the Canadian Buffalo reserve, and set forth into the night over the mines and wire at the northern limits of the Siegfried Line. The 7th Brigade took Zyfflich while the 8th Brigade "landed" at Zandpol and Leuth. The water was by that time at least three feet deep over most of the flood plain beyond the Rhine bunds [steep flood banks], and rising to lap the main Nijmegen-Cleve road. Those troops which had assaulted their objectives on foot in the early stages were swiftly marooned, sharing the second floors of houses and the roofs of barns with surviving livestock and the enemy.

ii.

The 9th and 10th of February were critical days at the extremities of the entire northern front. On the 9th the U.S. 1st Army was once more in Schmidt with its troops bearing down irresistibly upon the Roer and Urft river dams. It was too late. Holding their positions to the last moment, but not beyond it, the Germans opened the sluices. A cataract of water surged through Düren in a great wave to join the flooded Maas at Roermond. On the morning of February 10th the British forces committed to the Rhineland battle knew that Operation Grenade would not take place, that the U.S. 9th army was immobilized for an unpredictable period, and that they would fight alone.

At once the enemy began to move reinforcements from the Cologne plain to confront the 30th Corps in its attempts to burst through and out of the Reichswald area. For the Germans the time for strategy had passed; all that they could do was to fight from day to day, without thought for the future. Troops were committed piecemeal to the battle as they arrived, for the situation was desperate. Five hundred thousand refugees were reported to be pouring into Berlin as the victorious Russian armies drove on through Silesia. This news was as alarming to the enemy as it was heartening to the British. Yet the morale of the enemy was high, and there was no inclination at this stage to underestimate the fighting capacity of men making a last stand before the Rhine.

For at least two weeks it seemed certain that the Battle of the Rhineland would be isolated, with the British and Germans locked in a death struggle in forest, bog, and flood, and almost surrounded by water. The tremendous barrage fired to launch Operation Veritable had successfully eased the assault battalions onto their first objectives, but beyond those points it was clear by the end of the second day that the enemy was resolved to fight bitterly for every yard of German soil back to the Rhine.

In the extreme north the Germans had also called their last water resources to their aid. The main Rhine dikes had been breached at the outset, and the weight of flood water swiftly collapsed the Quer Dam and threatened the essential British axis [main line] of advance, especially on the stretch of road from Wyler to Kranenberg. To reinforce this flood the enemy blew the northern gates of the Spoy Canal, and with that the whole area north of the Cleve-Calcar road became a lake, lethal with submerged obstacles at unpredictable and varying depths.

The troops of the 15th Scottish were at once forced onto the railway line through Kranenberg, but even that was under water by February 12th, and the main axis was under three feet of water with the troops and vehicles of elements of three divisions piled up in appalling confusion as the 43rd Division strove to get through.

Partly as a result of this immense flooding of the Rhine and Roer, the Maas and Niers continued to rise steadily, hampering the bridging operations and the forward movement of supporting troops, armor and artillery.

In attempts to counter the floods Royal Engineers blew the dikes northeast of Nijmegen on the advice of the Dutch, and sent two million gallons of water an hour in a counter barrage to roll back water with water. The enemy at once breached the dikes of the Alter Rhine, and it seemed to the troops struggling over the Nijmegen-Cleve road that they fought along the shores of an inland sea with the tide steadily rising. The spires of churches, the crowns and tattered sails of windmills, roof tops and telegraph poles, with here and there the branches of trees, stood out ominously from a wild waterscape as broad as the estuary of the River Plate. Over this waste of water, whipped to white horses by fitful wind, and under an incessant drizzle of rain, the Canadian 3rd Division developed a form of "naval" warfare piloted by British crews in ungainly Buffaloes, Weasels and amphibious jeeps. Navigating with land maps, taking bearings on steeples, and constantly attempting to avoid the elaborate wire and minefields of the hidden defenses, the Buffaloes, buffeted by the waves, taking in water across their blunt bows, moved steadily upon their objectives, answering bursts of spandau fire from windmills and roof tops with bursts from their Brownings and Brens.

The work of maintenance of the fleet of amphibious vehicles in addition to the immense labors to build ramps and bridges and roads, put a massive burden upon the engineers. In the midst of the waters men worked with wire cutters, their hands and arms blue and cold as they strove to release the tracks of the Buffaloes from the wire. Weasels were often at the mercy of the curious cross currents, and almost as many vehicles lay "hove to," stranded on wire or submerged obstacles, as moved to the attack. Now and then a vehicle heaved up out of the flood with its human cargo floundering, maimed in the water, after squatting upon a mine.

To protect the whole northern flank from enemy artillery, 3,500 tons of smoke supplies were brought forward, and 85,000 smoke canisters burned 500,000 gallons of fog oil to pour dense clouds of smoke across the water. Wainwright beach was a scene of immense activity, an improvised shipyard resounding to the clang of steel on steel as mechanics labored without rest, and sodden to their bones, to keep enough craft in service. For there was a danger that the assault troops would be as hopelessly marooned as were many of the enemy. It must be doubtful if ever before in warfare have men at the back worked so hard and tirelessly, and with such ingenuity, to supply and serve fighting troops. And they too worked often under fire.

The work of detecting and blowing up mines under water and of marking "safe" channels with improvised buoys, was in itself remarkable and highly dangerous, not alone on the main floods, but on the "dry" routes to the Materborn, Kranenberg, and Cleve. All along the line pioneers and signal men matched the efforts of the engineers, laying corduroy tracks over the slush of scores of dangerous trails, stringing and repairing cables and wire and somehow keeping supplies of ammunition and food on the move.

By nightfall on the first day the gunners had fired 500,000 shells, and as they manhandled and bulldozed the guns forward to new advanced positions, new supplies followed them, as it seemed, by countless minor miracles.

All forward tracks were given names, and all laterals were numbered, in the forest regions. Coded traces were issued to aid battalions moving forward on compass bearings by day and night, "navigating" the forest by following white tapes knotted at every one hundred yards, while flank parties struggled through the undergrowth to protect the main bodies. It was warfare of a remarkably blind nature, groping for—and often encountering—groups of enemy hand to hand in the darkness.

In the wake of the infantry the gunners were having a tremendous struggle, often surprising pockets of enemy, especially on the 51st Division axis. There on the road to Gennep the 63rd Anti-tank Regiment flushed the enemy out of a magnificent dug-out equipped with a piano, a grandfather clock—still ticking and showing the right time in spite of the bombardment—and pots boiling on the stove.

By the end of the second day Operation Veritable had become a tactical tangle, impossible to unravel, and the story of the battle can only be built up from a mass of fragments. Brigade orders were changed several times a day. Battalions seldom knew what they were meant to do for more than two or three hours ahead. Orders from the top had become meaningless, and in this situation the waging of the struggle devolved upon the shoulders of brigade and battalion commanders. Out in the front they knew what could be done, what must be done, and they did it. The elaborate movements and timings, the steady leap-frogging planned for infantry and armor, were so much waste paper. Reliefs were impossible. Brigades, let alone divisions, could not hope to pass through those in front, and those in front stayed in front, while behind them a wedge of men, armor, guns, carriers, cranes, bridging tanks, fascines, bulldozers, and a whole host of vehicles bogged down. Yet no one faltered, and slowly order began to grow out of chaos, and the patterns desired were attained.

Strangely, in these early stages, simplicity lay on the flooded northern flank. The fleets of Buffaloes sailed on, marooned friends and foes were steadily rescued. Gulls soared and swooped over the ragged "flotillas," wheeled hopefully above the numerous craft trapped by the underwater wire, the lonely men struggling to reach land in collapsible boats. Signposts sticking out their arms above the waters indicated the invisible roads to submerged villages. A small herd of Friesian cattle huddled on a mud bank in the yard of a half-submerged and shell-holed farmstead, and on a strip of land a foot deep under water a solitary black horse trotted up and down, up and down, whinnying sadly. Canaries still sang in their cages framed in glassless windows. A spotted dog rushed, barking furiously through a shattered barn. Above all was the crash and mutter of heavy guns, the harsh threat of spandaus, and the answering bursts of the Brens.

Over this battlefield the Stormont, Dundas and Glengarry Highlanders, piloted by British crews, reached the Spoy canal on February 10th and assaulted Duffelward and Rindern, closing in to the north of Cleve, and observing the wreckage of the town. On that evening men lay out upon the Rhine bunds on the banks of the last barrier between them and the heartland of Germany.

For five miles, the main road to Cleve lay under three feet of water, and DUKWS [trucks capable of floating in water] moved forward over the flooded tracks through Kranenberg.

From the high turret of a mansion standing on a piece of high ground in the midst of the floods to the northeast of Cleve it was possible, even before Cleve had fallen, to look far out over all this wilderness of war, and to discern the beginnings of order on the left. Elements of an enemy parachute regiment were marooned some two thousand yards away on a small island, helpless but still dangerous. Buffaloes and Weasels were busy taking blankets and food to troops isolated in the floods and to first-aid posts. Those unfortunates marooned for the night in their Buffaloes stretched tarpaulins athwart their "ships," posted look-outs, and prepared to make the best of it. The earphones of the radio telephones buzzed with messages. From somewhere out on the water a colonel asked insistently for "Control":

"Hello, Control! There are six very wet and weary men out here. We're coming in soon. Hot food and a fire. How about it?"

"Can do," said the voice of Control.

Nevertheless, in this strange manner the northern flank was swiftly covered, and patrols were out on the Rhine bunds, all at a very small cost in lives. Without the 79th Armored Division, without the vision and dogged persistence over many years of Major General Sir Percy Hobart—for he had conceived and made possible all this collection of "Funnies"—it is hard to imagine how this battle, and many others in Northwest Europe, could have been fought at all.

13: *THE BATTLE OF THE REICHSWALD*

i.

BY FOUR o'clock on the morning of February 9th the 44th Brigade had contrived, with a dogged determination beyond all praise, to heave itself into the forefront of the battle. The 2nd Battalion of the Gordons, coming under command, moved out of Nederijksche wood two hours after midnight to enter Nutterden seven hours later after battling with mines, felled trees, wire, and the hazards of the trail, rather than with the enemy. Kranenberg was clear and the way was open for an assault upon the twin hills of the Materborn feature, the essential preliminary to the attack on Cleve.

Under artificial moonlight the brigade had crossed the anti-tank ditch guarding the Siegfried defenses, and soon after first light the 6th Battalion K.O.S.B. [King's Own Scottish Borderers] had reached the narrow belt of the Reichswald immediately to the south of Nutterden. Brigadier Cumming Bruce, commanding the 44th, realizing that having got his brigade into the lead he would almost certainly stay there, reacted to the demands of the hour with energy and skill. In mid-afternoon he launched the 8th Battalion R.S.F. [Royal Scots Fusiliers] supported by Grenadiers against one side of the Materborn while the 6th Battalion King's Own Scottish Borderers in Kangaroos went in against the other.

The speed and power of these twin assaults surprised the enemy. Footholds were swiftly gained and secured, but a desperate and bitter struggle developed for control of this citadel defending Cleve and for the escarpment and woodland belt dominating the last section of the main road. Both sides knew that every hour counted. Enemy reinforcements of quality and supported by self-propelled guns were rushing to strengthen the Cleve garrison and block the Calcar road, and the chances of "bouncing" the town and pushing on with fast armored cars to Calcar were rapidly diminishing.

By last light on the 9th the King's Own Scottish Borderers and the Royal Scots Fusiliers were secure on the Materborn, but a hard core of enemy remained. At the same time a squadron of the 15th Scottish Reconnaissance Regiment attempted to advance south of Nutterden on the road to Hekkens through the forest. It was no easy matter to keep troops on the move in the darkness even with the help of artificial moonlight, but one battalion was established firmly on the road. A group of enemy moving forward to reinforce positions already lost fell into the hands of patrols of the Reconnaissance Squadron, and two officers and fifty men added new identifications to the growing tally. Seven battalions from three reserve divisions had already been encountered, and it was clear that the enemy was moving troops with all speed through Geldern and Xanten to the north. It was also clear that the furious artillery bombardment and the constant air strikes had disrupted enemy communications and spread confusion throughout their forward defensive positions.

Meanwhile throughout the 9th, the 46th and 227th Brigades had been steadily consolidating their gains, and rescuing their armor and vehicles from the mud. The chaplain of the 2nd Battalion of the Seaforths had taken advantage of the near impossibility of further forward movement to bury the battalion dead. The Glasgow Highlanders were readying to aid in the fight for the Materborn as soon as they could get there. The 7th Battalion of the Seaforths were totally involved in a battle against mud, mines, and flood. Towards evening it began to sleet, and then— mildly—to snow.

Soon after dusk the enemy shelling and mortaring became severe and accurate. A direct hit on the command post of the 2nd Battalion of the Gordons killed eleven men and wounded five, including two officers killed and one wounded, a savage end to a successful day, and a foretaste of the fire power still available to the enemy, and of the bitter struggle ahead.

It was at this hour, in these conditions of rising floods with the axis of the 15th Scottish beyond use, and with every way forward blocked with men, vehicles, mud and water, that the 43rd Wessex Division received orders to dvance out of Nijmegen, pass through the 15th Scottish, y-pass Cleve, and strike south towards Goch. It is nlikely that a more optimistic order has ever been given. t was based partly on the belief that Cleve had fallen, ut it also reveals a strange failure to appreciate the true onditions forward.

In a spirit, therefore, of "theirs not to reason why"— r how—the 4th Wiltshires led the 129th Brigade of the 3rd out of Nijmegen on the night of February 9th with he intention of advancing through the Materborn gap nd the slender neck of the Reichswald east of Nutterden. t was a night of bitter cold with the rain driving in sudden ierce squalls over the water from the northeast, a ghoul-sh night, of searchlights, flares, bursting shells and burn-ng buildings, revealing the desolation of water and bog as n a nightmare.

When the head of the brigade reached Nutterden on he fringe of the shambles of transport and armor and vas confronted with the rising floods, it was clear that a 1ew way forward must be found. Undaunted by the con-'usion, reconnaissance parties at once explored the pos-ible secondary routes. Air photographs had given the mpression of a secondary road with a concrete surface. 'n fact, the surface was of sand. The way was blocked oy felled trees, skillfully mined and covered by spandau ire, but the 4th Wiltshires pressed on with the 5th Wilt-hires and the 4th Somerset Light Infantry close behind.

The record of that night lives only in the minds of those who traveled that road, fighting in the pitch darkness with an invisible enemy, firing at gun-flashes, and steeling nerves against the murderous bursts of mortar bombs. The remarkable truth is that at first light the 4th Wiltshires reached the outskirts of Cleve near the junction of the Goch-Bedburg road. Southward lay the planned line of their main attack, for the divisional task was to roll up the Siegfried Line from north to south while the 15th Scottish pressed on beyond Cleve to Calcar.

But all this was no more than the rough outline of intentions in that drab dawn of February 10th when the 129th Brigade, having squeezed through the "eye of a needle" in the wake of the 15th Scottish Reconnaissance Regiment, suddenly attacked the enemy in Cleve. Fierce fighting had again erupted with the dawn on the Materborn when the brigadier of the 129th ordered the 5th Wiltshires and the 4th Somersets into the attack.

In the ensuing battle fought by the 15th Scottish and the 129th Brigade in and over and through the shocking rubble of Cleve, the confusion of the enemy proved even greater than the confusion of the attackers. So unexpected was the attack that the German garrison commander had no chance to deploy his reinforcements of men and guns. Fighting was intense, incoherent, unpredictable, and deadly, for the enemy paratroops, although very few of them had ever worn parachutes, or ever would, had been chosen for such a role and were of the highest quality youth still available.

All through the 10th and the night of the 10th/11th fierce fighting raged as isolated enemy groups fought for the shapeless rubble of Cleve and clung to the hear of the Materborn. Sporadic bursts of fire still came from the mounds of rubble until afternoon of the 11th. It was a Sunday. From dawn until noon the bark of spandaus answered bursts from stens as troops of the 15th Scottish advanced over the flooded main road, running in the shelter of their armor. On the western approaches the near suburban homes were burning fiercely like torches in the water. It was still dangerous to move unwarily, and it was not until early afternoon that the last burst of machine-gun fire from the armor silenced the last men in the last rubble heap, and Cleve was ours.

"What always will rankle in the minds of those who fought at Cleve is the oafish stupidity of the attack by Bomber Command," wrote Major General Essame.* It is a harsh but just comment, for if Cleve had not been bombed at all it is probable that the 43rd would have gone through with comparative ease.

The ruin of the old Swan Tower, which, it was said, had once been the meeting place of smugglers, stood above the hideous confusion like the hub of some shattered wheel, one of the very few recognizable objects on which the eye could focus. The normally peaceful waters of a canal rushed like a torrent in a narrow channel through the rubble, and a white goat led a section of infantry across the tangled wreckage of a bridge.

From a high point the Canadians could be seen landing

*The 43rd Wessex Division at War 1944-45.

at the village of Rindern, a mile or two over the floods to the northeast, busily consolidating their hold over all the outcrops sprouting from that desolation of water, littered with all the garbage of war, and with the Buffaloes moving against the trailing backcloth of the smoke screens.

The situation over the main axis was worsening steadily. The head of the 214th Brigade had reached Nutterden with the divisional commander refusing, in spite of a high fever, to hand over any of his responsibility at such a time. It was impossible to bring up the third brigade of the division. The news of all these difficulties had reached the 21st Army Group Commander, and he had at once resolved to see for himself. No fire engines rushing through the entrails of a great city at the peak of business, have ever made greater demands than those made by the Field Marshal and his transport that day. The water was more than two feet deep in places, and still rising. DUKWS were moving troops forward through Kranenberg, and the platforms of the railway station were as crammed with men as any suburban line station on a weekday morning. Hundreds of men were wrestling with transport, exhausting all their energies and ingenuity to keep traffic moving. Perhaps it is one of the tragedies of the exalted that, with the best will in the world, they can never discover life again as it really is, that they can never again share, or know, the common lot. To those struggling on blocked roads, and attempting to repair the additional burden of the Field Marshal's progress, it was a matter for relief that the Monarch and the Prime Minister had not chosen this day to see for themselves. It was a memorable Sunday.

But while there was darkness in the rear there was a glimmer of light forward. A special force of armor with the 7th Seaforths strove to attack towards Calcar against the enemy astride the road in strength. The 129th Brigade moved to secure the high ground east of Bedburg and thus to be a position to pinch out the Staatforst Cleve, opening the way to the Goch escarpment from the north.

In Cleve, the 15th Scottish, having played a prominent part in the forefront of the battle for the town, handed over to the Canadian 3rd Division and began to shake themselves loose. The original hopes of the Reconnaissance Regiment "to flood the country with armored cars" had become idle dreams; nevertheless there were hopes that men and armor might soon gain a grip on solid earth ahead.

Opposition was hardening fast when on the 12th the Scottish right flank linked up with the Welsh left some three thousand yards east of the Cleve-Hekkens road. Conditions forward were still frightful. The 9th Cameronians, attempting to dig in, struck water at 9 inches, and were very wet. Magnificent efforts were being made all along the line by the master cooks, and in the most unlikely places troops were heartened by the sight, smell and flavor of hot food. The good humor seldom faltered. A rifleman of the Cameronians, moving up from a reserve position, remarked: "It must be dangerous here, the Color Sergeant's wearing a steel helmet."

The period of alarms was at its height, with orders reversed within an hour or two of being given. In the woods south of the road to Moyland and Calcar fighting was intense.

ii.

The progress of the 53rd Division through the dank and dark Reichswald forest had in it something of the macabre, evoking flashes of vivid memory implanted in childhood by the legends of the brothers Grimm. By February 10th, roads assigned to the division had ceased to exist. Everywhere the sandy or muddied tracks had become impassable morasses until fortified with poles lashed together into corduroy bases by the pioneers. These in turn soon sank. All vehicles were banned in the forest, except jeeps, and even these often had to be abandoned. Battalion commanders habitually moved with their forward companies, and brigades strove to keep close up behind their battalions maintaining communications by means of liaison officers and runners—though "runners" is a peculiarly inept word to describe the dangerous activities of the men struggling through quagmires and dark undergrowth, everlastingly alert for enemy.

Danger lurked in scores of hide-outs, impossible to mop up in the early stages, and sudden death was imminent at every intersection of the trails. Enemy self-propelled guns and well-sited machine guns were able to crisscross the forest area with barriers of fire which might well have proved impassable to troops less resolved to gain ground and to struggle through to the light of day.

Immense efforts were made to bring up anti-tank guns using Loyd carriers with some success. In darkness, in confusion, in a somber wilderness lit by a kind of greenish twilight by day and submerged in the dark blackness of the tomb by night, companies, battalions, and brigades struggled on, their progress punctuated by sudden brief and deadly encounters. Small groups of men, usually in platoon strength, came face to face, and at such times the battle was to the bayonet.

The whole forest had the feel of some stagnant pool. Preliminary bombardment, while killing very few of the enemy, had toppled the crowns of scores of trees and shattered hundreds to matchwood. In such conditions the 53rd steadily progressed to cross the Cleve-Hekkens road, one of the two concrete roads running through the forest from north to south, and to press on towards the Cleve-Goch road, and daylight. P.I.A.T. mortar teams fought in pairs, stalking and attacking the enemy self-propelled guns with success, but only twelve bombs per company could be carried by troops already festooned with the chattels of war. Artillery support was of little value, but searchlights helped movement by night.

In the moments of rest men had some comfort from the tins of self-heating soup they carried, but there was not much time or opportunity for rest. The companies moved in tight formations with two platoons up. It was dangerous to straggle, and the tails of battalions were always in danger from determined nests of enemy awaiting their chances to strike.

On the 11th and 12th, enemy opposition stiffened all along the line, but now the leading battalions of the 53rd Division were in sight of the Cleve-Goch road, and with solid contact on the left. By the 13th the whole central mass of the forest had been cleared, and the weight of the 30th Corps attack had begun to turn, to bear down in a slow right-wheeling movement on the central hub of the 53rd, to the southeast, massing inexorably against the fortress town of Goch and the ramifications of its surrounding defenses. There was no doubt in any mind that Goch would prove a very tough nut to crack.

iii.

The 51st (Highland) Division in the right flanking role had the easiest road to travel and the hardest battles to fight. Inevitably the two things went together. The road ran southeastward from Mook to Gennep with a loop of the Maas flats on the right and the escarpment of the southwestern ridge of the Reichswald on the left. A light railway line, battered to uselessness by shellfire, ran in places tight up under the escarpment and the fringe of the forest. It was a dangerous road to travel, deeply cratered and mined, covered by mortar fire, and enfiladed by spandaus on either side.

The township of Gennep, protected by the formidable barrier of the Niers River in spate, was a vital part of the powerful defensive system of which Goch was the core. The opening of the road to and through Gennep was essential to the development of the battle, for while Gennep commanded the rail and road crossing of the Maas it was impossible for the British 2nd Army to bridge the river and to open up a main line for reinforcements and supplies. A major assault across the flooded Niers and the capture of Gennep was, therefore, a priority task of great urgency for the 51st Division. The secondary task was the clearance of the southern part of the Reichswald, the taking of Hekkens and Kessel, and the opening up of the good roads through the forest. On the whole right flank of the battle the enemy defensive line faced north in its natural defensive features rather than east.

On the morning of February 8th the 153rd Brigade advanced in the wake of the barrage down the road to the south from Mook, while the 154th moved south from Groesbeek to clear the southern fringes of the Reichswald and thrust with all speed upon Hekkens. Supported by the Derbyshire Yeomanry, and by the 107th Armored Regiment, R.A.C., with the Fife and Forfars under command, both brigades struck determined enemy opposition. Swiftly on their first objectives on the high ground in the forest, the 154th fought fiercely astride the Frasselt-Hekkens road all through the 9th and 10th. It was war with the bayonet and grenade, with P.I.A.T.'s and anti-tank guns attacking enemy self-propelled 88's and strong points. Mines were deadly and skilfully concealed. Every barn and building housed resolute groups of enemy armed with automatic weapons and holding their fire. Strong points silenced by heavy mortaring erupted suddenly into fierce action, the occupants directing deadly fire upon the

ils of advancing companies. In such conditions the kind
f leadership, commonplace thirty years before at Ypres,
as demanded and given. Company and platoon com-
anders, leading their men in furious assaults against
nemy strong points, were the first to die. On the 9th, the
th battalion of the Black Watch paused to bury its dead
hile armored bulldozers heaved the rubble of victory out
f the path of troops going through.

The half-tracks were blowing up on the Frasselt-Hekkens
oad as the 5th Seaforths strove to go through on Hek-
ens. Miraculously battalion cooks brought up hot food
t night, and the men were fortified with rum rations. By
he 11th the 5th Seaforths were down to two and a half
ompanies, and with two companies organized as platoons.
he battalion commander was wounded in the neck, and
he toll of officers had been heavy.

The slogans painted in large white letters upon the walls
f barns and houses revealed something of the despera-
ion of the enemy. Phrases such as *"Der Feigling ist ein
ump"* [The coward is a clod], *"Leben tot as Slav"*
Slavery is living death], together with the familiar,
Ein volk, ein Reich, ein Fuhrer" [One people, one
mpire, one leader], dissolved into dust at the impact of
he mortars and were heaved out of existence by the
rmored bulldozers. Whole villages disappeared without
race as the Seaforths, Black Watch, and Camerons bore
lown upon Hekkens and Kessel, and the 53rd Division
vheeled down through the forest and on the twin con-
erging roads behind them. On the 13th, the battered
eaforths were astride the Cleve-Hekkens road, making
vay for the 53rd Division to put in a fresh assault on the
iercely held road center of Hekkens. By that time the
3lack Watch and the Gordon Highlanders were fighting
rom house to house in Gennep, harassed by spandau
ire from all sides, and meeting heavy counterattacks.

iv.

It was not an easy passage down the river road to Gen-
iep; nor was the going simple through the deceptively
lose country on the fringes of the Reichswald flanking the
oad to the northeast. Here, where the forest peters out,
iving way to scrub and thin groups of trees, scores of
racks, and as many hamlets and farmsteads, interlace

the scrub and tree clumps, giving good fields of fire to the defenders, and a confused vision to the attackers.

Here was no vague invisible enemy. At the outset the 5th Black Watch and 1st and 5/7th Gordon Highlanders were in the midst of enemy groups, harassed by spandau fire and swiftly moving snipers, as they struck south out of the Reichswald to cut the road and comb the fringe of the forest on the left flank. On the road itself the Derbyshire Yeomanry led off with great dash, perhaps inspired by the fact of hard ground under the tracks of their armor. At once the road was covered with cross fire as every house and hamlet and strong point manned by resolute men threw down gauntlets of fire in the face of the attackers.

All through the 9th and 10th, scores of fierce platoon and patrol actions blazed from end to end of the road and over the network of villages on the flanks. Ambushed at half a dozen points, the men of the Derbyshire Yeomanry dismounted from their armor to go in furiously with grenades against an enemy immovable by other means. By the morning of the 10th, they had jumped the road crossing to the north of Gennep to assault the large village of Ottersum.

All three battalions of the 153rd Brigade had fought their ways through ambushes and road blocks, the 5/7th Gordons, bloodied in a terrific fight at the first road crossing, swept on devoid of cover, giving tongue at sight of the enemy, and literally in full cry. They reached Ottersum close behind their supporting tanks, and the spearhead of the reconnaissance squadron.

The enemy defense of Ottersum was a foretaste of the battle ahead, and it was clear that the whole line of the Niers River was held in great strength. The first to make the crossing was a lieutenant of the Black Watch, leading his platoon with great skill and courage in assault boats and infiltrating under cover of darkness to the outskirts of Gennep without disturbing the enemy deep in his dugouts. In his wake the whole company got across to hold on grimly against spandau, machine-gun, and mortar fire while behind them in Ottersum the battle raged with grenades and automatic weapons from house to house, from cellar to roof top. Artillery support, serving to alert the enemy, was more of a menace than an aid in an operation that had become fluid and confused, blazing spasmodically at hidden strong points all along the line of the attack. Prisoners were few. The 5/7th Gordons advancing down the main road in an attempt to seize the main bridge into Gennep saw it blown before their eyes. That night under heavy shelling the battalion crossed the river in Buffaloes. Accurate artillery fire now proved vital in breaking up counterattacks coming in furiously against the Black Watch and Gordons in attempts to hurl them back into the river.

All through the night of the 12th Guards worked under murderous shelling and mortar fire directed by an enemy knowing the range of the target to inches, yet by morning they had thrown 110 feet of Bailey bridge across the Niers and opened the way for the armor. By that time the main axis of the 51st Division had collapsed, demanding eight hours of dangerous labor before it could be restored.

Nowhere was the Royal Engineer contribution to the battle more evident than in the maintenance of these roads, so necessary to the 51st. All through the days and nights the bridge-builders and the road crews worked incessantly on construction and maintenance. By night searchlights illumined the crossing-points of the Maas, sparkling like necklaces over the water, and threw huge shadowed caverns of darkness under the escarpment of the forest above the Mook-Gennep road. The din of battle was incessant; and in an uproar which seemed at times to embrace all nature, huge vehicles bore their vast and varied loads forward to the brink of battle. Under the escarpment the men manning the armored bulldozers and the plate-layers toiled incessantly, and the light railway grew literally before one's eyes.

All along the north bank of the Niers, the 51st and 53rd Divisions were closing up, and a bitter fight raged over all the region of the Hekkens cross roads. In Hekkens village not one brick stood upon another, and armored bulldozers, heaving the rubble from the way, wiped all sign of Hekkens from the face of the earth.

To the left the anti-tank guns supporting the Cameron Highlanders blazed away at enemy artillery O.P.'s [observation posts] and smashed the church steeple of Kessel, while the 3-inch mortars of the Argyll and Sutherland Highlanders hurled their bombs into the midst of enemy groups across the Niers. Armored bulldozers moved into action, guns blazing, to fill an anti-tank ditch barring the way to the 5th Seaforths; it was clear that the pressure building up on the north bank of the river was irresistible. Grimly the Argylls moved down the road to Kessel to assault across the Niers in Buffaloes. Behind them came the Seaforths. On either flank were the Black Watch, and the enemy shell fire was deadly and accurate at all possible crossing points.

But the heart of the battle was in Gennep and to the south on the line of the railway and in the flanking woods. Here the enemy built up counterattack after counterattack, his assaults bringing him at times within yards of battalion headquarters. It was essential for the British to anchor their right flank tight on the Maas, and this they did at a point where the river loops eastward at the village of Heyen. Yet it was in the narrow ways of the shattered township that the fighting was the most furious and deadly. Spandau fire blazed from cellar, attic, and rooftop; snipers sniped with ruthless efficiency, and the mortar bombs splintered the rubble-dusted air with hidden death.

No form of warfare makes greater demands upon the physical and nervous resources of men; no form of warfare demands higher qualities of courage, of morale, and resource. The 5/7th Gordon Highlanders and the Black Watch were equal to the task. Led always with steadfastness, often with great skill, and at times with heroism beyond the normal demands of brave conduct, moving from house to house, from cover to cover, knowing always the deadly high pitched whine and sickening thud of bullets in flesh, coming from all angles, men slowly but inexorably cleared the enemy from Gennep.

The same lieutenant who had first led his platoon of the Black Watch across the Niers in assault boats led also the Black Watch in the fight for Gennep when his commander and second in command were killed. That was leadership at its most resourceful and heroic best.

v.

By the 13th of February, the 51st Highland Division had anchored the right flank on the Maas at Heyen and cleared Gennep of the enemy. The first phase of the Battle of the Rhineland was at an end, and the battle of the Reichswald was won. In the center the 53rd Division had cleared the whole of the main forest region, and the good laterals were open from north to south. But even the good roads had sustained the worst ravages of war, and there was a stretch out of Hekkens, a main road, bearing the sign, "The Liver Mile." Every yard of this corduroy was a jolting torment for men and vehicles, but it was passable. Roads and tracks everywhere presented a shambles of bogged tanks, bulldozers, A.V.R.E.'s and vehicles of all kinds. Movement of vehicles remained an intolerable labor, but was no longer impossible.

On the left the 43rd was poised for its southern thrust, outflanking the still powerful enemy defenses east of the Cleve-Goch section of the main railway line.

Meanwhile the 15th Scottish was heavily engaged on the Calcar road, still unable to make much impression on an enemy as unyielding as a wall of steel and resolved to bar the way. Enemy reinforcements were pouring in, supported by first class artillery. The worst was yet to come. Across the floods north of the Cleve-Calcar road the Canadians had anchored their left securely on Emmerich. The floods showed no signs of abating, and the levels of the Maas and Niers rivers continued to rise.

That was the situation on February 13th. The jaws of the enemy had been forced open, but the hinges of the jaws still held, and the constriction of the front remained acute. From Cleve to Goch is a distance of eight miles, and in that area, bounded by the Nijmegen-Cleve road on the left, by the Gennep-Goch railway line on the right, and backed by the Maas, four divisions plus two armored brigades, a brigade of the 79th Armored Division, a great mass of artillery and supporting troops, were crushed together like a phalanx in a shambles of mud, flood, and shattered timber.

Through four days and nights from the 13th to the 17th, the battle raged all along the line with a growing intensity, especially along the line of the Niers River and on the approaches to Goch. South of Gennep the enemy held on to the last man in trenches twelve feet deep, and could only be moved by assault with grenades. Counterattacks supported by self-propelled guns came in again and again, the first savage counterattacks experienced by the 51st Division since Normandy. Enemy strong points continued to fight until overwhelmed.

By the 15th the attack was closing in with irresistible force on the road to Asperden, astride the railway line, and astride the Cleve-Goch road. The 43rd Division was rolling up the enemy line from the north, and from three sides the attack on the Goch hinge was building up to its furious climax.

14: THE SECOND PHASE—GOCH-CALCAR

i.

THE 15TH of February was a key day. The waters of the Maas and Niers had reached their peaks, and no further flood possibility remained to the enemy. Even the weather showed signs of improvement, and there was a glimmer of hope for the U.S. 9th Army waiting impatiently at the turbulent barrier of the Roer. If no more rain should fall, even that broad torrent must soon abate.

On the right flank of the Canadian 1st Army engineers of the British 8th Corps viewed the receding waters with relief. They had worked like beavers to construct and to open a bridge to span the Maas at Gennep. Hundreds of feet of Bailey pontoon had been rising and falling with the erratic floods over the approaches; now the pontoons began to subside, resting upon the squelching earth. A small sign bore the legend: "Gennep bridge-4008 feet." When it was finally opened to heavy transport at dawn on the 20th, it represented a major achievement of engineering under atrocious conditions, and murderous enemy fire. Seven bridges then spanned the Maas on the Canadian front to feed men, shells, and supplies to the troops ahead.

In the pale sunshine of the dawn hopes began to rise all along the line. Men whose horizons of life were bounded by the hour, by a few yards of grey landscape, the ominous shells of farmsteads, the rubble of villages, began to scour themselves of the grime of battle, and to get their second wind. North of Gennep men stood under the showers of mobile baths knowing a luxury greater than anything they could remember in all their lives. Battalions, temporarily out of the line, cleaned up and cursed as they strove to get the muck out of their rifles. But it was not given to any visitor to know how they felt; how they felt was known only to themselves, and perhaps not even to themselves. Life had taken on new meanings, and only the abnormal was real, the sudden explosion which took away a man's arm in the act of eating—or his life, the incessant murmurous whisper of death, the strange orchestra of a hundred weapons each of which, unknowing, men came to know. The men in the forward positions had lived in an uncharted wilderness for more than a week. They were the P.B.I. [Poor bloody infantry], and though they bemoaned their lot, it is doubtful if many would have exchanged places with others in less danger, less mud, less everlasting misery in which there was a kind of happiness, perhaps unattainable elsewhere.

At noon the Canadian 2nd Corps began to come into the battle behind the 15th Scottish on the left, to drive on to Calcar while the British 30th Corps wheeled southeastward upon Goch. On the right flank the British 52nd (Lowland) Division struck south along the line of the Maas through Afferden, and east towards Weeze. The going was very hard. Nine enemy divisions were now identified in the battle, one Panzer division, one Panzer grenadier, three infantry, and four paratroop divisions, and supported by good artillery, self-propelled guns and mortars. Outgunned by a margin of perhaps ten weapons to one, and almost helpless against air attack, the enemy gunners yet managed to meet the attackers with the heaviest fire most of them had ever experienced. This was the enemy version of "We shall fight on the beaches . . ." It had the feel of a fight to the death; there was no give anywhere.

The 15th Scottish, striving to make good their positions in the woods flanking the Cleve-Calcar road opposite Moyland, had fought themselves almost to a standstill. The 10th H.L.I. had advanced to within a mile of Moyland village, and captured the high ground to the southwest, but again and again the counterattacks came in supported by self-propelled guns. Enfiladed by heavy machine guns from the uncleared woods on their flanks and with one of their companies overrun, they held on grimly for three days and nights while the 4th Canadian Infantry Brigade forced a way through on their left.

Since the day of the fall of Cleve, the 15th Scottish had fought by day and night on that stretch of road and in the flanking woods. Under artificial moonlight by night, and with creeping barrages lifting three hundred yards every twelve minutes, and helped by directional tracer, they battered away. Fighting or not fighting there was no rest by night anyway.

The 9th Cameronians attacking all through the night of the 15th with the 10th H.L.I. [Highland Light Infantry] in support, met a terrible counterattack against their right flank in the mists of dawn, and were overrun. Only steadfast courage on the part of every man saved companies from disaster.

The 7th Seaforths, in a night attack on the Moyland road, surprised the enemy and "dug themselves into shallow holes and prayed" one hundred and fifty yards short of Schloss Moyland. They had suffered heavy casualties for three days and nights. They had sand in their rifles, and sand in their guts. On the 16th they lost eleven men to their own artillery.

On the right of the Seaforths that morning the 9th Cameronians were moving on a square of woodland known as "Ian." It must be cleared at all costs, said the brigadier. The shelling, mortaring, and spandau fire was deadly, but at first light on the 16th, tanks were coming up in support, and the Calgary Highlanders were going through. The pincers were closing in on Moyland from three sides, and the Typhoons were diving down out of a clear sky on the Schloss, once the summer palace of Frederick the Great.

Such was the position when the Canadians took over on the left flank to open the way through to the Hochwald, and the 15th Scottish Division leaving a brigade under Canadian command, turned south for the attack on Goch. It would not be any better at Goch, but it would be different.

In all this warfare in which armor had found it costly and often impossible to attempt to spearhead infantry, the armored personnel carriers called "Kangaroos" had proved themselves, and their crews had been worthy of the vehicles. They had carried infantry into battle all along the line, often producing men behind the enemy forward defenses, and gaining initial advantages that would have been impossible otherwise. The Kangaroo crews, overworked and vulnerable, had suffered heavy casualties. In the early stages this had been hard to avoid, for harassed commanders did the best they could. It was said of the Kangaroos that "nothing since the substitution of the musket for the crossbow has been comparable (with them) in modern warfare." It may not be an exact tribute, but it is a just one.

ii.

To the men of the infantry battalions in the line February 15th was little different from any other day, and no less dangerous. It was a day of intense fighting from north to south. The differences were that letters were arriving, that wounded were getting back more swiftly, that hot breakfast was not a thing dimly remembered, that orders began to take effect. There was a chance of minor comfort out of the line of battle, to shave, to bathe, even to sleep. Above all there was a sense of form, of order out of chaos, not perhaps discernible to the troops advancing upon some target known as "Shrimp" or "Toad," or squatting in the mud and scrub of "Clapham Common," but to the brigadiers and major generals. At last they had begun to see daylight. Battalions passed through battalions, brigades through brigades, and even divisions, through divisions. There was more room to maneuver. The roads were drying out. The weary dedication of hundreds of men working for days on the lines of communication almost in states of coma, gave way to the expression of feeling, to curses and bad temper.

All this began to have an effect forward. The 43rd Division, launched virtually in error on the road to Cleve, had broken loose, and having outflanked the main Siegfried defenses east of Bedburg, was rolling up the enemy from north to south. But "rolling up—" the division's own phrase—is not a good description. The enemy had to be scraped up, dug up, rooted out almost man by man. When on February 17th the 43rd Division overlooked the battlefield of Goch from the escarpment to the north, they had advanced ten miles from north to south, and had performed a major role in the development of the battle. Thanks to that, the 15th Scottish came down on their left without much difficulty, ready to spearhead the attack on Goch from the north.

Through all this time the 53rd Welsh Division had suffered the appalling discomforts of the Reichswald forest, fighting its way through a tangled wilderness of dripping misery without landmarks. After a week it seemed to

many battalions that they inhabited the entrails of some
evil noisome beast, heaped with the rotting half-devoured
carcasses of its prey, and from which there was no escape.
But on the 15th, the 1st Battalion of the East Lancashires
on the extreme right made contact with the 51st Highland Division, and the 53rd covered the left flank of the
Highland Scots in their assault upon Asperden.

A deadly and ferocious battle plain for all to see was
building up on all the western approaches to the inner
fortress of Goch in an arc from Kassel running south
through about 90 degrees to the 52nd Division fighting on
the Afferden-Rempeld-Groote Horst road. Neither dusk,
nor night, nor dawn was free from savage counterattack.
No village on all that tight perimeter was secure. Every
gain had to be held grimly against constant attack and
under heavy mortaring, shelling, and incessant sniping.

Everywhere the noose was tightening round a tract of
town and country that resembled an inferno, shuddering
incessantly to the impact of explosions, shot through with
great spouts of smoke and flame, and thunderous with
appalling uproar.

The 32nd Guards Brigade, under command of the 51st
Division, smashed its way through between the 51st and
52nd to capture Hommersum and Mull on the 15th,
reaching Hassum on the 16th, and threatening Siebenger-
wald. It was the worst fighting the brigade had ever known,
and severe losses on the line of the Kendal forced them to
withdraw.

On the extreme right the Reconnaissance Regiment of
the 52nd Division probed out from Afferden to Rempeld,
while the infantry cleared the thick woods flanking the
road. On the night of the 16th, the Royal Scots and the
H.L.I. with the K.O.S.B. in support assaulted the last of
the enemy in the southeastern fringes, and with the dawn
faced a prospect as dismal as any they had ever known.
On their right two hundred yards of flood water aug-
mented an immense anti-tank ditch running due east from
the Maas. Seven hundred yards ahead across open fields
stood the ancient moated Kasteel Blijenbeek. That seven
hundred yards of open ground was to be a graveyard for
the Churchill tanks of the 24th Armored Brigade, and for
the men of the 4th Battalion K.O.S.B. From behind the
anti-tank ditch enemy self-propelled guns picked off the
tanks, while mortars and heavy machine guns aided by

medium artillery, ably directed from observation posts in the Kasteel, made the open ground impassable for men.

From the ground the enemy position was impregnable. The shells of our twenty-five pounders and 5.5.'s bounced off the reinforced walls. Again and again desperate attacks were easily beaten off, bringing only demands from the enemy that the attackers should surrender. Such was the spirit of the garrison of Kasteel Blijenbeek, a spirit which survived until Spitfires destroyed the castle and its garrison with 1,000 pound bombs. But it was impossible to extend the 30th Corps front another yard to the southward, and it was not until March 1st, with the position hopelessly outflanked by the American advance, that elements of the 52nd Division Reconnaissance Regiment finally got across the anti-tank ditch. Between that line and the line of the Niers the enemy defenses were almost solid.

It would be an exaggeration to say that Kasteel Blijenbeek was typical of the powerful enemy defenses surrounding the fortress of Goch, but it would not be a great exaggeration. Five British infantry divisions and two armored brigades, supported by massive artillery and overwhelming strength in the air, in an arc from north through west to south bore down in relentless pressure upon a tight perimeter of concrete pill boxes with walls two feet thick, reinforced with 4-inch steel plates all linked in with anti-tank ditches and fortified villages in a chain of strength that would only be broken by being blasted off the face of the earth, and by the bold and ingenious use of the varied engines of war provided by the 79th Armored division.

Men brooding upon that prospect on the night of February 17th, on the eve of the battle for Goch, thanked God, not only for the infantry, but also for the "Funnies" of the 79th Armored Division. Now men realized clearly the changed nature of this war, that there could be no end other than the destruction of the enemy, and that it seemed beyond the wit of man to make it otherwise.

For the enemy defending Goch there could be no hope; the only possible line of withdrawal lay along the railway line to the east, for the road south through Weeze to Geldern was closely threatened. The Allies were fighting to destroy the German army west of the Rhine, and the Germans had accepted that battle. There was not much

point, as Hitler had said to von Runstedt, "in trans
ferring catastrophe from one place to another." And the
smell of disaster was upon Goch.

iii.

It was estimated that three enemy divisions reinforce
the garrison troops in the fight for Goch. Against them
was the task of the 51st Highland Division to clear the
town south of the river Niers. The 53rd Division would
maintain the positions on the escarpment between the
river and the line of the Goch-Cleve railway. The 43rd
Division would maintain the position left of the 53rd and
would secure eight crossings of the formidable anti-tank
ditch immediately south of the escarpment. The 15th
Scottish would then pass through to take Goch north of
the river Niers.

All the approaches to the town were covered by dikes,
anti-tank ditches, trench systems and pillboxes, and the
whole area, as the final attack opened, was like the
crater of a volcano in eruption. It seemed impossible that
a single square foot of air could be free from screaming
metal, yet on the night of the 17th/18th the 43rd Divi
sion gained and held crossing points over the anti-tank
ditch. No man knows how. It was achieved by a kind of
dogged madness by men who had passed through the
barrier of ordinary fear to survive or to die in a limbo
known only to those who have experienced such things
and to each man differently.

Mattresses of rockets had reduced the township of
Asperden to a heap of smoking rubble, and left an after
math of fiendish din. Incongruously in that place a pri
vate soldier played quietly upon a piano while his colonel
sat on a box under a wavering wall having his hair cut.
Mortar bombs burst at short intervals spaced by the in
cessant whine and rattle of spandaus and rifles. Some
men shaved. Some urinated. The battle was not yet per
sonal, but it was unpleasant to wait. From that point
down the road and across the railway line the Black
Watch and the Gordon Highlanders led the direct assault
of the 51st Division from the northwest, the subalterns
leading their thin columns of men, humped with the tools
of war, silent and with tight lines under the nostrils.
Column after column disappeared into the smoke to probe
into the lethal acrid rubble heap of the town of Goch.

It was half past seven o'clock on the night of the 18th when the 5th Black Watch approached the outskirts of the town, moving forward stealthily in the darkness. It was for the 1st Gordons coming in behind them to touch off the inferno of a defense that blazed from every house, crater and rubble heap. It seemed then that Goch erupted into a conflagration of war without shape or coherence, blazing out far beyond the outskirts, and which raged for three days and nights of incessant dust, din and death.

At three o'clock on the afternoon of the 18th the 8th Royal Scots had led the 6th K.O.S.B. and the 6th Royal Scots Fusiliers on the road from the north, and by midnight they, too, were inside the town confronted by a factory with enclosed overhead footways spanning the road. Through that night the 6th K.O.S.B. had fought for their bridgehead over the main anti-tank ditch, won it and held it under terrific machine-gun fire and shelling, and enabled the Kangaroos to shuttle the infantry forward. On the 51st Division axis a bridge was also secure across the anti-tank ditch, and in the dawn of the 19th the "Funnies" were lumbering forward blindly to the shambles, the Crocodiles searing the eyeless sockets in the rubble heaps of homes. But the immense weight of air bombardment had effectively closed the way for armor beyond the fringes, and inside the infantry fought alone.

Early on the 19th, a company of the Black Watch led by Major Brodie assaulted the hospital building and captured the garrison commander and his staff. With that Goch had officially surrendered, but it made no difference. Probably no one knew, nor cared. There were no communications and not much need for them within the vortex of the Goch inner perimeter, nor over all the wilderness of trench, concrete and dikes beyond. Even a week after the last German had fired a shot in the dust heap of Goch, no man moved or walked by day with impunity in that desolation, acrid with the stench of cordite, and sour with vomit and the putrefying offal of men.

Day after day the slow processes of death and destruction gnawed away at the outer defenses. The petard tanks, with the spouts of their huge mortars as wide as the funnels of tug boats, lumbered up through the swirling smoke of battle to within one hundred yards of the concrete forts and pillboxes, belched their bombs upon them, tearing out great jagged holes for the Crocodiles to sear out the enemy with bursts of flame. That was the task, the blasting and burning of a hundred strong points. But there were times when infantry, unable to call these great weapons to their aid, rushed up under cover of smoke to hurl grenades through weapon slits, and even to clamber upon the roofs, seeking the apertures of chimneys and ventilators.

The trail of war was increasingly marked by the roasted bodies of men in armor, men in aircraft, men in pillboxes, men in cellars, their charred torsos swollen, rigid and terrible to see. And it seemed that the stench of burning flesh was as clinging in the nostrils as that of burning rubber.

But inside the town of Goch it was a more personal matter. Brave men, plunged into that hideous cauldron of explosions, and by the night of the 19th, two brigades, the 153rd and the 44th, were fighting inside the town, stumbling through fire and smoke in choking misery, half blind with smarting eyes and unaware of minor wounds. Every crater and rubble heap and cellar was a potential death trap, mined and booby trapped, and under incessant fire without coherence. No armor could penetrate that shocking rubble heap. Yet inside it men kept their heads, sorting out the strands of that maze of shattering sound and echo, planning their struggle, section, platoon, company. Whole companies cut off and leaderless found new leaders, and many survived.

Dutch-piloted Mitchells of the R.A.F. added to the death and dust that day, inexplicably mistaking Goch for Weeze, and adding to the infantryman's loathing of saturation bombing of towns. The bombing, said the infantry, frightened no one, killed very few, and presented the enemy with almost impregnable defensive positions in an impassable and formless shambles.

Slowly the battle for Goch, which was a score or more of battles, expanded on the flanks, drawing the noose astride the Goch-Weeze road, the Goch-Calcar road, and on the 21st, the last of the enemy withdrew along the railway line to Udem, leaving Goch to the pitiless revenge of their artillery and heavy mortars.

As to facts, there are only simple facts. On the 20th, A company of the 1st Battalion the Gordons was wiped out but for one N.C.O. and four men. The ambulances were struggling forward under cover of smoke to seek out and remove the wounded. The War Diaries read soberly enough, for what can they say of it: "Black Watch fighting fiercely all through 20th and 21st at times completely surrounded. . . . 'Houses lousy with enemy . . .' 22nd: Three more officers killed . . ."

The men manning the Kangaroos carrying the men into the battle ran a gauntlet of fire from bazookas, heavy machine guns, spandaus, self-propelled guns, mortars, and grenades. Visibility was seldom as much as fifty yards. The miracle is that so many survived.

In a cellar of Goch, in the midst of appalling din and with all the earth shuddering and heaving to violent impacts, a major, his face tattooed with blood specks and yellow with iodine, read out a message, "Have you sent back your leave personnel?" It stretched men's faces in grimaces of laughter, and while they laughed the building above them disappeared, heaving every man in the cellar into a heap, still laughing, still alive.

A huge man in a white overall and with a red cross on his chest like a crusader strode through the rubble and lifted wounded men to shelter. A priest crawled about in the crypt of a shattered church, muttering something about communion wine.

On the 21st the battle had abated, and the sun shone upon the hideous carcasses of the place. The railroad tracks of the marshalling yards reared up in a chaos of tangled metal like snakes out of a pit. Everywhere the engineers prowled about their dangerous business of detecting unexploded mines and bombs. The arch of the great red-brick gate house still stood on the lip of a giant crater at the heart of the town, and the sun glinted on the metal lettering of the words "Hitler Jugend." Two slender twisted pipes of steel, all that remained of the bridge, spanned the torrent of the river Niers, and deep in the cellars of the houses hampers of food were ready packed for flight, and bottles of fruit stood in rows.

With the fall of Goch the last great bastion of the main defenses of the Siegfried Line in the north had been overwhelmed. On the roads out of the town to the southeast and to the northeast the battle was raging, down towards Weeze, east towards Udem, and in the north towards Calcar. Another and another "Goch," until the end. There were no illusions now. There would be no bursting through into the open. Eleven German divisions were wedged into the last bridgehead in the north, in the tract of country bounded by the Calcar-Udem-Kervenheim road, the Winnekendonk-Kevelaer-Geldern road, and held within the narrowing triangle of the roads converging upon Wesel. These were the desperate remnants of the German army in the north. It would go on like this day after day, a pitiless killing match. It was astounding, when men had time to reflect upon it, how the enemy contrived to move troops and maintain men and guns in the fight under incessant bombardment from the air, strafed by Typhoons at every road junction and assembly point, and under constant artillery fire. Even the Wesel bridge, the last escape route, defied all the efforts of British and American bombers to destroy it.

iv.

In the north the enemy, reinforced by a newly arrived *Panzer Lehr* division and an infantry division, had maintained a tremendous resistance in the battle the Canadians had inherited from the 15th Scottish on the Calcar road. The great red-brick pile of the Schloss of Moyland still standing, pock-marked by shot and shell and shattered by the rockets of Typhoons, had become the symbol of it. Six days after the Seaforths had come within one hundred and fifty yards of it to dig themselves in and pray, the castle still held out. But on February 22nd a dirty white flag was hoisted above the main turret, and half a dozen white cloths fluttered from the window sockets and embrasures to the south.

The capture of the Schloss of Moyland not only marked the end of the second phase of the Rhineland battle; it seemed to mark, also, the end of an era. The bright sunshine shone upon the dusky red bricks of its mellowed walls and revealed the desolation of the surrounding lawns and parklands, laid waste by the violence of the fighting. Two antlered deer, cast in bronze and mounted on stone plinths, flanked the bridge over the outer moat. The swollen body of a dead horse lay in the drive. At the main entrance to the house stood two small sixteenth-century cannon, and inside was a vast confusion of wreckage. In the great principal bed chamber, where the curving walls were embellished with paintings of flamboyant nudes, the cooking stoves of a French Canadian company roared under pans of frying fat. Here Freder-

ck the Great, at ease in the canopied bed on the raised
dais, had once held the morning levee. In the magnificent-
y appointed bathrooms of the state apartments, groups
of soldiers washed and shaved for the first time in a week.
A record of "The Barber of Seville" was on the turntable
of the phonograph in one of the drawing rooms, but it
vas difficult to imagine that anyone had listened to music
ince the dawn of February 8th.

The place had been a treasure house, and in scores of
ooms all the bric-à-brac of an exquisite home of princely
vealth lay jumbled in confusion. In the cellars of the
castle, Ilse Marie, Baroness Steengracht von Moyland,
at upright in the midst of her white-faced servants,
eeming the lone survivor of a world long since dead. It
vas impossible to believe that a way of life such as hers
had persisted until a week ago; impossible to imagine
hat such a life would ever again be possible.

Forward of Moyland, the Canadians had come within
one thousand yards of Calcar, but the town held firm. It
vas vital now to break through across the Calcar-Goch
oad at a point between Goch and Udem, some five miles
o the east of Goch, and to capture a spur of the scimitar-
curved ridge covering the Hochwald and Balberger forests. This was the central core of the last great defensive
barrier running from the west bank of the Rhine near
Rees, forward of the forests, and south to Geldern.

The front was still greatly restricted, but in the south
he fall of Goch had enabled the 30th Corps to turn
down towards Geldern. On February 23rd and 24th, the
53rd Division with a brigade of the 15th Scottish cover-
ng its left flank, and the 52nd Division on the right, was
meeting tremendous resistance in front of Weeze in conditions that showed few signs of improvement. In the cen-
er the 43rd with elements of the 15th Scottish and the
armor of the Coldstream Guards battled doggedly to within twenty-five hundred yards of Udem. All complained
bitterly of water problems. The 53rd hit water at a depth
of eighteen inches and could not dig in; the 15th Scottish
ound it difficult to wash and shave; the 9th Cameronians,
half-bogged in a stagnant marsh under heavy shelling by
day and night, recorded thankfully the issue of a double
ation of rum on the night of the 23rd.

In Goch itself on that day, the 7th Battalion The Black
Watch buried their dead while their 1st Battalion waded

across a river three feet deep on the road to the south

For the 51st and 15th Divisions, Operation Veritable was nearing its end. To all but those taking part, all was quiet on the Canadian 1st Army front. As the Canadian Army regrouped for the final phase on the Rhineland battlefield, the focus had moved sharply to the U.S. 9th and 1st Armies, at last across the swollen Roer and soon racing for the Rhine.

15: *GRENADE*

i.

PRECISELY AT a quarter to three on the morning of February 23rd the guns of the U.S. 1st and 9th Armies roared out their challenge behind the swollen Roer. While the staccato pattern of the gun flashes danced in macabre confusion over the bivouacs and paraphernalia of a quarter of a million armed men, the bursting shells piled chaos upon chaos in the rubble of scores of towns and villages. Already in all the littoral of the river from Julich to Düren it would have been difficult to find two stones the one upon another, and the sight of a standing wall was astonishing.

Forty-five minutes later the assault troops of the 1st and 9th Armies launched their assault craft upon the still turbulent waters of the Roer, and the barrage lifted. It had been little more than a token, the harsh cry of havoc that unleashed the dogs of war. Ten divisions of the 9th Army, organized in three army corps, faced the Roer between Julich and Düren. To the south, fourteen divisions of the 1st Army had awaited eagerly the signal to obliterate the last of the enemy between them and the Rhine.

The final plans for the launching of Operation Grenade had been reviewed at a conference on February 17th. It had been decided that unless one inch or more of rain should fall, or there should be an unlooked-for increase in flooding, the attack would go in on the 23rd. The U. S. 9th Army, crossing the Roer between Roermond and Düren would drive north through München Gladbach to the Venlo-Wessel road to link up with the British. It would clear the area on the left bank of the Erft to Düs-

seldorf. At the same time the U.S. 1st Army would cross
the Roer south of Düren to protect the right flank of the
9th Army with its left while the center moved on Cologne.

One felt then, and one feels in retrospect with all the
inner records of those days available, that no one in those
impatient American armies bothered to measure rainfall
in that last week. Whatever the conditions, somehow on
that morning of the 23rd the assault troops would have
crossed the Roer. The conditions were grim. The river, a
full eighty yards wide, flowed at five knots. A few enemy
guns contrived to add to the difficulties of the men on the
water, the inevitable mortars took a toll, but it was clear
that the strength of the enemy defenses had been sapped
and that little more than token resistance faced the U.S.
armies. By noon on the first day under cover of the U.S.
29th Tactical Air Force putting on its greatest effort of the
campaign, the assault force was secure on the eastern
bank, and a heavy pontoon bridge was in place behind
them. In twelve hours sixteen battalions were enlarging
the bridgehead, and six class-40 bridges (capable of carrying armor), four class-5 infantry-support bridges, and
a number of foot bridges and ferries were operating in
support. It was a tremendous example of drive, energy,
engineering skill and ingenuity, and only the rubble of the
ancient city of Julich and the valley of the Roer impeded
the progress of the troops. No more than four enemy
divisions and scattered garrison troops remained to face
two armies and to block the way to the Rhine. The entire
enemy reserve of seven infantry and three armored divisions had already rushed north to reinforce the parachute
army in its suicide struggle against the Canadians and
British in the Rhineland battle.

While the bulldozers shovelled paths through the rubble of the Roer towns, the 9th Army built up its strength
in the bridgehead, ready to burst out. On its right flank,
the 7th Corps of the U.S. 1st Army was racing for the
Erft. By February 26th the 9th Army had three corps on
the general line Oberemdt-Opherten-Holzweiler-Venrath-
Erkelenz. The 16th Corps on the left seized Gladbach
against a beaten enemy, and with that the old British
sores of Roermond and Venlo were at last eliminated
without a battle. There was barely time or space for the
remaining enemy to pull out from these, his last bridgeheads on the Maas.

A week after the assault crossing of the Roer, the 13th Corps in the center had entered München Gladbach, the largest German city to fall into Allied hands, while the 19th Corps on the right was racing for the Rhine at Neuss opposite Düsseldorf. The flank-protecting role of the 1st Army's seventh corps was no longer necessary.

On March 1st the Supreme Commander joined his 9th Army commander, General Simpson, in München Gladbach and had to put on his tin hat against the shell splinters of anti-aircraft guns attacking an enemy jet aircraft overhead. The Americans were jubilant. The assault of February 23rd had sparked off the race for the Rhine from Wessel to the Swiss border. While the 7th Corps turned south on Cologne the 3rd Corps in the center drove for Bonn, reaching Euskirchen on March 4th. The 5th Corps on the right was almost upon the Rhine at Remagen.

The news of these things had destroyed the last of General Patton's slender store of patience, and with Bradley's blessing his third army accelerated its advance astride the Moselle upon Trier. The path through to the Rhine was almost open. Patton had been swift to recognize that this was a chance for the repetition of the pattern of August, 1944. Again the Canadians and British were fighting the German armies yard by yard on the left flank in a battle of "the hinge." It was for him again to break through with his armor, and as early as February 20th he had pressed General Bradley to let him go. "All of us in high position," he wrote to Bradley, "will surely be held accountable for failure to take offensive action when offensive action is possible."

With some difficulty Bradley restrained him, pointing out that the major thrust in the north had been agreed on, but of Bradley's sympathy there is no doubt. "Regardless of what you and I think of this decision," he wrote to Patton, "we are good enough soldiers to carry out these orders."

By the end of February, Patton was beyond restraint, and the will to restrain him did not exist. It was rumored that he towed his Rhine bridge behind him wherever he went. The fact that Hodges' 1st Army was beating him to the Rhine filled him with envy, but that Montgomery's army might beat him to a bridgehead was more than he could bear. He need not have worried on that account.

Montgomery had carefully planned every detail of his
set-piece crossing, and fixed the dates. Nothing would
move him an hour forward or an hour back.

In the 1st week of March, Patton had his armor on the
move through the Eifel on his left flank, and by the time
the 1st Army's 7th Corps had swooped upon Cologne to
clear the whole city within forty-eight hours, the 3rd
Army was gathering momentum to clear the country
west of the Rhine from Mainz to Koblenz.

Even General Simpson, commanding the 9th Army
and under 21st Army Group command, showed signs of
restlessness in early March. On the 2nd, his spearheads
had reached Neuss, and by March 5th his army had
cleared the Rhine bank from Düsseldorf to Mors. He had
advanced some fifty miles with 7,300 casualties, and
complained to the Supreme Commander that he had
seven divisions he couldn't use. Why couldn't he make
a surprise crossing of the Rhine?

But Montgomery was adamant. "He preferred the
planned assault of the Rhine on a broad front between
Rheinberg and Emmerich."* It seemed even that the
Field Marshal had an *idée fixe* about crossing the Rhine;
to "jump a bridgehead," in the unlikely circumstances
that such a possibility existed, was in some way undigni-
fied, and not in the book of rules.

The possibility did seem unlikely in the extreme. On
March 3rd, following the fall of Krefeld to the 9th
Army, the commander of the German *1st Parachute
Army*, General Alfred Schlemm, received the first of a
series of orders from the Führer. In no circumstances
was any bridge over the Rhine to fall into Allied hands,
and yet the bridges must be kept open to the last moment
to ensure supplies to the troops on the west bank. Failure
meant death. When, soon afterwards, the Americans
came dangerously close to the Homberg Bridge, Schlemm
wirelessed orders to blow it. The colonel in charge of the
bridge hesitated, whereupon Schlemm replied that if the
bridge was not blown immediately, he would personally
shoot the colonel and "anyone else he found near it."

Meanwhile on March 7th the U.S. 9th Armored Division of the 3rd Corps approached Remagen. Their orders
were to move southward, but when the great Ludendorf

*Pogue, *The Supreme Command*.

Bridge was seen to be still intact Brigadier General Willam Hoge, commanding the 9th Armored, ordered his men to seize it without hesitation. The story of how the 9th Armored grasped this unlooked-for opportunity of war has been amply told.* It was a magnificent effort, and it sent Bradley into transports of delight. At that time General Bull of SHAEF was with Bradley, and he suggested that the Supreme Commander should be consulted before further forces were committed to the bridgehead. General Eisenhower himself has left a record of the ensuing telephone conversation.

"I was at dinner in my Rheims headquarters with the corps and division commanders of the American airborne forces when Bradley's call came through. When he reported that we had a permanent bridge across the Rhine, I could scarcely believe my ears. He and I had frequently discussed such a development as a remote possibility, but never as a well-founded hope.

"I fairly shouted into the telephone: 'How much have you got in that vicinity that you can throw across the river?'

"He said: 'I have more than four divisions, but I called you up to make sure that pushing them over would not interfere with your plans.'

"I replied: 'Well, Brad, we expected to have that many divisions tied up around Cologne and now those are free. Go ahead and shove over at least five divisions instantly, and anything else that is necessary to make certain of our hold.'"†

In the light of the 21st Army Group's harsh and sustained battle in the north, the Remagen episode illustrates not only how inexorably the emphasis was moving away from the north, but how great was the discrepancy at this stage between British and American strength. While the Americans had more divisions than they knew what to do with the British were scraping the bottom of the barrel. Two divisions were moving up from Italy to reinforce the Canadians and the 2nd Army. In the north on the day that the 9th and 1st Armies had burst out across the Roer, the Canadian 1st Army began to regroup for the third phase of its struggle to destroy the enemy in the north. Operation Grenade had exploded to such pur-

*Ken Hechler, *The Bridge at Remagen*
†Eisenhower, *Crusade in Europe*

pose that it had stolen all the thunder. The eyes of the world had moved elsewhere, and once again it seemed often to the Canadians and the British that they fought alone in a kind of isolation.

General Eisenhower paid a great tribute to Field Marshal Montgomery when he wrote: "Progress was slow and costly (for the British and Canadians) and opposition became stiffer as the Germans began moving their forces from the Roer into the path of the Canadian advance. Montgomery was not too displeased by this transfer of German weight because of the promise it held that, once the American attack began, it would advance with great speed."

It is difficult to imagine Generals Bradley and Patton "not too displeased" in a similar situation, and it must be remembered that this war was fought before a world audience. From February 23rd the Canadians and British fought out their long and bitter battle against the finest troops remaining to the enemy in the diminishing bridgehead narrowing upon the apex of Wesel. As the ground grew less, the battle increased in fury, and the last day was worse than the first. The audience had long since left their seats.

ii.

The regrouping of the Canadian 1st Army in the three days from February 23rd to 26th took place against the background of a struggle in which the antagonists were locked solid. There was not a yard of give over all that narrow front, and the operation by which General Crerar planned to smash his way through was aptly named "Blockbuster." It was for this that the army regrouped its forces.

It would be tedious to attempt to unravel the day-by-day battle in all its horrible monotony of death and discomfort. It might tend to confuse rather than to illuminate. Nevertheless the realities of these days should never be forgotten, or hidden behind such phrases as: The Canadian 1st Army regrouped. There is always a feeling, however illogical, that this implies some pause. The truth is far otherwise. While a large scale reorganization and movement of men and armor, of artillery and the many specialized implements of war, all involving great tonnages of transport and supplies, began to move over utterly inadequate roads, the battle raged with a fury demanding all the energies of those involved. It was not enough to hold; it was necessary to go forward, to insert wedges into the enemy's hardening barriers of defense.

At six o'clock on the morning of February 24th, for example, the 53rd Division, supported by 13 field regiments, Royal Artillery, 6 medium regiments, 1 heavy regiment, 2 heavy anti-aircraft regiments, and by the 8th Armored Brigade, and Flails, Crocodiles, Kangaroos, and A.V.R.E.'s of the 79th Armored Division, attacked southward from Goch against the town of Weeze. By noon of that day two battalions of infantry were astride the Goch-Weeze road some 4,000 yards short of the town and its anti-tank ditch. The flame-throwing Crocodiles, moving in support of infantry and armor, had done their deadly work in the villages of Hohenhof and Host, villages that had long since ceased to function as villages and were now outposts of great strength. The 71st Brigade got a company into a village called Rottum, and it seemed well named.

At a quarter past five on the morning of the 25th, twenty-four hours after the attack had been launched, it was brought to a standstill one mile short of Weeze. Enemy counterattacks had inflicted heavy casualties and severe losses in tanks of the 8th Armored Brigade. The way back, and the way forward, was littered with dead and the debris of war. Every way forward or back over the whole front of the 1st Canadian Army was a shambles of destruction, thick with smoke and stench, and shot through with flashes of the guns, and the reeking blasts of incessant explosions.

While the 53rd was fighting itself to a standstill on the road to Weeze from the north, the 52nd Division was blocked on the road from the west, and with one of its units engaged in a hand-to-hand struggle with the last defenders of the keep of Kasteel Blijenbeek. It was no better on the road to Udem.

On February 26th the regrouping of the Canadian 1st Army for Operation Blockbuster had been achieved, and a slight, but general improvement, of the forward positions had been won. On the left the Canadian 2nd Corps comprised:

Canadian 4th Armored Division
British 11th Armored Division
Canadian 2nd Armored Brigade
Canadian 2nd Infantry Division
Canadian 3rd Infantry Division
British 43rd Infantry Division

On the right the British 30th Corps:

Guards Armored Division
6th Guards Armored Brigade
8th Armored Brigade
34th Armored Brigade
British 3rd Infantry Division
15th (Scottish) Infantry Division
    (to be relieved by 3rd British)
51st (Highland) Infantry Division
52nd (Lowland) Infantry Division
53rd (Welsh) Infantry Division

In addition there had been a redistribution of units of the 79th Armored Division.

The inter-corps boundary would run right of the Canadian 2nd Corps through a point near Kervenheim to include Sonsbeek.

That was the line up for the last battle. The plans had been worked out in detail, and the outline of the Intentions gives an idea of what remained to be done, and how, roughly, it would be done.

The intention was to break through between Udem and Calcar, produce two armored brigades on the Hochwald ridge, and exploit through to Xanten.

Phase one was timed to begin at half past four on the morning of the 26th. Two brigades of the Canadian 2nd Infantry Division would secure the high ground immediately to the south of Calcar, while a brigade of the 3rd Infantry Division, and two armored Regiments of the 4th Canadian Armored Division secured hill spurs and features to points south of Udem. The 3rd Canadian Infantry Division would then capture Udem while an armored group closed in from the northeast.

These things having been done, it was hoped, within the compass of a single day, the 11th Armored Division would advance southeast, capture Sonsbeek, and position its leading brigade on the high ground to the north of the town.

The way would then be opened for the Canadian 4th Armored Division to advance east astride the road and railway running between the Hochwald and Balberger forests. The Canadian 2nd and 3rd Infantry Divisions would follow up to protect the flanks of both armored divisions. Xanten and Wesel would then be within striking distance.

Such was the nature of Blockbuster, and its opening was supported by 19 field regiments of artillery, 8 medium regiments, three heavy regiments, 1 Canadian rocket unit, and all the air support available.

16: ALL QUIET ON THE NORTHERN FRONT

i.

INEVITABLY THE focus of interest had moved to the right at the end of February. Names like Düsseldorf and Cologne, even München Gladbach and Krefeld, were recognizable in the ears of the world, carrying with them the certainty of victory. Udem, Weeze, Sonsbeek meant nothing, and but for a wife of Henry VIII, it would have been difficult to arouse interest in Cleve. Goch was no more than an ugly word.

Not unnaturally, a sense of excitement gripped onlookers, not only far from the battlefields, but on them, and it was difficult even to persuade any information about the left flank out of the headquarters of the 21st Army Group. Nothing was happening on the left. The regrouping had been successful; all was going according to plan.

The British 2nd Army was deeply involved in the planning of the Rhine crossing and, with the 12th Corps, was far more interested in mysterious exercises on a section of the Maas than in the battles to the right or the left. Canadian 1st Army Headquarters seemed depressed, and not without reason. Their great fight on the left flank in Normandy had passed almost unnoticed. Their unimaginative investment of the channel ports had been dreary. Even their long-sustained struggle for the Scheldt Estuary had been overshadowed by the final assaults on Walcheren. And now, after months of plodding up the left flank, living in polder lands in dreadful conditions, they approached the climax of their greatest battle at a moment when all the world looked the other way. However unfortunate it may be, the audience had become an important factor in the Second World War; the more important because in the nature of things its eyes could never penetrate beyond the spotlight to the dim figures writhing in the smoke.

The first phase of Blockbuster had gone well. The high ground south of Calcar had been seized without difficulty, and forward troops had reached the outskirts of Udem. But the enemy defenses swiftly hardened. Before noon on the first day, the armor had begun to bog down. Before dusk the Canadian 8th Infantry Brigade suffered 25-percent casualties, and seventeen tanks had been lost to enemy anti-tank guns, Panzerfaust and Panther tanks. Before the dawn of February 27th no one had any illusions about Blockbuster. It was going to be a grim and bitter fight to the finish. No one doubted that. The enemy defense was no brittle crust which might crack wide open. It was hard right through.

Udem was cleared on the 27th, and eight civilians crawled up out of the rubble putting on an act of dubious welcome for which the troops had no time and no response. They were no longer liberators, or if they were, they didn't feel like that. The streets of Udem were the accustomed shambles. Out of a window aperture overlooking a road deep in tangles of wire, wood, dust, and stone, a succession of large plates crashed into the rubbish.

"The washing up, sir," a young soldier said.

"You just chuck it out of the window?"

If he had said "Why not?" it would have been difficult to find a good answer.

Late on the 27th the Canadian 4th Armored Division began to penetrate the Hochwald lay-back positions, and had elements on the threshold of the dangerous gap between the Hochwald and Balberger forests. It looked like a death trap.

Counterattacks came in again and again and maintained with an almost demoniac violence, not only of men, but of heavy mortars, self-propelled, and medium guns. Nothing like this had been encountered before anywhere on the western front. By the end of the second day, one hundred tanks had been put out of action, more armor than any enemy Panzer division could have mustered.

The Canadians pressed on, yard by yard, clinging to a grip on the spine of railway running through the gap. Meanwhile the Canadian 2nd Infantry Division, moving down into the Hochwald to protect the left flank of the Canadian armor, ran into the garrison withdrawing from Calcar and prepared to fight its way through the Marienbaum at all costs. Calcar itself was yielded in the end almost without a shot, but the price was paid in blood on the road.

On the right flank the 11th Armored Division had been fighting its way to the south round the flank of the Balberger wood to capture the high ground north of Sonsbeek well ahead of the Canadian 3rd Infantry Division, whose role was to capture the Sonsbeek plateau. It was becoming clear that the enemy paratroops were resolved to hold a hinge position on which they might swing their troops away from the inevitable advance of the British 30th Corps. Their doom was being spelled out on their left flank.

Nowhere was the fight more desperate than in the narrow gap between the Hochwald and Balberger woods. There an assault battalion of paratroops, supported by self-propelled guns and heavy mortars, sold the pass inch by inch at a high price.

ii.

Even the British 30th Corps was unusually reticent in the last days of February, for the ebullient disposition of its commander normally spread a sense of excitement at the dullest moments. In 30th Corps Headquarters it was impossible to avoid the conclusion that Operation Veritable, in its closing stages, had become a grim and deadly grind. The battle had never got going, and it would not get going. Three weeks of savage fighting through the mud and sodden entrails of the Reichswald and its neighboring strong points had at least brought some simplicity into the pattern of the battlefield. The Canadian main route now lay through Calcar towards Xanten, thence at the last to converge upon Wesel. The 30th Corps main route struck down almost due south from Cleve, through Udem, while on the extreme right the 52nd Division was to draw a wide noose round the flank and swing up the

Geldern-Issum-Alpon road upon Fort Blücher and Wesel.

From a study of these things, it appeared that the heart of the enemy defense west of the last lay-back position must be on the road Kervenheim-Winnekendonk. Veeze and Kevelaer still held, but were no longer of great importance. But progress was dreadfully slow. On February 27th the 52nd Division at last began to break out of the Afferden area to relieve the 51st Division. On March 1st the Reconnaissance Regiment gained a small bridgehead over the anti-tank ditch which had held their southern flank, and with that the 1st Commando Brigade, coming under command, moved south along the banks of the Maas from Afferden to Well. It was hard going even here, and beyond Well the enemy still held on. Perhaps that is as good a measure as any of the tenacity of the Germans with their backs to their "last ditch."

With this the Weeze-Kevelaer line shook loose, and the 3rd Division swooped down and through to link with the Americans at Geldern. The Hochwald gap was undoubtedly the last remaining strong point, and well covered by the enemy positions based on Kervenheim and Winnekendonk. The 11th Armored Division had been slowed by heavy fire from Kervenheim in its advance on Sonsbeek, and there were no signs of enemy withdrawal as the British 3rd division cut the Udem-Weeze road on February 27th and faced east. The *7th Parachute Division,* stiffened up by many of those who had managed to fight their way out of Goch barred the way. Every thicket and farmhouse held enemy; every narrow stream was a lethal barrier.

iii.

On the morning of Wednesday, February 28th, Tactical Headquarters of the 185th Infantry Brigade of the British 3rd Infantry Division, was established in an isolated farmhouse forward of the Udem-Weeze road, and some 4,000 yards short of the village of Kervenheim. The farmhouse lay sheltered under the lip of a shallow sandy bowl. Thin rectangular belts of trees divided the flat brown patches of arable land in the foreground. Probably because of its isolation and because at the last there had been very little fighting, the house had not suffered much damage. Three enemy tanks, seemingly undamaged, on the fringes of the woodland testified to the fact that the enemy had

been surprised and overwhelmed in sleep by a strong
reconnaissance patrol in the hour before dawn. A few
shreds of enemy clothing and equipment lay about in the
farmyard and round the tanks, but these were the only
signs of struggle or flight.

Taken as an isolated incident, it might have seemed to
confirm the views of corps and division that nothing
—or very little—was happening, or about to happen, of
any note. But it would have been dangerous to read too
much into the fact of a small group of enemy surprised in
their sleep. For days and nights the enemy had been battered mercilessly by artillery and aircraft, denied all hope
of relief, of rest, of victory, or even of escape. It was astonishing, not that some were "punch drunk," or exhausted, but that so many continued to fight with a desperate
and fanatical violence in the last flare up of their nervous
energies.

The lip of the sandy bowl hid the farmhouse from the
rear, and on the gentle downward slope behind the ridge a
battery of Bofors was already in position. Behind them
the guns of a field regiment of artillery were deployed in
the low scrub, and a company of machine gunners had
also taken up their positions on the flanks.

At noon on February 28th a sense of tension began to
be evident in and around the farmhouse. It heralded the
approach of a zero—or H—hour. It was apparent, passing through the gun lines.

In the farmhouse yard a captain of the Coldstream
Guards stood nonchalantly beside his armored scout car,
and discussed with his corporal driver the question of
what he should wear as leg covering. It seemed that the
captain liked to wear a "lucky" pair of jodphurs on days
when he considered the omens propitious.

"The question is, Collier," he said, "will it be a walk-
in?"

Possibly the captain had been influenced by the fact
of the abandoned tanks. Nevertheless, there was nothing
callow about him.

The corporal was non-committal; one felt that he liked
to leave these decisions to his master. The exchange
sounded flippant, but it had a grave undertone. These two
men, the eyes and ears of a squadron of tanks, had been
together through many battles. They moved with the
tactical headquarters of infantry battalions, often in

a dangerous isolation, spotting targets, disguised strong points, enemy armor and self-propelled guns, and "whistled up," as they said, their own armor. A great deal depended on their alertness, their courage and their accuracy.

Many times they had sniffed the morning air, as they did on this morning of February 28th, for "omens," and the captain's choice of garb for his legs had become a matter of importance. Corporal Collier was not too happy when the captain, suddenly jaunty in decision, opted for jodphurs. It was, he felt, too early for such optimism.

The captain's name was Cresswell. He wore the ribbon of the Military Cross. Having ordered up the jodphurs he went swiftly into the farmhouse. Three jeeps with their drivers awaited their masters, and were spaced out carefully, having discovered on many occasions the accuracy of enemy mortars. The crackle of war, of rifle, spandau, and machine-gun fire, was incessant, but sufficiently remote to be ignored. The more thunderous undertones of artillery had become a part of the background, as unnoticed as a ship's engines on a long voyage, and yet to which the ears of all are constantly tuned.

The big farmhouse kitchen, which occupied almost the entire ground floor of the building, was sparsely furnished. A large kitchen table stood off center towards the far end of the room, and there were two smaller tables, probably with the chairs, the props of brigade. The Brigadier sat at the kitchen table with the Brigade Major on his left, studying a map intently. The Intelligence Officer sat facing the Brigade Major with his own map out in front of him, and his notebooks ready. The Brigade Major had a set of headphones and a mouthpiece on the table beside him, and the Intelligence Officer had a field telephone. At a small table in the corner of the room two signal lance corporals sat facing each other wearing headphones, their faces completely absorbed. Half a dozen officers were gathered in the room, exchanging greetings and light badinage, yet attentive to the slightest gesture of the Brigadier. It was almost time.

All that was known about the country ahead was on the 1:25,000 maps. Lives depended on the accuracy of maps, and the accuracy with which men read their signs. Patches of woodland filled spaces between the lines of tracks, and enclosed tracts of open field or pasture. Here and there were farm buildings and the isolated dots marking some hamlet. Thin blue lines marked the courses of dikes or streams. The most definite of these lines was called the Muhlen Fleuth. It was known to be twenty-four feet wide and too deep in many places for wading.

Such a stream might not appear at all on the 1:25,000 maps of corps. Minor obstacles were the business of brigadiers, lieutenant colonels, and lesser commanders, looming very large in the lives and deaths of N.C.O.'s and privates.

"If they can get a bridgehead right off the mark, the rest may be easy," said the Brigadier.

The low murmur of conversation hushed upon the instant, and a burly lieutenant colonel, commanding the 1st Battalion Royal Norfolk Regiment, studied the Brigadier's map. "They" were the K.S.L.I [King's Shropshire Light Infantry] on the left, and the Warwicks on the right. The moment these two battalions secured the flanks, the Norfolks would go through in the center to assault and capture the village of Kervenheim. That was the brigade objective.

Kervenheim looked like the linchpin of the last of the enemy's heavily defended positions west of Hochwald. The area bounded by Kervenheim-Weeze-Kevelaer-Winnekendonk looked ominous. If Kervenheim went, there would not be much future for the enemy in the area.

"One minute to go," said the Brigadier. He leaned his left arm on the table and watched the sweep of the second hand on his wrist watch. It was exactly 1359 hours—one minute to two o'clock.

Precisely on the stroke of two o'clock an avalanche of uproar engulfed the farmhouse. The Bofors were firing flat from within one hundred yards. Behind them and to the flanks the whole orchestra roared out its shattering pattern, and two thousand yards ahead two battalions of infantry began to move forward from their starting lines, leaning on the barrage as close up as they dared.

It was impossible for a moment or two to think under the vicious screaming din of the Bofors. The Lieutenant Colonel of the Norfolks studied the position with the Brigadier, their heads close together. Each battalion had a squadron of tanks in support, and the Flails, Crocodiles and A.V.R.E.'s of the 79th Armored Division.

The Warwicks came through on the telephone, going

in, two hundred yards from the river, the Muhlen Fleuth. The red and blue lines, the arrows and circles, on the Brigade Major's map, indicating the positions of our own troops and of the enemy, at once seemed alive.

"Barrage lifts in one minute, sir," shouted an artillery officer.

Suddenly the deluge of din gave way to the sharp intake of silence. The C.O. of the Norfolks drank a mug of tea and munched a sandwich. A tall, well-built major with ginger hair came into the room, saluted smartly, his mouth immediately breaking into a wide grin.

"Good leave, Charles?" asked the Brigadier.

"Grand, sir."

The thunder of the guns began to rise again to drown for a moment the fierce mutter of the machine guns. On the headphones the fierce noises of the battle had a strange remote reality, bringing back the noises of bursting shells, a dangerous undergrowth of sounds.

At 1445 hours the Warwicks reported one company over the river, and one company at the bridging point. A.V.R.E.'s and tanks were moving up.

Again the thunder of the guns rose.

"Right. Off you go, Peter!" said the Brigadier.

The C.O. of the Norfolks rushed out, and was away in seconds with Captain Cresswell's scout car after him, bounding, lurching, skidding over the mud tracks, towards the battle. One thousand yards ahead the Norfolks formed, trailing off in companies skirting the woodland, stringing out in lines towards the river. The Flails moved steadily over the flat open ground, their chains lashing the earth, and behind them the A.V.R.E.'s bore huge Facines and were followed by Petard tanks. All the array of mechanical warfare moved steadily across the open tract of plowed fields between the woods, the Churchill tanks of the Coldstream Guards covering the infantry.

"This is Prince Charlie six . . . Prince Charlie six . . . Report my signals. Over," said Captain Cresswell into his radio telephone.

Five hundred yards ahead bursts of flame welled up out of the earth like blood and hovered there. A crimson mist hung over the woods, and the earth began to leap up in gray spouts from enemy shell bursts. Typhoons swooped like wild birds, patterning the brazen sky with rocket trails, and out of the ditches on the edge of the wood the men of the Norfolks rose up, crouching, half-running, towards the vortex.

But it was too soon. The Warwicks and the K.S.L.I. were in the midst of the enemy, and the right flank was dangerously open. The Norfolks halted at the rim of the woods, waiting the word to go forward. It was nearly five o'clock. The C.O. had gone back for orders. Soon the sky would darken. The Norfolks lay on the edge of a wide plain of open land surrounded on three sides by woods. A troop of Churchill tanks, their besas [machine guns] blazing, moved on a small village half-hidden in a copse which must be on the river bank. A lone tank supported a section of infantry moving in swift bounds upon a farmstead in the midst of outbuildings on the far edge of the plain.

Almost imperceptibly the battles on the flanks began to spill over and to envelop the center. Captain Creswell spotted the muzzle flash of a self-propelled gun threatening the lone tank and the infantry section. A hare sat motionless, ears flat, and small birds flew madly in zigzags, hemmed within the invisible cage of battle. The small village, half-hidden in a copse, erupted into flame, and enemy machine guns searched the woods with fire, crackling through the trees like flames fanned by the wind to consume dry bracken. The machine-gun fire pressed the waiting Norfolks close against the wet earth, urgently to dig narrow slots for shelter.

The sun was almost down, and a slender rift of gold showed in the western sky. The infantry section came running out of the farm, urging seven prisoners at the double across the open ground. Over that open ground two stretcher-bearers toiled slowly with their burden of a wounded man, the sticky brown soil heavy on their boots. The high-fluffing sound of enemy shells ruffled the darkening sky.

"We ought to be moving," said Captain Cresswell. "If we're going to move."

The barrage in support of the attack of the Norfolks was due. The Typhoons and Spitfires dive-bombed within four hundred yards on the right in the last flight before night.

Out of the crimson murk of smoke and flame, hedged in by spouting columns of earth, a pitiful cavalcade stumbled from the farmstead, the old and the young—a man with a dog in the lead, a woman, children, goats, geese—bewildered, overtaken by war. In this alone, war had not changed. In this fashion, in all the long history of warfare, peasants had stumbled from their homes.

iv.

The Norfolks lay dispersed in the woods all night in the shallow slots they had cut for themselves, two men to a slot, sitting, knees up, face to face, heads slumped forward under tin hats. In the ditches at the roadside on the edge of the open land, others lay in blankets behind the Bren carriers. Two hundred yards out three sections had dug in after dusk. Patrols would be out all through the night. Something had gone wrong, and nobody knew what; nor would they ever know.

Gusts of wind fanned the flames of the small burning village to moments of brilliance, and the cage of war had a more intense definition, lit with many fires, explosions, gun flashes, and the occasional Very light. The sky was restless with the drumming and shuffling of shells, and a sustained barrage was concentrated upon Weeze.

The C.O. of the Norfolks held three order groups in the night. An angle trench had been dug, and in this, ankle deep in mud, under a piece of tarpaulin supported on boxes and anchored by spades, the company commanders huddled round the massive figure of the C.O. He wore a paratrooper's jacket over a thick sweater, and with a red-spotted scarf round his neck. A hurricane lamp shone upon the map and on the shadowed, grave faces of the company commanders, their cheek bones highlighted. The C.O. had wanted a night attack, but the tank commander did not.

The battalion cooks brought up hot stew and tea in containers at about nine o'clock, and out on the edge of the plain Captain Cresswell directed the efforts of a task to pull a damaged Flail tank out of the ditch. An hour later a post corporal found his way to the wood with a small sack of letters, and two men sorted them by candlelight in a slot. No one would read a letter that night, and in the morning many would be dead.

The last order group took place under the tarpaulin soon after midnight. A decision had been reached. At a quarter to four the battalion would move over the Muhlen

Fleuth and forward some one thousand yards to the rim of the woods outside Kervenheim. They would dig in and attack under a barrage at nine o'clock.

At half past three the cooks toiled forward again through the livid night with thick sweet porridge, sausages, hunks of bread, and more tea. A three-quarter moon shone brilliantly in a clear sky. The wood became inhabited with shadowy figures crawling up out of their slots, stretching aching limbs, glad of the hot breakfast.

A man said "Rabbits"—it was the 1st of March [an English superstitition, to say "rabbits!" on awakening the first of the month]. Half an hour later the leading companies began to move. The second in command, the ginger-haired major with the broad grin, stood at the roadside bordering the wood. Steadily the platoons filed past, a silent procession of human pack animals, their faces framed in woollen mufflers, like visors under the tin hats. On their backs a pack, a short spade, a pick, rifles slung.

The second in command greeted each platoon commander, " 'Lo, Harry, g'morning." " 'Lo, Charles, g'morning."

The flames of the burning village bronzed the trail of faces as they plodded through. On the outskirts of the village in the purple-gray before dawn, an old man stood with his back to the road, unmoving, his head bowed. A middle-aged woman grasped the arm of an aged woman, a bundle of skirts, a wizened, shrivelled face under a thin covering of gray hair drawn taut. The two women stumbled over the fields away from the marching troops. A few yards in from the road a man buried his dead.

Beyond the river the road was open to the dark line of woods, close up on the left and perhaps three hundred yards distant on the right. Bursts of tracer and flares shone suddenly upon a roof top in the right-flanking woods, and illumined a desperate encounter. A large house stood out silhouetted in the trees, and tracer hitting the roof was ricochetting and soaring high. The crash of machine-gun and small-arms fire rose in a crescendo. It was ominous. It should not have been there.

One hundred yards ahead the road came under heavy fire from self-propelled guns and mortars, and the Norfolks crouched, running under cover of the armor and the Bren carriers. It was not the battle of the Norfolks. Their way lay straight ahead to a line of woods marked by the

burning shell of a farmhouse. They went forward in bounds
of about fifty yards, strung out. A man bearing the heavy
tube of a mortar sucked great gusts of the morning air
into his lungs.

At five o'clock the twin beams of searchlights made
artificial moonlight, forming a huge "V" in the sky, dense
black between the broad incandescent bands, the outer
edges fringed with purple to merge into the flames licking
up from the woods, the farms, hamlets. For more than
twelve hours this road, the road back, would be almost as
deadly as the road forward, and over it the double-decker
jeeps would bear their burdens of wounded out of the
battle, the medical corps men sheltering the maimed
bodies with their own.

At a quarter to five a message reached battalion tactical headquarters from the Warwicks. The message reported much that was already known, and something that
was not: a farmhouse and outbuildings, known as the
Muserhof on the right flank and covering the approaches
to Kervenheim was strongly held by enemy. The Muserhof
position gave the enemy a magnificent field of fire at an
oblique angle to dominate the open western approaches.
It looked bad on the map.

v.

Soon after five o'clock in the morning the Norfolks dug
themselves in on the forward edge of the woodland belt,
facing Kervenheim at a distance of about half a mile. A
Company was on the right, B Company in the center, and
C Company on the left. D Company was in reserve.

Battalion headquarters made use of an old pit, or
cellar, in the shelter of a smouldering, roofless farmhouse, and reinforced it with sandbags and rubble. The
rest of battalion headquarters dug in as deep as they
could in the time available. The burning farmhouse had
provided a beacon in the last stages of the march and revealed the dark tunnel of trees arching over the road.

The K.S.L.I. were within fifty yards on the left and one
of their patrols made immediate contact. The left flank
was secure. Patrols made use of the remaining darkness
to probe into the outskirts of Kervenheim, and towards
the Muserhof. The moon was still up in a sky filled with
scudding cloud, and the moaning of heavy shells. It was
peaceful until dawn. The sunrise was very beautiful, the

eastern sky filled with feathery clouds stained scarlet. The heavy-clouded sky in the west was the dusky color of ripe peaches. This was the last sight for some. Heavy bursts of enemy mortar bombs fell in the woods, and the 88's tore out the top of a strip of woodland like a frieze. The tree bursts and the heavy mortaring were deadly, but not more deadly than the persistent, accurate sniping at very short range.

It was an uncomfortable time for the Norfolks from half past six until half past eight when the 25-pounders began to range on the target ahead. One battery, ranging short, sent three successive salvos almost on top of battalion headquarters.

Captain Cresswell had "whistled up" the squadron of the Coldstream Guards, and an observation tank moved out forward of the wood on the right, trying to spot the muzzle flashes of the enemy self-propelled guns. It was heavy going for tanks. Two Churchills churned up the mud in a shallow dike thirty yards behind battalion headquarters, and tore up the signal wires in their tracks when they got going. It was deadly in the open for the men laying signal wires.

From dawn onwards the medical corpsmen were busy bringing the wounded out of the woods, running wherever the mortar bursts were thickest, seeming themselves unaware of danger.

At twenty minutes to nine the barrage opened, and the steeple of Kervenheim Church stood out dark and black above the smoke. At nine o'clock C Company went in on the left with B Company in support and a troop of tanks. Company A attacked on the right, and with that a tornado of heavy machine-gun fire ripped over the open plain out of the Muserhof and tore through the woods like the lashing of steel whips. Crawling, crouching, striving to move forward in bounds, A Company tried to worm its way right-handed and onward to close the Muserhof, answering the tremendous concentration of spandaus and mortars with Brens, small arms, and their own mortars. The supporting tanks of the Coldstreams could not keep with the infantry. Two tanks bogged down five hundred yards short. The last word came from the observation tank: "It's awfully bare . . ." A direct hit on the tank ripped off the end of the sentence.

At eleven o'clock the remnants of A Company regained

the dangerous shelter of the woods. The tank commander had been killed. A boy, red faced, and wide-eyed with a kind of wonder hung with his left arm round a medic corporal's shoulder, trailing shattered legs. A pale-faced, ginger-haired lad hung on the corporal's other shoulder, his left arm swinging loose. Slowly they came back, a steady cavalcade of wounded. Hour after hour the air-bursts of the 88's, the mortars, and the heavy machine-guns, lashed at the woods, and across the open ground. The armored carriers, and the double-decker jeeps, the stretcher bearers, went forward and back, steady and steadfast, and the Norfolks pressed their attacks.

On the left two companies had got into Kervenheim supported by Lieutenant Melikoff in his Churchill tank, and with a troop of tanks in close support. It was not just fighting in a village, but fighting in a fortress, with every house and backyard not simply a place hiding enemy, but a carefully thought-out defensive position. Machine guns were mounted on every roof, manned by desperate men to whom the abnormal had become the only reality: there was only war, and only now.

A tremendous counterattack drove the Norfolks out of Kervenheim within the hour. Lieutenant Melikoff, wounded in the head, and his tank bazookaed, somehow managed to fight his way out. Halfway through the morning B Company had lost all its officers, and a battered remnant of the company at last regained the woodland line. It was about noon when D Company went in with the reorganized remnants of C and B Companies. By two o'clock it was as certain as anything could be that they would hold in Kervenheim. Hidden nests of enemy seemed to be everywhere, and the fire from the Muserhof had not abated. Nevertheless, the enemy must yield to the inexorable pressure.

In the rear, Brigade "Tac" [Tactical Headquarters] moved up to the wood in which the Norfolks had spent the night. Brigade "Main" moved up to the farmstead in the sandy hollow. Divisional "Tac" moved up. The Norfolks would spend the night holding the river line through Kervenheim. The Lincolns were going through. The British 3rd Infantry Division was moving down on Winnekendonk, its right flank tied in with the 53rd Division. By nightfall on March 1st the triangle of which Kervenheim ' ad formed the eastern apex had fallen. Weeze and Kevelaer, and the last of the river Niers line could not be held, and indeed it must have been the confusion of enemy fighting their way back through the woods that had so disrupted the right flank of the 185th Brigade attack.

The Muserhof position finally fell to the 53rd Division, and above all to the personal courage of tank commanders and infantry. At six o'clock on the evening of March 1st Captain Cresswell and his driver, Corporal Collier, stretched their weary legs for the first time in many hours. Lightly armored and vulnerable, they had worked tirelessly under fire, spotting the muzzle flashes of enemy self-propelled guns. The black steeple of Kervenheim Church stood out black and solid above the smoke and flame of the village. There was a mist of driving rain. Sporadic fighting would go on in and around Kervenheim all through the night. Neither Captain Cresswell nor Corporal Collier spotted the muzzle flash of the enemy self-propelled gun which put a shell within half a dozen yards of them. It blew off Collier's left foot and wounded the captain.

It had not been a day for jodphurs.

17: *THE END OF VERITABLE*

i.

THE BATTLE of Kervenheim was one of the scores of pieces which went to make up the picture of Operation Veritable. It helped to fill in a small, but important, triangle of the struggle and to open the way for the final phase. From March 2nd when the last of the enemy rearguards had been forced to abandon the Kervenheim-Winnekendonk line, the bridgehead began to shrink rapidly to intolerable proportions.

The fury of Operation Blockbuster, concentrated upon the Hochwald and Balberger forests, had not diminished; but the pressure on the flanks increased alarmingly for the enemy. The 43rd Division, in contact with the Canadian 2nd Division in the Hochwald, advanced steadily, supported by Flails and flame-throwing Crocodiles, to reduce Marienbaum. On the right the enemy still clung to Sonsbeek and the high ground to the north. On the flanks the battle for the Hochwald lay-back would be won and lost.

Between the 1st and 4th of March the battlefield was rapidly "tidied up." The 1st Commando Brigade on the extreme right flank of the 52nd Division made contact with the U.S. 17th Cavalry Reconnaissance Regiment, and the mopping up of the last of the enemy between the Maas and the Goch-Geldern road opened the way for the 52nd Division to swing eastward.

On the 4th of March the 53rd Division, nearing the end of its long commitment, cleared Geldern and moved east in solid contact with the U.S. 16th Corps on the road to Issum.

The British 3rd Infantry Division, having moved swiftly through Winnekendonk upon Kapellen, turned northeast to make contact with the Canadian 3rd Division still fighting desperately hard in the Balberger Forest. Heavily cratered roads, innumerable mines, blown bridges over minor waterways, and tank obstacles, all covered by an enemy whose resolution had stiffened in the face of imminent disaster, held up the Guards Armored Division in its efforts to go through, and exacted a heavy toll in armor and men. The whole terrain was jammed tight with enemy and obstacles, and the enemy fire power, concentrated on very narrow frontages, had become devastating. There was still no room for armor to maneuver. No obstacles would be by-passed, and whenever armor attempted to advance alone it lost heavily. That was even more true at the end than in the beginning.

By nightfall on the 4th, tremendous pressure had been brought to bear upon the Hochwald and Balberger positions, but it was not until Sonsbeek fell on the 6th, and Marienbaum yielded to the 43rd Division on the left, that the last of the enemy seemed to vanish, and the way was open between the forests. There had been no give at all, and the enemy rearguards had fought with incredible ferocity to cover the last withdrawal to the shrinking bridgehead.

The British 3rd Infantry Division, and the 11th Armored Division, were pinched out, and the 52nd Division relieved the 53rd Division on the right. Five divisions, some of them with a frontage of little more than one thousand yards, converged upon the site of the catastrophe Hitler had not sought to evade.

Every kind of lethal obstacle filled that last narrow triangle of land, bounded by Xanten on the left, though Veen, to the Issum-Alpon road, with its apex on Wesel. The natural defenses of railway, canal, dike, and woodland had been greatly strengthened, thick with mines and wire, with concrete emplacements and machine-gun nests, and with deeply entrenched positions in the woods. The formidable defenses of Xanten blocked the left flank. Alpon, no less heavily defended, blocked the way through on the right. At the heart lay Veen, barring the way through the center.

Behind this last enemy position, packed tight with mortars and self-propelled guns, the Wesel bridges remained open, defying all the efforts of the Allied Air forces to destroy them. Wesel itself and the eastern and western approaches to the bridges were deluged day and night with one thousand bombs. Direct hits were reported, but still the bridges held, and some sort of traffic was maintained.

Such was the last battlefield, defended by twenty thousand paratroopers, dedicated to the last stand. As late as March 7th, no order to the enemy had been given to withdraw, and on the following day, when the U.S. 1st Army began to pour its troops over the Remagen bridge, the line Xanten-Veen-Alpon still held.

ii.

From the artillery observation posts on the ridge east of the Hochwald Gap, the whole battlefield lay spread out in a magnificent and terrible panorama within the compass of the human eye. It was thus possible to watch the last act played out to its inevitable end.

From the 6th to the 10th of March, the battle raged with frightful intensity on a front no more than eight miles wide, the antagonists locked together at every point, almost immovable until, at the last, the tattered remnants of an army withdrew behind fanatical rearguards.

Had the weather permitted the Allied air forces to play full parts in support, it is difficult to imagine how any of the enemy could have survived. As it was, the pounding by artillery and bombing within the confines of that narrow triangle was awe-inspiring. Through all the 6th and

7th, with fighting by day and night enclosed in a diabolical inferno of fire, scarcely a yard had been gained. A tremendous assault against the western outskirts of Xanten had been repulsed and driven back. Veen with its lethal strips of forest on the left-center seemed impregnable, and on the right the 52nd Division faced formidable obstacles covering the approaches to Alpon.

It is almost impossible, to evaluate one section of that narrow battlefield against another, but Xanten was the undoubted key, for with its fall the whole of the enemy right and center would be outflanked.

Immediately to the south of Xanten the railway lines from Cleve and Goch converged to a single track, which again split into two behind Veen, both lines joining the Geldern-Wesel line astride the Xanten-Rheinberg road. These lines, together with a complex system of small canals, dikes, and rivulets, added greatly to the defensive strength of the Veen positions.

On the British right, the line of the Winnenthaler Canal interlaced with the stream of the Muhohl to provide a natural defensive barrier in front of Alpon and the whole of the right-center.

For the enemy there was nothing more to be sold for blood. This must be the end, for a break-through anywhere must open the way to Wesel, and cut the last possible line of withdrawal. Thursday, March 8th, had the feel of a day of reckoning. Left, right, and center, the 43rd, the 52nd and the 2nd, 3rd and 4th Canadian Divisions, had gathered themselves for major attacks concentrated with all their strength, supported by an immense weight of artillery. There was the knowledge, too, that the end must be very near, that it was beyond the strength of flesh and blood to withstand so great a battering. To the 43rd and the 2nd and 3rd Canadian Divisions it seemed a very long road back to Cleve: it was longer still for the enemy, and with nothing at the end of it but death, surrender, or retreat across the Rhine. And at any moment retreat might become impossible.

The 8th of March was a day of heavy cloud masses, but with good visibility. A white smoke screen streamed across the northern flank of the battlefield to shield the 43rd Division from enemy guns beyond the Rhine. Shells from batteries of 5.5's crashed into the town of Xanten so that the dark shroud in which the town was hidden flickered incessantly with bursts of flame and the flash of enemy fire. The lovely church and spire of Xanten, raised on a slight hill, seemed to be riding the heavy cloud banks as the smoke of battle swathed its base.

The villages of Wardt and Vynen had already fallen to the 43rd Division, and the spires of their churches stood out dark and clear against the white smoke screen. Thin lines of bushy-topped poplars spaced the lush pasture lands of the valley to the fringes of the Staatforst de Hees, covering Veen. In that small forest, stuffed with mines and ammunition dumps, a fanatical group of paratroopers were fighting to the last on top of a powder keg. Crocodiles, Flails, tanks, and men moved in eccentric fashion over that landscape like pieces moved on a board.

Behind the small forest three tall factory chimneys revealed the position of rail sidings, and in the midst of a great turbulence of smoke and flame Veen itself lay hidden at the very vortex of the tremendous struggle. Again and again the fringes of the Staatforst de Hees leapt into running flames as the Crocodiles, moving with the Canadian infantry, burned and carved a way yard by yard.

The whole of the middle distance was lit hour after hour with the constant flicker and flare of running fires and explosions and the flash of guns. At intervals farmsteads and ammunition dumps blew up in billows of heavy smoke shot through with flames, and men like ants ran and fell, moving forward and back.

Indeed from that high ridge, immune from the enemy guns concentrating all their power on the battle itself, it was easy to see everything, and yet to see nothing. There was, as always, no way of knowing the reality of the last days without going down onto that terrible stage.

By nightfall the 43rd Division had forced its way through to the southern half of Xanten, and hung on grimly. Nevertheless the intensity of the battle of the left did not abate. The defenders of Xanten, forced to withdraw, reinforced the defenders of Veen, and fought back with savage counterattacks supported by cataracts of mortar fire. The Staatforst de Hees still held. Veen still defied capture.

Meanwhile on the right the 52nd Division was involved in a desperate struggle to encircle Alpon from the North. It was two o'clock in the afternoon when the 156th Brigade attacked in a wheeling movement to the north of the town in an attempt to cut the lateral railway and the last line of retreat for the enemy in that quarter. The Guards in support of the left-flanking battalion found the way blocked by heavy cratering, and could not keep up with the infantry. At the same time confusing reports of the American advances close up on the right flank hampered the fire plans of the gunners of the Mountain Division.

By dawn on the 9th the Royal Scots Fusiliers had succeeded in outflanking the town, but at a high cost. On their left the 6th Cameronians had suffered terrible casualties with two companies cut off, and a third in serious trouble. Nothing except death would move the enemy. At last the 6th Cameronians, their ammunition exhausted, and subjected to devastating fire from Spandaus, mortars, and self-propelled guns firing over open sights, were overrun. They had lost four officers and one hundred and sixty-nine men in their attempts to cut the railway line to the east of Alpon.

In the opinion of the historian of the 52nd Division, the 6th Battalion Cameronians "took the brunt of the German fury in holding open one of their last lines of escape." It may be some measure of the quality of this fight to the bitter end that similar claims could be justly made for units of all the divisions involved.

Haus Loo, it was claimed, was the last enemy stronghold to fall on March 10th, but there was sporadic fighting at many points, even in the area south of Xanten, all through the 10th as the enemy rearguards strove to gain a few more hours of time to cover the withdrawal of all that remained in men and materials of General Schlemm's *Parachute Army*.

At last on the night of the 10th a series of deep rumbling explosions told all those who still fought on that the Wesel bridge was blown. At twenty minutes to eleven on the morning of March 11th, an air observer confirmed that the great railway bridge had been destroyed by the enemy, and from Nijmegen to Neuss the 21st Army Group had closed the Rhine.

iii.

The "bag" of prisoners, equipment, and materials of war, was much less than had been expected, yet the eleventh hour had already sounded before General Schlemm finally received permission to withdraw the *1st Parachute Army*. Early in March, when the madness of continuing the fight west of the Rhine might have been apparent even to a madman, General Schlemm had appealed to his Army Group Commander, Colonel-General Blaskowitz, for his support. It was as a result of Blaskowitz' personal intervention that an emissary from the Führer's Headquarters reached General Schlemm's Headquarters west of the Rhine on the morning of March 9th. This officer, a lieutenant colonel unaccustomed to the front-line realities of warfare, had been carefully subjected to a considerable ordeal by gunfire to ensure that his judgement of the desperate position should not be at fault. Thus it was that on the night of March 9th the remnants of the *1st Parachute Army* had begun an orderly withdrawal over the battered concrete and steel of the Wesel railroad bridge.

In the last stages of the battle the enemy had mustered more than 1,000 guns, and 717 mortars, to subject the Canadians and British to the heaviest volume of fire experienced in the campaign.

The battle yielded a total of 51,618 prisoners, 29,379 of them to the U.S. 9th Army, and 22,239 to the Canadians and British. They came from eighteen divisions and many hastily organized battle groups. Of these at least fourteen divisions and a high proportion of the battle groups, had fought the Canadians and British in the North.

In addition it was estimated that the enemy had lost a total of 38,000 killed and wounded. The remnants of the *1st Parachute Army* had withdrawn across the Rhine leaving behind some 90,000 men killed, wounded or prisoners.

The Allied losses had not been light. The U.S. 9th Army in its rapid advance had lost 7,300 killed and wounded, and the 1st Canadian Army 16,000 killed and wounded, two thirds of them British.

By the fortunes of war the Canadians and the British on the left had held the hinge, as they had done in Normandy, taking the full weight of the enemy defensive battle, and opening the way for the brilliant drives of the American armor on the right. By its Battle of the Rhine-

and the Canadian 1st Army had cleared the road to Cologne for the U.S. 1st Army.

By the fortunes of war, also, the Allied Supreme Commander's "broad front" policy, sustained from the beginning against all argument, had triumphed. By the end of March General Eisenhower had closed the Rhine over its entire length, and achieved his intention to destroy the German armies west of the Rhine. Few would deny that Adolf Hitler, refusing all the pleas of his commanders to withdraw, had been his most powerful ally in this achievement.

Sources used for BATTLE FOR THE RHINE

United States Army in World War II. The European Theatre of Operations. The Supreme Command, by Forrest C. Pogue. Office of the Chief of Military History, Department of the Army, Washington, D.C., 1954.

United States Army in World War II, Three Battles: Arnaville, Altuzzo, and Schmidt, by Charles B. MacDonald and Sydney T. Mathews, Office of the Chief of Military History, Department of the Army, Washington, D.C., 1952.

United States Army in World War II. The European Theatre of Operations. The Lorraine Campaign. Office of the Chief of Military History, Department of the Army, Washington, D.C.

Roosevelt and Hopkins; an intimate history by Robert Emmet Sherwood. Harper, 1950.

Crusade in Europe by Dwight D. Eisenhower. Doubleday, 1951.

The Second World War, 1939-45 by Major-General John F. C. Fuller. Duell, 1949.

The Second World War. vol. 6, *Triumph and Tragedy* by Sir Winston Churchill. Houghton Mifflin, 1954.

A Soldier's Story, by General Omar N. Bradley. Holt, 1951.

War As I Knew It, by General George S. Patton. Houghton Mifflin, 1947.

Top Secret, by Ralph Ingersoll. Harcourt Brace, 1946.

The Struggle for Europe, by Chester Wilmot. Harper, 1952.

The Execution of Private Slovik, by William B. Huie. Duell, 1954.

The Green Beret, by Hilary St. George Saunders. Collins, Canada, 1949.

Normandy to the Baltic, by Field-Marshal The Viscount Montgomery of Alamein, K.G., G.C.B., D.S.O. Houghton Mifflin, 1948.

Operation Victory, by Major-General Sir Francis de Guingand, K.B.E., C.B., D.S.O., Scribner, 1947.

Defeat in the West, by Milton Shulman. Dutton, 1948.

The German Generals Talk, by B. H. Liddell Hart. Morrow, 1948

Mountain and Flood, 1939-46. Divisional History of 52nd Division, by George Blake, Glasgow, Jackson Son & Co., 1950.

Borderers in Battle. The War Story of the King's Own Scottish Borderers, 1939-45, by Captain Hugh Gunning. Martin's Printing Works, Berwick-upon-Tweed, 1948.

The Canadian Army, 1939-45. An Official Historical Summary, by Colonel C. P. Stacey, O.B.E., A.M., Ph.D., Director, Historical Section, General Staff. Published by authority of the Minister of National Defence, Edmond Cloutier, King's Printer, Ottawa, 1948.

Operations in North-West Europe from June 6th, 1944 to May 5th, 1945, despatch submitted to the Secretary of State for War, June 1, 1946, by Field-Marshall The Viscount Montgomery of Alamein, K.G., G.C.B., D.S.O. Supplement to the "London Gazette," September 3, 1946 (No. 37711)

Report by the Supreme Commander to the Combined Chiefs of Staff on the Operations in Europe of the Allied Expeditionary Force, June 6, 1944, to May 8, 1945. London. H.M.S.O., 1946

History of the Second World War, United Kingdom Military Series, *Grand Strategy,* Volume v. August, 1943-September, 1944, by John Ehrman. London. H.M.S.O., 1956.

Grand Strategy, Volume vi. October, 1944-August, 1945, by John Ehrman. London. H.M.S.O., 1956.

North-West Europe, 1944-45. The Achievement of Twenty-First Army Group, by John North. London. H.M.S.O., 1953.

COUNT FIVE AND DIE

by Barry Wynne

How Allied resistance leaders were deliberately sacrificed to Gestapo torture—the true story of our D-Day deception plan, "Operation Stampede." Long buried in classified files, this is one of the most blood chilling stories to come out of the war.

". . . One of the great untold stories of World War II."

> Gen. William J. ("Wild Bill")
> Donovan
> *Director, Office of Strategic
> Services*

Paperbound: 35¢

BALLANTINE BOOKS, INC.
101 Fifth Avenue • New York 3, N. Y.